Wm C Smi[...]
14 Camerouth [...]
622 - 6009
1980

D0918365

The
YONGE
STREET
STORY

1793-1860

The YONGE STREET STORY

1793-1860

An Account from Letters, Diaries and Newspapers

F. R. Berchem

McGRAW-HILL RYERSON LIMITED

Toronto   Montreal   New York   St. Louis   San Francisco
Auckland   Bogotá   Düsseldorf   Johannesburg   London
Madrid   Mexico   New Delhi   Panama   Paris   São Paulo
Singapore   Sydney   Tokyo

TO PAT,
Whose ideas encouraged this story.

ACKNOWLEDGEMENTS

The author would like to express his appreciation of the considerable help and advice that he received from Mrs. Patricia Hart of Richmond Hill Public Library. Also to the several Historical Societies and Associations and Archives which made their material so readily available.

THE YONGE STREET STORY: 1793-1860

Copyright © F. R. Berchem, 1977. All rights reserved. No part of this publication may be reproduced, stored in a retrieval system or transmitted, in any form, or by any means, mechanical, electronic, photocopying, recording or otherwise, without the prior written permission of McGraw-Hill Ryerson Limited.

1 2 3 4 5 6 7 8 9 0 AP 5 4 3 2 1 0 9 8 7 6

Printed and bound in Canada

Canadian Cataloguing in Publication Data

Berchem, F. R., 1931-
The Yonge Street story

Bibliography: p.
Includes index.
ISBN 0-07-082567-X

1. Toronto, Ont. — Streets — Yonge Street — History.
2. Ontario — History — To 1867.* I. Title.

FC3097.67.B47   971.3'541   C77-001535-2
F1059.5.T6875Y648

Table of Contents

"LIEUTENANT-COLONEL JOHN
GRAVES SIMCOE 1752-1806
FIRST LIEUTENANT-GOVERNOR
OF UPPER CANADA 1791-1796
FOUNDER OF THE CITY OF
TORONTO JULY 30TH 1793"

Chapter One

The Simcoe Years (1791-96)

Roads by themselves are not the stuff of exciting history. They need to have the colour from the characters associated with them to make their story sparkle. Where would the tale of the CPR be without that old Scots scalawag, Sir John A. Macdonald, and his cantankerous Caledonian countryman, Donald Smith, who later became Lord Strathcona? What were the canoe routes without the vigour of the voyageurs and the Nor'Westers? Travel and adventure go together, and travel goes with roads.

Well-trodden pathways marked the waygoing of generations before the Roman legions unrolled their stone roads on the map of Europe. 'Before the Roman came to Rye . . .,' wrote G. K. Chesterton, 'the rolling English drunkard made the rolling English road' — and he went on to describe how

> I knew no harm of Bonaparte
> And plenty of the Squire,
> And for to fight the Frenchman
> I did not much desire;
> But I did bash their baggonets
> Because they came arrayed
> To straighten out the crooked road
> An English drunkard made.

Whatever may have been the domestic road-making habits of the merry English rustic, his military countrymen abroad built roads that ran straight and deliberate to form strategic links: thrusting avenues of aggression, not wandering lovers' lanes. Such a road was Yonge Street, the creation of Upper Canada's first lieutenant-governor, Colonel John Graves Simcoe.

John Graves Simcoe was very much the soldier. Courageous, forthright, determined, and ambitious, he was a professional military man, in some ways ahead of his time — which was before 'Old Beaky,' the Iron Duke of Wellington, insisted on a more professional outlook in an army whose officers would stray into battle wearing top hats and waving umbrellas. In the field, said the duke, the latter were not only ridiculous but unmilitary.

Neither of these labels could be attached to Simcoe, although his voluminous correspondence outlining his schemes and the methods for their development tended to be at times tedious, even pompous. So much so, that he was told of: 'The general complaint of His Majesty's Ministers [is] that you will not take enough of responsibility on yourself, that by not doing it you give them great trouble and subject yourself to frequent great inconvenience.'[1] However irritating his numerous proposals may have been, they could not be called ridiculous.

He learned his military business the hard way. Serving during the American War of Independence, he was wounded while leading the Grenadier Company of the 40th Regiment at the battle of Brandywine Creek in September 1777. He was given command of the Queen's Rangers in the following month, was wounded twice more and taken prisoner; he escaped, and then, his health broken by his wounds, returned to England as a lieutenant-colonel in 1781.

During his service he saw and appreciated the value of green-clad, woods-wise troops for North American warfare where the precise drills so carefully rehearsed for battle on the plains of Europe were of little use. Although he may have respected their methods, John Graves Simcoe — monarchist, old Etonian, and country gentleman — had no enthusiasm for American republican habits, and avowed that 'there is no person, perhaps, who thinks less of the talents or integrity of Mr. Washington than I do . . .his natural avarice and vanity, two principal ingredients in his character.'[2]

Simcoe might well have dismissed as mythical republican rubbish the story of young George and the Cherry Tree, but not the axe that did the deed. Amid the detailed correspondence that he poured forth as lieutenant-governor of Upper Canada is a requisition that contains typical Simcoe observations: '[Axes] made in America, tho' not so neatly fabricated are of infinite more value to the several persons who use them. It is Customary with the Manufacturers in America to warrant the Quality of the tools they make for six months, and take back or replace those that are found insufficient. This ought to be adopted in England. . . . The axes sent to this Country [Upper Canada] are so carelessly fabricated as to be totally incompetent to any Service whatever. . . .I think that Fifty will be the smallest quantity that the Queen's Rangers can possibly execute their public employment with the ensuing year; but should they not be of the prime quality I shall be obliged to purchase them in this Country.'[3] 'Execute' was probably not the best word to use in connection with axes being used in the public employment; but, in his zeal, Simcoe would have been totally oblivious to fine

QUEEN'S RANGERS c.1793
Raised: December 1791
Disbanded: November 1802

points, as he was then on one of his favourite hobby-horses, a newly raised Corps of Queen's Rangers for service in Upper Canada.

Upper Canada had been separated from Quebec and made a province in 1791, and even before taking up his residence as the first lieutenant-governor of the new province, Lieutenant-Colonel Simcoe was proposing to the secretary of state that 'there should be a Corps of Troops raised independent of those of the Line, & who should be employed to the civil purposes of the Colony, in the construction of the various public works, of Buildings, Roads, Bridges, & communications by Land & on the Waters, that this Corps should also take upon itself as soon as it shall be duly instructed therein, the navigation of the King's Vessels on the Lakes for the various purposes of which they may be required.'[4]

Shortly thereafter, the king was pleased to direct that a corps of infantry be raised particularly for service in Upper Canada, and Sir George Yonge, the secretary at war, wrote to Simcoe that the king had further consented to the corps wearing a green uniform of the same pattern as that worn by the late Corps of Queen's Rangers in the American war.[5] When Simcoe finally arrived at Niagara toward the end of July 1792, the reincarnated Queen's Rangers had been raised and established in Upper Canada, ready to hew the paths for settlement and communication.

It is hard to say what priorities Simcoe might have given to the various claims of civil and military tasks. However, with France's declaration of war on England in February 1793, and with the fear that America might take advantage of this to harass England in North America, military considerations came first with him.

He did not hear of the outbreak of war until the end of May 1793, when his immediate concern became the western or upper posts at Michilimackinac (Mackinac), Detroit, Niagara, and Oswego. These were posts that, although located in territories belonging to the American Congress, were occupied by British garrisons and traders.[6] Even before coming to Upper Canada, he had flatly stated his opinion that if these posts were given up, then 'the loss of Canada ultimately and not very remotely must follow.'[7]

His particular fear was Detroit. At this time, the great North West Fur Company was starting into its most vigorous phase, determined to hold the fur trade in Canadian hands. Benjamin Frobisher, a partner in the company, said that many of the traders depended upon Detroit for the supply of provisions, especially corn, the staple food of the trade. Should the Americans possess Detroit, they would have it in their power to ruin the Canadian competition.[8] He proposed a transport route along what was then known as the Toronto Carrying Place, which ran from the mouth of the river Humber to the river Severn (Matchedash); such a route would connect Lake Ontario with Lake Huron and bypass Detroit.

Simcoe realized from the outset that the scrapping between the American Congress and the Indians, which had continued since the acquisition of the North Western Territory by the States in 1787, could ruin the Detroit branch of the fur trade for Canada.[9] The welfare of the merchants engaged in the trade did not, however, worry him greatly. Typical of his class and profession, he had not much liking for merchants, and was not likely to exert himself overmuch in their behalf. Canadian retention of the fur trade he wished, but preferred that the Indians bring their furs to those who might settle in his new province, rather than to the agents of merchants in distant Montreal.[10]

Simcoe seems to have disliked anything that might have interfered with his personal ambition and schemes for Upper Canada. There was something of the old Roman proconsul in this upright, unbending soldier who saw the building of his province as a purely personal matter. He would have liked to see a hereditary aristocracy established. Settlers he might encourage and tolerate if they would benefit his plans. His view of merchants was dim. The Provincial Marine, the sailors who manned the small government ships on the Great Lakes and who were not liable to military authority and discipline, he described as 'the most profligate men I have ever heard of.'[11] He did not place any great trust in Indians even if his wife did think that some amongst them looked like 'the figures painted by the Old Masters.'[12] He quarrelled continually with his military superior, the governor of Canada in Quebec, Lord Dorchester, an able soldier who was constantly splashing cold water on his subordinate's enthusiasms. Simcoe did not put much faith in any military support from the Loyalists, who had come north from the American states, although he kept his greatest disgust for their former countrymen, from Washington down to the lowest official.

He found the Americans — filled with the rude bluster of democracy and possessed of greedy, grasping, aggressive, republican habits — too close a threat for comfort at his headquarters in Navy Hall, Niagara. He decided to move to a location that would be more suited to his purposes. A man of action, Simcoe moved determinedly and promptly, convinced that he would sway others by the arguments with which he swayed himself.

Upon hearing of the outbreak of war with France, another nation of damned republicans, he wrote on 31 May, 1793, to Alured Clarke, Lord Dorchester's representative in Quebec, offering him some lengthy 'Observations upon the Military Strength and naval Conveniency of Toronto which I propose immediately to occupy . . . upon minute Investigation I found it to be without comparison the most proper situation for an Arsenal. . . .The Spit of Land which forms its Entrance is capable of being fortified with a few heavy Guns as to prevent any Vessel from entering the Harbour or from remaining within it. . . . .I have good Information that a Road is very easy to be made to communicate with those Waters which fall into Lake Huron. . . . .In regard to Lake Huron, tho' it is not so immediate an object of Attention, yet I consider it ultimately of the most extensive and serious Magnitude.'[13]

Having stated his purpose, Simcoe proceeded as he had planned. On 30 July, 1793, he embarked in the topsail schooner *Mississaga* with his family, household goods, (notably a 'Canvass house' of remarkable aspect that had been the property of the late Captain James Cook killed in a squabble with Hawaiian natives), and a company of the Queen's Rangers. They arrived safely in Toronto Bay. Lord Dorchester, unimpressed, commented somewhat sourly, 'I know not what is meant by a Port in Upper Canada.'[14]

Undeterred, Simcoe proceeded to follow up his suggestion that he have authority over the naval armament upon the upper lakes, and expressed a hope that 'Lord Dorchester will think it proper to place the naval arrangements under my controul.'[15] Lord Dorchester didn't think it proper.

So much, thought John Graves, for Dorchester, and took it upon himself to change the name of Toronto to York, in celebration of the grand old Duke of

York's success in an action against the French in Holland, of which news was received in Upper Canada at the end of August 1793. It gave the lieutenant-governor an opportunity to introduce some pageantry to his newly established headquarters. On 24 August, Mrs. Simcoe described how 'the Gov. ordered a Royal Salute to be fired in commemoration of this Event & took the same opportunity of naming this station York. ....There was a party of Gibbeway Indians here who appeared much pleased with the firing. One of them named Canise took Francis [Simcoe's son] in his Arms & was much pleased to find the Child not afraid but delighted with the sound.'[16] It was to such martial sounds that young Francis would die at the seige of Badajoz, during the Spanish Peninsular War; he was buried on the battlefield, aged twenty-one.

MISSISSAGA   ONONDAGA

From a photograph in Toronto Public Library, Simcoe Papers: reproduced in Ontario History Vol. LIX, March, 1967.

To forestall the anticipated rumblings from Dorchester, Simcoe explained to a long-suffering Henry Dundas, the secretary of state for home affairs, that he was occupying York in his capacity as *civil* governor of Upper Canada and so was free from the military authority of Lord Dorchester. He also took the opportunity to stress York's importance to Upper Canada: 'It is requisite for the safety and security of the Province to occupy the different Posts I have intimated York, Long Point and London to seperate and to command the Indian Nations. The ready access which the former of these Posts has to Lake Huron, and from thence to the

"24 August, 1793 : The Gov. ordered a Royal Salute to be fired ......
The Missisaga & Onondaga fired also & the Regt. ...... It was a damp day &
from the heavy atmosphere the Smoke from the Ships Guns ran along the water
with a singular appearance." (Mrs. Simcoe's Diary)

mouth of the French River, by which the north west Trade from Montreal passes into Lake Huron may probably be of great Military importance, and there is little doubt but the produce of the Lands on this Communications (and on the River Thames) in case of Detroit being ceded to the United States, will in no distant period be sufficient to supply the North West Trade with such provisions as it may, and which the Merchants concerned in that Trade constantly represent as the principal Utility, as far as they are concerned of our retaining possession of Detroit.'[17]

Remembering what Benjamin Frobisher had said in 1785, this was obviously no very original idea. It was also unlikely that Simcoe would waste much time in promoting a tradesman's thoroughfare for the North West Company's men, whom their rivals in the Hudson's Bay Company dubbed, with rather unbecoming sneers. 'the pedlars from Quebec.' It was simply one more arrow in Simcoe's quiver of arguments for building up York and developing a route to Lake Huron. From this he could establish his pet military project for Upper Canada: a triangle of bases, with London as the capital on the forks of the river Thames, York on Lake Ontario, and a base on Lake Huron linked to York by a route north.[18] Dorchester, however, quickly quashed any ambitions for London, and Simcoe had to concentrate his hopes upon the creation of York and a route to Lake Huron.

The aspect of York and the land beyond did not encourage any impressions of rustic, picnic idylls, grand though it may have been. It offered little more than gloomy forest, plague, and pestilence. Joseph Bouchette, who was captain of the *Mississaga* and who surveyed Toronto harbour for Simcoe in 1793, said that he could 'distinctly recollect the untamed aspect which the country exhibited when I first entered the beautiful basin. Dense and trackless forests lined the margin of the Lake, and reflected their inverted images in its glossy surface.'[19] Bouchette, like most sailors, preferred his scenery from the ship.

Ashore the forest stretched unbroken, if not trackless, along the Toronto Carrying Place; it was picturesquely described in misleading, Rousseau-like raptures as 'a perpetual gloom of vaulted boughs and intermingled shade, a solemn twilight monotony.'[20] It was also damp and depressing. Mrs. Simcoe found the mosquitoes bothersome and the rattlesnakes repulsive, and noted her husband's ill-health: the aches from his old wound were aggravated by the climate, and he suffered from severe headaches and fevers.[21] One uncharitable grouch, finding York an abysmal hole for humanity, saw in the lieutenant-governor's ill-health retribution for having dragged his staff and officials to such a dismal dump.[22] The winters were ice hells and the summers so hot that one suffering British sentry declared that only a strip of paper separated the land from the fires of damnation.

The land at Toronto and Matchedash had been bargained for in 1787 by Sir John Johnson, superintendent of Indian Affairs and Dorchester's preference for the position of lieutenant-governor of Upper Canada; he had already negotiated with three Missisauga chiefs at Quinté in September of that year. The agreement was made final, perhaps in the presence of Lord Dorchester, at Toronto in August 1788. The land was exchanged for the sum of £1700 in money and goods, the latter including brass kettles, mirrors, 5 boxes of guns, 200 pounds of tobacco, and 96 gallons of rum.[23]

The inspiration for the Toronto Purchase seems to have come from a somewhat shadowy — some seem to think shady — individual, the chevalier Philippe de Rocheblave. One of twenty children in a French noble family, he had fought for the British during the American War of Independence, commanding the post at Kaskaskia (Fort Gage) where he was captured. Imprisoned in Virginia, he escaped and returned to Quebec. When his hopes for a grant of land on the Rideau River came to nothing, he petitioned Lord Dorchester for a grant at Toronto, including the island and the Carrying Place to Lake aux Claies (also known as Lake La Claie or La Clie and later as Lake Simcoe). Rocheblave felt that he was due some compensation for his misfortunes during the American war, and he pressed his claim hard. It was referred to a special committee of the privy council in the summer of 1787, and was taken up in 1788 for consideration;[24] but, with the decision to divide Quebec into Upper and Lower Canada in 1791, Rocheblave's hopes were again dashed.

Whether he was a man of vision, or a rogue with an eye to the main chance, or both, has long been debated, but he lost no time in urging his schemes upon Simcoe after his arrival in Upper Canada as lieutenant-governor in 1792. In a long-winded, sometimes high-flown discourse in French, Rocheblave told Simcoe that Toronto had 'the unusual advantage of possessing a harbour in front on Lake Ontario and a harbour in the rear on Lake Huron.'[25]

Simcoe, as already noted, was quick in latching on to that idea without saying anything about the source of his information. He had his own ambitions and plans for Upper Canada and was not much impressed by some of the liberal notions on education and law held by Rocheblave, an aristocrat tempered by the realities of North American life. Simcoe was not particularly interested, either, in Rocheblave's argument that the Toronto Portage from the mouth of the Humber River to Lake Huron would give the Montreal merchants a head start in the fur-trade competition. It would, Rocheblave claimed, get them into the upper country west of Lake Superior before their New York rivals, who would have to go from Oswego to the Niagara Portage and then through Lake Erie to Lake Huron. The fortunes of Lower Canadian merchants, however, were not a concern of the consul of Upper Canada.

A product of Eton and Oxford, Simcoe was no doubt well drilled in the history of classical Rome — or else it was well beaten into him in the manner of his time. His ideas for his beloved Queen's Rangers certainly followed the old Roman colonial pattern. Discharged soldiers would be given an allotment of land, and these disciplined veterans, loyal to the Crown, would provide a stable, trusty nucleus on which to develop the outpost towns of the new province. It didn't work out: the temptation and opportunities to desert were too strong on the isolated frontier.

Who were these men by whom Simcoe set so much overoptimistic store? Many of them had seen active service with the original corps of Queen's Rangers, the 1st American Regiment, during the War of Independence; they had headed over the border to New Brunswick, away from the republican taint, once the war was over. Remarkable characters, too: Lieutenant Charles Dunlop, who had been an ensign in the old corps. (in 1777 at the age of thirteen) and at fifteen had led a stirring cavalry skirmish; Ensign James Givins, chosen for his considerable skill in Indian languages; Captain John McGill, who had been taken prisoner with Simcoe in the American war and who had offered to let 'Johnny' Simcoe escape by getting into his bed. (a scraping key foiled their plans.) McGill, however, did not in the end serve with the newly raised Queen's Rangers, being offered instead the post of commissary of stores and provisions for Upper Canada.

McGill was one of the many Scots who sought to make their mark in America at that time. Captain David Shank of the Rangers was another, as was that hardy Highland nut, Captain-Lieutenant Aeneas Shaw, who, upon hearing of the formation of the new corps in Upper Canada, made up a detachment in New

Brunswick and marched it on snowshoes to Montreal in the winter of 1791-92.

The men of the Queen's Rangers were provided by drafts from regular British regiments of the line, such as the 73rd Foot, and from volunteers in Canada, about fifty of whom were added to the corps, many of these being United Empire Loyalists lately from America.

In July 1793, some one hundred of these Queen's Rangers under Captain Shaw sailed in batteaux from Niagara, which Simcoe renamed Newark, followed by the schooner *Onondaga* and the sloop *Caldwell* with another division of the corps.[26] Upon arrival at Toronto they found a population of two Missisauga Indian families and the trading post of Jean-Baptiste Rousseau at the mouth of the Humber. Their first achievement was to clear ground near the site of the present Canadian National Exhibition and to build Fort York in 1793 for their accommodation.

In their brief history, from 1791 to 1802, the Queen's Rangers could claim no battle honours for their colours, but they did leave a lasting memorial in laying the foundations of York. Toronto's streets today bear the names of many of these Rangers: McGill, Shaw, Givins (misspelt Givens); and from Simcoe's friend, Surgeon James Macaulay of the Queen's Rangers in the American war, come James and Terauley streets, with Hayter and Louisa streets being named for members of his family.

Lord Dorchester chose to describe the work of the Rangers as Simcoe's 'Provincial Projects'.[27] They may not have been the stuff of glorious military legend, but they made a great contribution to Upper Canada. Perhaps their most notable achievement was in clearing the way for the road that Lieutenant-Governor Simcoe named Yonge Street after Sir George Yonge, the British Secretary at War from December 1783 to July 1794.

Inspired by the stories that he had heard about a trail connecting his newly created York with Lake Huron, Simcoe set out from the mouth of the Humber River on 25 September, 1793, to follow a route to Machedash Bay. With him went Lieutenant Pilkington of the Royal Engineers; Lieutenant Darling of the 5th Foot; Lieutenant Givins, Queen's Rangers; Alexander Macdonnell, sheriff of Home District, who kept a diary of the journey; the surveyor, Alexander Aitken; two Lake aux Claies and two Matchedash Bay Indians; and a dozen soldiers of the Queen's Rangers.

They went by horse as far as the end of the Carrying Place on the west branch of the Holland River near present-day Kettleby. From there, five canoes were used to slither, rather than float, down the shallow, swampy stream to Lake aux Claies; it was reached on 29 September after a stop the night before near the encampment of the Ojibwa Indian, Old Sail. He it was who told Simcoe of another route leading south from the east branch of the Holland River by which the swamps could be avoided.[28]

Huts of the Queen's Rangers, 1794 - from a drawing by Mrs. Simcoe.

With his customary habit of scattering new names like birdseed, the lieutenant-governor called Lake aux Claies, Lake Simcoe in memory of his father, Captain John Graves Simcoe, Royal Navy. (He had died from pneumonia when in command of H.M.S. *Pembroke* in the fleet that was on its way to attack Quebec in 1759. He was buried at sea, off Anticosti Island in the Gulf of St. Lawrence.)

It was no easy paddle even in the deeper waters of Lake Simcoe; freshening winds delayed the passage across Kempenfeldt Bay so that the head of Lake Couchiching, at the northern end of Lake Simcoe, was not reached until 1 October. The island at the entrance to Lake Couchiching was named Francis's Island for Simcoe's young son. After camping at the head of the lake, the canoes were headed into the rapids and shoots of the Severn River, where John Vincall of the Rangers cut his toe with an axe during one of the portages.

From the mouth of the Severn the party entered the bay named Machedash by the Indians in apt description of its 'marshy places', but re-christened Gloucester Bay with no great degree of imagination by Simcoe. That evening, the fourth of October, they encamped near the post of a rather colourful trader named Cowan, located on the east side of the bay, opposite the site of today's Fesserton.

Cowan was a successful, independent trader, probably of Scottish origin, but known locally as Jean-Baptiste Constant. He spoke fluent French as a result of being captured by the French as a boy at Fort Pitt in 1758. He was believed to have been settled at Matchedash Bay since 1777,[29] trading his furs at Michilimackinac and owning a post at La Cloche on the mainland, opposite Little Current on Manitoulin Island. On Simcoe's recommendation, Cowan was later employed as an official Indian interpreter; he lost his life in the wreck of the

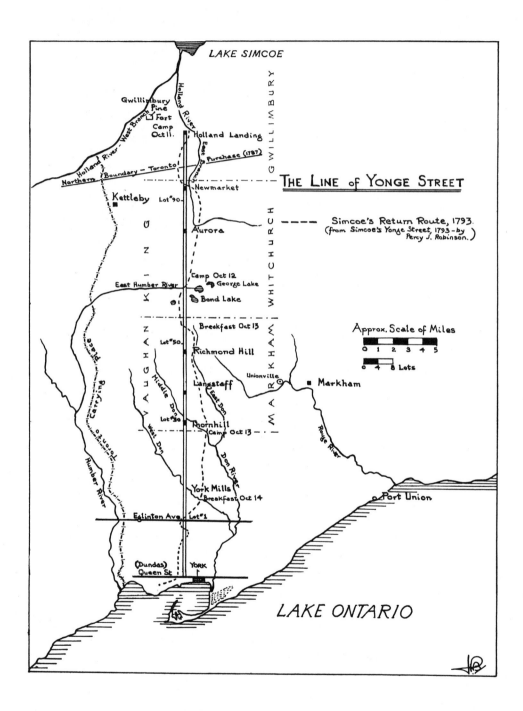

LAKE SIMCOE

Gwillimbury Pine

□ Fort
Camp
Oct 11.

Holland Landing

Purchase (1787)

Holland River – West Branch

Northern – Boundary – Toronto

Newmarket

Kettleby   Lot #90

THE LINE of YONGE STREET

– – – – –   Simcoe's Return Route, 1793.
(from Simcoe's Yonge Street, 1793 – by
Percy J. Robinson.)

Aurora

Camp Oct 12

East Humber River   George Lake

Bond Lake

Breakfast Oct 13

Lot #50

Richmond Hill

Approx. Scale of Miles
0 1 2 3 4 5

0   4   8 Lots

Unionville

Langstaff   ■ Markham

Lot #30

Thornhill
Camp Oct 13

Middle Don

West Don

Don River

East Don

Rouge River

York Mills
Breakfast Oct 14

Humber River

Port Union

Eglinton Ave. Lot #1

(Dundas)
Queen St   YORK

LAKE ONTARIO

Speedy on Lake Ontario in 1804, on his way to the trial of an Indian accused of murder.

On the morning of 5 October, Simcoe went in one of Cowan's large canoes, worked by five of his Canadian employees, to view the harbour at Penetanguishene, the 'Place of the White Rolling Sands'. He later wrote to Dundas that 'a gale of wind prevented my perfectly attaining this Object, but under the shelter of the Islands I went sufficiently close to satisfy myself, The Engineer and Surveyor, who accompanied me, that it was a safe and commodious Harbour, and capable of containing Vessels of as great Burthen as can be supposed to sail upon Lake Huron.'[30] Should 'Pennatangushene' develop in importance, he entertained ideas of calling it 'Gloucester'.[31]

"The Indians lost their way & when they had Provisions for one day only, they knew not where they were. The Gov. had recourse to a Compass & at the close of the day they came on a Surveyor's line & the next Morning saw Lake Ontario. Its first appearance, Coll. Simcoe says, was the most delightful sight at a time they were in danger of starving & about 3 miles from York they breakfasted on the remaining Provisions." — on 14 Oct. 1793 — (*Mrs. Simcoe's Diary* for 25 Oct.)

Having accomplished this purpose of finding a suitable base on Georgian Bay or Lake Huron, Simcoe began the return to York on 6 October. Kempenfeldt Bay was crossed on the tenth, and on the eleventh the party set off from de Grassi Point. Ranger Vincall's foot was now giving so much trouble that when the Holland Landing Place at the old pine fort was reached early in the afternoon, Macdonnell, Givins, and Vincall were left there to wait for horses to be sent from York. The site of the old pine fort was called Gwillimbury after Mrs. Simcoe's father, Major Gwillim.

Simcoe and the others continued on foot 'by the new route' that he had been told about by Old Sail.[32] This trail wound south through what is now Aurora, Richmond Hill, and across branches of the Don River at Thornhill and York Mills. The weather turned wet and miserable as they stumbled on in a south-south westerly direction toward the bay and then west to the fort. They were back at York shortly before three o'clock in the afternoon of 14 October.

Simcoe was delighted with what he had found. He expounded with enthusiasm on his discovery, and straightway started in to develop it as he thought best for Upper Canada. Henry Dundas was again the recipient of a flood of notions on 'Provincial Projects': 'I have directed the Surveyor early in the next Spring to ascertain the precise distance of the several Routs which I have done myself the honor of detailing to you, and hope to compleat the Military Street or Road the ensuing Autumn — The importance of this Communication is evident.'[33] The winding trail that he had travelled from Holland Landing down the east branch of the Holland River to the Don and its branches was to be the basis for his 'Military Street or Road': Yonge Street.[34]

On the subject of the development of military roads, Simcoe had already forcibly expressed his ideas to Dundas: 'Another exception was thought proper to make on the Military communications; as it is intended that they shall be carried on, in as straight a line as possible. Its determined that such a line should divide the several Townships, and for the speedy settlement of the Country, and the future maintenance of the Road that no person should be allowed a Lot thereon who was not a bonafide settler, and that the Reserves which would have fallen in this line agreeable to the general plan, should be distributed among the rear concessions.'[35]

It is apparent that although Simcoe may have wished to attract trade along the York to Lake Huron route, his prime interest was in a military thoroughfare, and settlers would be essential for its upkeep. If anything, however, his schemes discouraged settlement. By emphasizing that maintenance duties would be firmly imposed upon settlers along his military roads, he drove them away from such thoroughfares to settle back in the comparative obscurity of the townships.[36]

The Yonge Street project was speedily begun, and during February and March 1794, the deputy provincial surveyor, Augustus Jones, started at the Holland Landing with a small detachment of the Queen's Rangers to run the line of the

May 1794 : Alexander Aitkin with a party of Rangers lays off 111 lots on both sides of the street from Eglinton Avenue to the Landing .... By 18 May, 4 miles of road had been opened north of Eglinton Avenue, but no bridges built.
(*Simcoe's Yonge Street*; 1793 — Percy J. Robinson.)

new road to York. In May, Alexander Aitken, the surveyor who had accompanied Simcoe on the journey to Matchedash Bay, took a party of the Rangers to lay off 111 lots on both sides of the Yonge Street line, numbering them from one at what later became Eglinton Avenue. By the middle of the month some four miles of road had been opened north of Eglinton to Lot 17, a quarter of a mile north of what is now Sheppard Avenue.

Opening the road was a bone-jarring, monotonous slog. This unromantic task meant the marking and felling of trees along the surveyed line through heavy forest. Dull though it may have been, and uncomfortable to boot in the close dampness and gloom, it was for such a job that Simcoe had planned his Rangers.

The threat of war and Lord Dorchester disrupted the harmony of the lieutenant-governor's plans before 1794 was through.[37] The Indian war over the boundary between American and Indian territory in the Northwest (what is now Ohio, Indiana, Illinois, Michigan, and Wisconsin) had reached a critical stage by 1794. Simcoe was acutely aware of the danger of a clash between battle-fired American troops and the British garrisons at the western posts, such as Detroit, if these were approached closely in Congress's march against the Indians. He urged a course of action upon a sceptical Lord Dorchester: 'The necessity of occupying Matchadash and Long Point, become to me every hour more evident, in particular as I know of no other Posts, in which our shipping could find shelter, should the Army of the States occupy Detroit.'[38]

Simcoe had his sympathizers at home, such as the marquis of Buckingham, who expressed his concern in a letter to Lord Grenville on 6 August, 1794: 'I fear very much for Colonel Simcoe's situation, if *all* the posts, and particularly Detroit are immediately ceded. Old Michilimackinac is abandoned, and a small post established in an island near it, within their [the American] line; that island must be struggled for, as I understand that it has the only secure anchorage at the mouth of the Straits. He [Colonel Simcoe] is very sanguine in his hopes that the communication will be opened and settled by families from York [Toronto] to the Lake Huron by Lake Simcoe to Matchadash Bay before winter, which will entirely divert the course of the fur trade.'[39]

Simcoe saw Upper Canada as a front line of defence to be held at whatever cost. Dorchester saw only an outpost to be withdrawn from in the defence of Lower Canada in the event of any serious threat to Quebec, which provided the vital link with the sea routes to England. Dorchester had instructed Simcoe to arm the Provincial Marine on the Lakes,[40] but Simcoe, as we have seen, was not enthusiastic about that organization, preferring that it remain secondary in importance to a land-based military force. Simcoe's warnings on the American threat were generally dismissed by Dorchester as being overstressed.

In the summer of 1794, however, even Dorchester began to show some alarm as the American forces under General 'Mad Anthony' Wayne approached Detroit in their march against the Indians. He sent several troops of militia to support the Queen's Rangers in Upper Canada.[41] The Queen's Rangers in turn were withdrawn from their road-clearing activities and dispatched to bolster the garrison at Fort Miami on the Maumee River flowing into western Lake Erie. This was a fort that Dorchester had instructed Simcoe to re-build, much against the latter's will.[42]

The popular view of Wayne's army has sometimes been of a motley collection of irregulars advancing in a much-as-you-please fashion against an assortment of feathered braves — an image coloured by legends of Washington's ill-fed, determined ragamuffins at Valley Forge. In fact, however, it was a 'well-drilled, well-fed army of 1800 United States regulars and 1500 frontier militiamen and twenty howitzers.'[43] Small wonder that Simcoe was worried.

This threat to Detroit faded with Wayne's decisive victory over the Indians on 20 August, 1794, at Fallen Timbers, a site within cannon shot of Fort Miami. Nevertheless, Simcoe's plans for Yonge Street's development by the Queen's Rangers had suffered a sharp setback. Matters weren't helped by Dorchester's letter of 7 October, 1794, forbidding Simcoe to use the Queen's Rangers for any civil purposes. With the withdrawal of his Queen's Rangers from the road-clearing job, Simcoe had to look elsewhere for help, in this instance to a rather remarkable character: William Berczy.

Born in 1744 at Wallerstein in Swabia, Johann Albrecht Ulrich Moll became better known in Canadian history as William von Moll Berczy. He claimed connection with the Austrian noble family of von Moll through an uncle who was for forty years minister of the House of Brunswick at the court of Vienna.[45] His adopted surname of Berczy seems to have derived from a popular abbreviation of Albrecht. Berczy appears as something of a latter-day Leonardo da Vinci; his talent for drawing had been developed by good teaching, and he was an architect, bridge designer, and writer much travelled in Europe.

" In November 1794 William von Moll Berczy (1748-1813), colonizer, road builder, architect and painter, brought the first settlers to Markham township. This group had originally emigrated from Germany to New York State, but moved to Upper Canada in 1794 and acquired extensive lands in this area. In 1795-6 sickness and famine reduced their numbers, but those who remained or returned to their holding laid the foundation for the rapid development of Markham township after 1800. Berczy, having exhausted his resources on the settlement, went to Montreal in 1805 where he achieved some success as a portrait painter. "

Erected by the Ontario Archaeological and Historic Sites Board.

An independent, vigorous individual, he disliked the narrow ways of the old regime in Europe. When he brought his group of settlers from Germany in the summer of 1792 to colonize and develop New York lands held by an English company headed by Sir William Pulteney, he often found himself at odds with established authority. As a result of these clashes, he found it difficult to gain credit and support for his proposals for settlement.[46] Nonetheless, in spite of a lack of an established framework of discipline and authority such as that within which Simcoe functioned, Berczy seems to have had a definite capacity for leadership, based more on personality than upon rule books.

Originally, he had agreed that his settlers would cut a road from Northumberland, Pennsylvania, toward the Genesee River and Lake Ontario. Berczy, however, had trouble with local authorities who badgered his settlement near Williamsburg, New York. Simcoe, in Upper Canada, ever alert for news of experienced settlers disgruntled with life in republican America, was kept well informed of these events. He wrote to Lord Dorchester on 2 December, 1793, that 'the Agent, Bertzie, is now in Jail, as I apprehend for overdrawing on his Employers, and it was with difficulty that Mr. Williamson escaped from falling a victim to the dissatisfaction of the German Settlers.'[47].

This Williamson, who was in danger of being scragged by Berczy's loyal followers, probably to Simcoe's delight, was Pulteney's representative in New York. Another of the tribe of ubiquitous Scotsmen, a former captain in the 25th Foot, he seems to have emigrated to America at some time in the late 1780s and, being the promoter of the wagon road that Berczy's Germans opened to Genesee, was heavily involved in land speculation. His first settlement in New York was quite simply and obviously named Williamsburg. Like many of his countrymen, Williamson tired of capering about in foreign parts and returned to Scotland in about 1800.

The prospect of large free land grants in the newly opened British territories to the north must have seemed a much more attractive alternative to what Berczy's group could expect in the United States. Simcoe liked to imagine the American settlers being oppressed by 'land jobbers'[48] and for his part, needed people to develop his new province; it was probably no accident that his brigade major, Littlehales, visited the Genesee settlement in the summer of 1793.[49]

After his break with the agents of Pulteney's enterprise, Berczy formed an association with the German company of Bremen-New York merchants. On 20 March, 1794, the German company petitioned the lieutenant-governor of Upper Canada with exorbitant hopes of being granted one million acres of real estate 'for the present and for more in the future . . .if possible situated on Lake Erie and from the Indian Lands extending West and North so as to comprehend the quantity.'[50] At the same time, Simcoe was protesting, perhaps too loudly to be believed by Lord Dorchester, that he had 'hitherto . . .taken no measures to forward this Emigration.'[51]

By any standards the German company's demand was presumptuous and excessive, perhaps the age-old trick of asking for the ridiculous in the hope of at least getting more than might normally be given; no harm in trying. Whatever the case, on 17 May, 1794, at a meeting with Berczy and his associates, the Executive Council of Upper Canada doled out the sizeable but customary grant of a 'tract of land to the extent of sixty-four thousand acres.'[52]

Berczy then wasted no time in writing to Simcoe for a clear set of guidelines for his followers, dropping a none-too-subtle hint in asking for 'Conditions to which they must submit themselves by settling this and other Tracts in future Time and they hope that it will be taken into Consideration the heavy Expences which they must undergo if they will effectually Succeed in the settlement of this and other Townships.'[53] Simcoe would hear quite a lot about those 'heavy Expences' as time went on.

This was followed up with a personal visit to Simcoe at Niagara early in June 1794, when the settlement terms were discussed. Simcoe, in pursuit of his own interests, here proposed that Berczy exchange the lands to be granted between Lake Erie and the river Thames for a tract of equal extent on Yonge Street in the rear of York, the intended seat of government.[54] Berczy agreed to this, and being pleased at the way in which his meeting with Simcoe was going, he revealed to the lieutenant-governor that he and his associates had already purchased land in Upper Canada in addition to the recent grant. This land comprised three townships and had been purchased from Andrew Pierce of Southbury, Connecticut; after obtaining the land in March 1793 from the government of Upper Canada, Pierce had had difficulty in raising the stipulated number of settlers. Simcoe, however, informed Berczy that he was already aware of the transaction.[55]

In the main, following Simcoe's plans for the development of the province, land would now be taken up in Markham Township, and Berczy's German settlers would become another road-building labour force. By the latter part of June the arrival of 'Bertzie with the Germans from the Genessees' was daily expected.[56] The migration was not to be as simple as it sounded.

Berczy, whose Williamsburg settlers were under an injunction not to leave New York State, evaded his opponents with clever stratagems. His followers were divided into several groups, some making their way on foot to Queenston, and others with the women, children, baggage, and transport to the mouth of the Genesee River where they embarked in boats for Niagara. Some of his original settlers may have deserted Berczy at this time; local people, however, joined in his trek for various reasons of their own, the most obvious being the chance to get free land in a place where, they hoped, government restrictions were as yet lax. With so many small groups moving through different locations, the local authorities were confused and outflanked, and Berczy's migration to Queenston, there to prepare for the final move to York, was successful.

Who were these settlers who would follow the Queen's Rangers in cutting the northward trail of Yonge Street? Berczy's detractors described them as the sweepings of the streets, the rabble of Hamburg. But no urban degenerates could have faced the rigours and uncertainties that beset Berczy's followers. Some 210 people, a mixed group of North Germans and Dutch, Hanoverian peasants, Swiss tradesmen, and families from Denmark and Schleswig-Holstein, went with Berczy to Genesee. Of this lot, about 186 made the move to Upper Canada, arriving at the end of June 1794, at Queenston above Niagara; from there they proceeded across the lake.

after a drawing by C.W. Jefferys.

"These Germans came on this summer, furnished with every thing to make their situation comfortable and enable them to improve their land to advantage, and no doubt in a short time will make a fine settlement."

(Letter from New York, 20 November, 1794.)

It was an organized move made by people who knew what they were about: 'Berczy had gained experience as a frontiersman, and he brought many of the necessities of life with him. They had horses, household equipment, axes, and tools. Their wagons were made with boxes that could be used as boats.'[57]

Such an influx of settlers along the newly surveyed line of Yonge Street could have sparked incidents with Indians not yet ready to accept such an invasion of their territory. A letter to Littlehales on 31 August, 1794, relayed information from the deputy surveyor, Augustus Jones, that 'during his survey in the winter, about the month of March, being at the house of an Indian Trader, John Culbertson by name, some Chippawas and Missassagas came and inquired of Wapinose, a Mississago, the business of the Surveyor—Wapinose made answer that he came to open a line for the benefit of trade, and that both parties would find the advantage from it in a short time. The Chippawas and Missassagas then said they had no knowledge of the sale of those lands, and at length began a dispute with Wapinose for accompanying the Surveyor.'[58] (Culbertson, or Cuthbertson, had a trading post at the south end of Lake Simcoe opposite present-day Nantyr.)

The same letter had news of a more disturbing nature. William Bond of the Queen's Rangers had settled upon a lot on the east side of Yonge Street where a branch of the Humber ran from its source near what is still known as Bond's Lake. In August 1794 he received word that 'three Mississagas or Chippewas came to the man he had left upon his lot making an improvement (about twenty miles in the rear of the town of York), and robbed him of all his provision, and even the shirt from off his back.'[59] The writer of the letter then noted that 'Mr. Bond in consequence of which says he shall write to his associates not to come into the Country.'

However much Bond may have been put out by these goings-on, nothing deterred Berczy and his associates from proceeding as planned. In his 'Narrative', Berczy tells how he began his 'exploratory journey' in late July 1794, 'and examined the land along Young [sic] Street, a road newly laid out towards Lake Leclay now called Lake Simcoe, as far as the spot destined for the building of Quilin-burg another new town in contemplation.'[60]

Simcoe may have been pleased with this forwarding of settlement in Upper Canada, but a good deal of umbrage was expressed in the United States, ever ready at that time to discover low cunning in every British scheme in North America. The *Gazette of the United States* of Philadelphia on 25 July, 1794, complained that 'the conduct of the British and the governor of Upper Canada has been carried of late to such a length, that their intentions to this country can no longer be concealed. We noticed in a former paper, that they had decoyed to their settlements a number of families who were under the most strict obligations to Mr. Williamson, who had advanced them an enormous sum.'[61]

At a time when relations between England and the United States were sensitive, and Jay's Treaty was being negotiated to settle the question of the western posts, these were fighting words. No doubt there were good grounds for such complaints, because Simcoe, with his distaste for American ways, could see no great wrong in luring settlers to Upper Canada. Simcoe, in fact, probably felt a glow of triumph at his one-upmanship over the republican ranks — a glow that blinded him to the possibility that he was just as likely to be a victim of 'landjobbers' and land-hungry opportunists, even if they were experienced in frontier life.

The cautious Dundas, faced with mounting American annoyance, became lukewarm, then chilly, in his response to Simcoe's enthusiasms, and warned him that 'there is every appearance of Settlers coming from thence [U.S.] in sufficient

Council-Office, Dec. 29, 1798.

YONGE-STREET.

NOTICE is hereby given to all persons settled, or about to settle on
YONGE-STREET, and whose *locations*
have not yet been confirmed by order of
the PRESIDENT in council, that before such
locations can be confirmed it will be expected that the following CONDITIONS
be complied with :

First. That within *twelve months* from the
time they are permitted to occupy
their respective lots, they do cause
to be erected thereon a good and
sufficient dwelling house, of at least
16 feet by 20 in the clear, and do
occupy the same in *Person,* or by a
substantial *Tenant.*

Second, THAT within the same period of
time, they do clear and fence *five*
acres, of their respective lots, in a
substantial manner.

Third, THAT within the same period of
time, they do open as much of the
Yonge-Street road as lies between
the front of their lots and the middle of said road, amounting to one
acre or thereabouts.

JOHN SMALL, C. E. C.

numbers, and of their own accord, without going out of your way to entice or allure them.'[62]

Simcoe was understandably miffed at this reaction to what he considered his patriotic efforts; it is perhaps true, however, that his zeal to settle his province led him to ignore many of the motives and realities of settlement. He was certainly naïve in his belief that settlers would flock in, attracted by the advantages offered by the benign rule of a beneficent Britannia — a Britannia whose servants would be regarded with increasing bitterness and distrust by Berczy. The majority of settlers undoubtedly came for the obvious attraction, large grants of free land; and who can blame them at a time when the greatest form of financial security was the possession of land?

To settlement along Yonge Street, however, Simcoe did attach some strings; they were evident in an announcement made by the acting surveyor general, D. W. Smith, in July 1794: 'Notice is hereby given to all persons who have obtained Assignments of Land ...on Yonge Street, leading from York to Lake Simcoe, that unless a Dwelling House shall be Built on every Lot under certificate of location and the same occupied within one year from the date of their respective assignments such lots will be forfeited.'[63]

The settlers on Yonge Street were required to clear the road along the quarter-mile frontage of their lots to the halfway mark of its sixty-six feet width allowance and to provide the means of transport.[64] The Yonge Street frontages were kept, it has been said, for settlers favoured by Simcoe, but in any event, with such conditions for occupancy of lots, the pattern of development along the road was bound to be erratic.

As Berczy would find to his cost, the British government in its tardy fashion also concocted some notions on the granting of land,[65] of which Simcoe did not seem to be aware at the time. A tighter rein was put on the procedures for granting land after Simcoe's departure from Canada in 1796, but even during his regime, when conditions were not met, landholders' pleas for consideration received scant sympathy. With Dorchester ever ready to scoff at his difficulties, Simcoe could not afford the luxury of leniency.

Simcoe made an arrangement with Berczy whereby the latter agreed to develop Yonge Street upon the withdrawal of the Queen's Rangers to garrison duty in August 1794. As Berczy described it in his 'Narrative': 'Near mid-way on Young Street between Lake Ontario and Quillinburg the provincial Government had reserved four lots of 200 acres each situated equally on both sides of the road, through which the River Don runs, to be sold for raising a fund to be employed towards making Young Street a practicable road for wagons. These four lots [Nos. 31 and 32 east and west sides of Yonge] he [Simcoe] offered me for that purpose.'[66]

The condition that Berczy accepted was that within one year from 15 September, 1794, he would lay out Yonge Street in the same manner as Dundas

Street, Simcoe's east-west military thoroughfare.[67] The existing part of Yonge Street would be improved, and the new road would be opened from Lot 29 as far as the pine fort at Holland River.[68] At the end of August, 1794, the able-bodied men from Berczy's group of settlers with an additional sixteen hired axemen from New York State established themselves in an encampment on the west bank of the Don near today's Queen Street.[69]

Although Simcoe grumbled openly in disgust at the withdrawal of the Queen's Rangers to be employed 'in the Protection of the Barrier Forts', he hinted in his official letters that he would succeed in spite of the bumbledom of his superiors: 'The Road to Hollands River was meant to have been opened this year. It is already sufficiently so, for the families who intended to reside there to go to their respective allotments, which are laid out in two hundred acres, adjacent to the Road, and bounded by it, and expressly granted on the Condition of absolute occupation and building.'[70]

Berczy's start was auspicious, and during October Yonge Street was improved between York and Lot 29 where the Johnson family had settled. It was not an easy task: 'From York to No. 28 the Road is difficult to finish being the mountainous part of that Country. The Road till now is cut out till No. 33 or 34. At No. 31 it is absolutely necessary to make a middling large Bridge over the Creek which crosses the Road and where now . . .Horses and Chattles must pass with Difficulty, the Banks being high and the soil soft and muddy wher Creatures falls in very deep.'[71]

Progress from there may be measured in a letter written by Berczy to the acting surveyor general, David Smith, at the end of November, 1794: 'Till now I have finished on Yonge Street only till Lott No. 36, but . . .I will this winter continue the work on Yonge Street the more as I have already begun to build and cleare on Lotts Nr 53 & 51 East of Yonge Street of which the settler oppen now the Road so far as to bring through a slaide. . . . .That piece of Road from York till Johnson I have great deal altered and till now reduced so far that I would already send 3 wagon loaded with goods & provisions till Johnson. . . .It was a great deal work to do and I hope that with some not great expences that piece of Yonge Street can be entire perfectioned next Spring . . . .The piece of Yonge Street from No 29 to River Holland which I have engaged to oppen on my own expences shall soon be performed as good as Circumstances will possibly admit.'[72]

Yonge Street, then, was cleared sufficiently to be used as a wagon road as far as Lot 35 in the region of Langstaff and partly cut to the area of Bond's Lake where Bond's hired man had been harassed by Indians. The job was a private venture, and Berczy, as can be seen from his remarks, was increasingly concerned with 'expences'. Summing up his activity, he noted that 'the remainder of October all November and part of December [1794] I employed in making Yonge Street practable with the assistance of my settlers and not at a small expence.'[73]

Sir,

Mr Secretary Littlehales having informed me, that my Report of the 15th of August, was approved by His Excellency the Lieutenant Governor, and it having been submitted therein, to complete the Survey between York & Lake Simcoe, to the extent of the Purchase from the Indians, you will proceed to York for the purpose of Surveying so much of that Tract, as is comprehended within the Township of York ......

(Survyr Genl the Honble D.W. Smith to Surveyor Augustus Jones, 27 November, 1795).

His Excellency was pleased to direct me, previous to my surveying the Township of York, to proceed along Yonge Street, to survey and open a cart-road from the harbour at York to Lake Simcoe ...... Mr. Pearse is to be with me in a few days' time with a detachment of about thirty of the Queen's Rangers, who are to assist in opening the said road.   (Surveyor Augustus Jones to Survyr Genl the Honble D.W. Smith, 24 December, 1795).

A wagon road meant in reality little more than a narrow path following the most natural route, marked only by the stumps of the trees that had been cut down to clear the way. Nevertheless, it was a beginning, and Simcoe, who was not so much concerned with 'expences', would write enthusiastically on 10 November, 1794, to the Duke of Portland, Dundas's successor as secretary of state: 'The Trader [Cowan] who lives at Matchadosh has had Cattle driven to him this Spring from York in six days & nearly half the road on Yonge Street is allotted to settlers.'[74]

And in the following month, with an eye to the importance that official circles attached to the prospects of trade encouraged by settlement through his province, he announced on a bouyant Christmas note to the Committee of the Privy Council for Trade and Plantations: 'It is with great pleasure that I am to observe that Seventy families at the least are settling in [York's] Vicinity, and principally on the Communication between that Town and Holland River, which falls into Lake Simcoe.'[75]

In an earlier, exhaustive effusion, he had emphasized to the committee that trade routes could flourish as settlement increased: 'By a road of two & Thirty miles thro' an excellent Country for Agriculture, [York] has a Communication with Hollands River, navigable for large Boats across Lake aux Claies or Sheeniong, (now Simcoe in respect to my Father's memory), to where by a Portage of five miles well adapted for settlement, (as I am credibly informed), it Communicates with a River which flows with few Obstructions into Matchadosh or Gloucester Bay . . .Lake Simcoe is capable of admitting any Vessels and its banks afford birch of sufficient size for the largest Canoes, an Object as stated to be of great importance to the Merchants [in the Fur Trade].'[76]

By late November, 1794, Berczy's followers had been settled in temporary huts or they shuddered in the shelter of tents as they suffered through the winter and attempted to build more permanent homes in budding Markham Township. Fevers, aches, and illness with only Berczy's well-meant but amateur doctoring were their lot.

Lieutenant-Governor Simcoe, at any rate, seemed well enough pleased by the way things were going. Berczy records in his 'Narrative' that 'in the latter part of November [1794] the Governor came for a short time to York as then I had already finished a great part of Young Street. . . .'[77] In token of his appreciation of Berczy's efforts, Simcoe offered him a position as magistrate, which was declined, and an appointment as captain in the militia. The latter commission seems not to have been officially recognized until 16 July, 1796.

A traveller in Upper Canada formed a rather rapturous impression of the Markham settlement and described it as follows in a letter: 'On the east side and joining the rear of these lots [along Yonge Street] is a settlement of near one hundred German families, on an excellent tract of land, much of which is open, white oak woods; these Germans came on this summer, furnished with every thing to make their situation comfortable and enable them to improve their land to advantage, and no doubt in a short time will make a fine settlement.'[78]

This rustic idyll, however, was not to become a 'fine settlement' but a bog of bickering and adversity and suspicion. Berczy's ideas for his settlement were not quite what Simcoe had in mind. Berczy was not tied to any notions of an imperial design, but followed instead the line of individual initiative. As a result of this he proposed to Simcoe that a canal be built to connect the Rouge, or Nen River as Berczy called it, and the Holland River, with wharves and storehouses at the mouth of the Rouge to handle the traffic of trade goods for Lake Ontario and Lake Huron. Simcoe listened with interest to the proposals and encouraged Berczy with an offer of land allotments on the Rouge to develop the scheme.[79]

Berczy's hopes were soon to be dashed when he learned from the surveyor general at Niagara in July 1795 that 'the lands given me by the Governor on the River Nen, were already granted in the greatest part to another person, two years before, and especially that part lying immediately at the outlet. . . .'[80] In spite of this unpleasant jolt, Berczy was 'still perfectly satisfied concerning the rectitude of the Governor's intentions,' but he blamed the British government for making rash promises that were misleading in regard to policies for land settlement.

Simcoe was basically an honest man, but as already seen in his attempts to encourage settlers away from the Americans, he was not overscrupulous in his efforts to realize his ambitions for Upper Canada. The suspicion that Simcoe's intentions were not as unselfish as Berczy imagined is hard to avoid.

No great insight was needed to realize that Berczy's idea, if carried out, might divert prospective trade routes and settlers away from York and Yonge Street to the area of Markham. Simcoe could not allow anything that might detract from his own grand design, and it is entirely possible that he deliberately and unfeelingly scuppered Berczy's scheme by reserving the land at the mouth of the Rouge for the government of Upper Canada.[81] Simcoe certainly became something of an 'elusive Pimpernel' whenever Berczy tried to have a meeting with him after this.

The parting of the ways had begun for Simcoe and Berczy. The breach widened during 1795 when cold, shortage of food and supplies, and finally mosquitoes spread illness among Berczy's labourers so that the contract to clear Yonge Street through to Lake Simcoe within a year could not be carried out. Berczy struggled gamely and desperately to keep his settlement going, but the odds continued to gather against him. 'Expences' became a nightmare. The government had provisions for its own forces, but these were not to be distributed as largesse to the settlers. Anything obtained from the government had to be paid for, and Berczy went to considerable lengths to obtain supplies and credit for his settlers. There is a mounting note of desperation in the appeals that he made to Littlehales and Simcoe: 'Your petitioner thinks it proper to state that many of his associates are almost starving, that since the month of September last none of them have had any flour. . . .'[82] Early in March, 1796, Berczy prevailed upon

Simcoe to give him an order on the king's military store of provisions for rice, peas, and pork, flour being scarce even in the garrison. In return, he gave a personal bond to the commissary and a mortgage upon his lands in the province.[83]

During that famine winter of 1795-96, about one third of Berczy's Markham settlers went back to Niagara. Simcoe's issue of government provisions in March 1796 to prevent starvation met with sour comments from Dorchester.[84] In all probability, he took the short view that much of the problem was Simcoe's own fault and he would not miss an opportunity to say 'I told you so' — after all, Simcoe had brought the settlers in before the province could absorb them adequately.

The savour of sourness spread in April and May of 1796 as Simcoe cancelled grants of land to leaders of township settlements because of irregular procedures. Some of these leaders had sold or rented their grants, others failed to meet conditions, and in some instances the red tape of the home government's belated attempts to establish clear rules for land occupation created hopeless tangles. The confusion signalled the end for Berczy's plans.

A report of the Committee of the Executive Council of Upper Canada, chaired by Peter Russell, the receiver-general, delivered the blow in July 1796: 'The Committee beg leave to recommend that the four Lots [31 and 32, east and west sides of Yonge] originally appropriated and under assignment for Mr. Berczy on Condition that he laid out Yonge Street in the same Manner as Dundas Street, and Compleated the same one Year from the 15th of September, 1794, may be sold for whatever sum they may bring and the Money applied for the expences incurred in opening Yonge Street — or they may be otherwise disposed of to reimburse Government, and as Mr. Berczy has justly forfeited his claim to those Lots from a failure in the Conditions, but has been at some Expence in endeavouring to carry them into Execution, until he was obliged to stop by the Sickness of the Labourers he had employed on that service — It is recommended by the Committee to Your Excellency to grant Mr. Berczy such a Portion of Land elsewhere in remuneration as Yr Excellency may judge proper.'[85]

By that summer of 1796 both Simcoe and Berczy found the taste of failure galling their enterprising spirits. Simcoe, who had intended that Upper Canada should become the 'Bulwark of the British Empire'[86] against any threats to English institutions in North America, saw his ideas for defence, settlement, and organization thwarted by his superiors and stalled by official indifference.

The manner in which his Corps of Queen's Rangers was used, or as he saw it, abused, was perhaps the sorest point. In October 1794, Dorchester had forbidden Simcoe to employ the Rangers in civil tasks. This veto, however, was moderated after the signing of Jay's Treaty between England and the United States on 19 November, 1794, whereby England would at last evacuate the garrisons from the western posts; it was a tardy proceeding that was not completed until the summer of 1796.

The ban on the Rangers performing civil jobs was lifted only on condition that the transport of government goods and stores would not in any way be hindered by such a concession. Simcoe, who tended to be bull-headed on the subject of his precious Rangers, would not consider this offer from Dorchester, believing that the home government would fully support *his* plans for the Queen's Rangers.[87] The government did not, and Dorchester then continued to draw upon the Queen's Rangers for military duties at Detroit and Niagara.

Simcoe persevered in spite of the restrictions resulting from the loss of his troops, and he pressed on doggedly with Yonge Street and his goal of opening 'the Road to Hollands River,' even though a year or more had passed since his original 1794 deadline. With Berczy's failure to accomplish much in 1795, Simcoe resorted to what few soldiers remained at York. Mrs. Simcoe noted in her diary on 28 December, 1795, that 'a party began today to cut a road hence to the Pine Fort near L. Simcoe.'[88]

This party was a group of the Queen's Rangers working under the direction of the deputy surveyor, Augustus Jones, who completed the opening of Yonge Street as far as Holland Landing by about 16 February, 1796. At that time of year it must have been a sodden, chilling, thankless task, but perseverance, discipline, or both, won out. Simcoe's road north from York to a connection with Lake Huron was now established.

A letter from Major Littlehales to John McGill, the commmissary, on 18 January, 1796, intimates that His Excellency, the lieutenant-governor, desired a sleigh with two weeks' provisions to be sent to Mr. Johnson's on Yonge Street for the Rangers who were opening the road to Lake Simcoe.[89] This was probably Asa Johnson, who at that time was settled on the west side, Lot 29, almost at what is now Thornhill. What a boon such provisions would have been to Berczy, if he could have obtained them without 'expence'.

Always one to press home a point, and to stress the need for the Rangers in those tasks for which he personally had envisaged them, Simcoe informed the Duke of Portland on 27 February, 1796, that 'the Road from York to the Head Waters of Lake Huron has been opened by the Soldiers. . . .'[99]

Although contemporary accounts described it as a road or a street, Yonge Street was in reality a pathway through the woods, winding along the land contours to avoid the swamps in the area of York Mills and Newtonbrook. North of Bond's Lake, or Pond as it was known, the way continued to be a 'pioneer route.'[91] The southern portion of the street, below Yorkville, was virtually impassable. Travellers from York had to head north along Parliament Street, which had been cut by the Rangers to Castle Frank in 1796, and then make a 'wide sweep' west to reach the navigable part of Yonge.[92]

Mrs. Simcoe relates that in March 1796 'an Indian & a Canadian came from Matchadosh Bay in five days [to York], & said they could have travelled the journey in four. We rode up the Yonge Street & across a pine ridge to C. Frank.'

And at the end of that month: 'Walked to C. Frank & returned by Yonge Street from whence we rode. The road is as yet very bad, there are pools of water among roots of trees, & fallen logs in swampy spots, & these pools being half frozen render them still more disagreeable when the horses plunge into them.'[93]

By June 1796, only about 145 of the Queen's Rangers remained in Upper Canada for Simcoe's work. By then, however, any remarks that Simcoe might have had to make on Yonge Street and his soldiers would have been Parthian shots. In December 1795 he had requested of the Duke of Portland that he be granted a leave of absence on the grounds of ill-health. Failing that, he said, his only alternative would be resignation. There can be no doubt that at the time Simcoe was a sick man; his ill-health was already evident in a portrait that Berczy is believed to have painted. How much of his illness was brought on by frustration and disappointment can only be guessed.

At least 'Authority' was graceful enough to grant the request for a leave of absence, although the Duke of Portland's letter of 9 April, 1796, bearing this news did not reach Simcoe until early in July. From then on, events moved quickly. Peter Russell, the receiver-general, was sworn in as administrator of Upper Canada and successor to Simcoe on 21 July. On the same day, Simcoe and his family left York. It is ironic that when he finally sailed from Quebec, his ship should pass in the St. Lawrence the vessel bringing back Sir John Johnson, the man who in 1792 had quitted Upper Canada in a huff at Simcoe's appointment as lieutenant-governor.

Berczy was now left at York without, as he said, obtaining anything positive in the way of assistance from Simcoe. Some of Berczy's notions on politics — perhaps more practical for a new, struggling colony than were Simcoe's — may have seemed dangerously liberal to the latter. Even had he been sympathetic, Simcoe's job was to serve the system that employed him, not to introduce political novelties. He had enough trouble foisting his other schemes on the home government without trying to sell it a blueprint for colonial administration.

It is difficult now to decide whether Simcoe was embarrassed by the difficulties that beset Berczy, or whether he deliberately sought to avoid him, having found him to be of less assistance to his schemes than he'd at first imagined. Certainly Peter Russell, who at the outset had been favourably inclined toward Berczy, changed his attitude when he was persuaded that Berczy's backers were American land-speculators. Russell, an Irish gentleman who had been military secretary to General Clinton, was not happy at the thought of such backers pushing people with their own republican sentiments into Upper Canada.[94]

After Simcoe's departure, Berczy continued his campaign to have his claims recognized. In October 1796 he set out for Niagara in the hope that he might at least obtain from the executive council 'the so long time withheld patent for 64,000 acres of land.' Instead, he wrote, he was informed by the president of the council 'that in consequence of an Act of the British Parliament it was out of their power to give to me or any of my settlers, a patent or possession of lands, before we had for seven consecutive years resided in one of the British Colonies without absenting for more than two months at one time — BEING ALIENS.'[95] His purchase of townships from Andrew Pierce was declared invalid, as was his commission in the militia: only an acknowledged British subject could hold the latter.

Berczy felt by the end of 1796 that he had been grossly deceived by the council whom he accused of falsifying a copy of the order that granted him and his associates a tract of 64,000 acres in May 1794. He resolved to go to England 'to prove the reality of the settlement which [he] had established in Upper Canada,'[96] but he did not leave until the summer of 1799. In 1802, after adventures that included being shipwrecked in the Bay of Chaleur and a winter trek from there to Quebec on snowshoes, he returned to Canada, a bitter and disappointed man. He eked out a living as a portrait painter in Montreal from 1803 until his death in 1813 during a journey to New York. The journey, undertaken in circumstances that seem mysterious and at a time of British-American warfare, brings to question Berczy's loyalties and motives.

For Simcoe, there would be no honours. In spite of the grandly named Lord Simcoe Hotel on University Avenue in Toronto, there was in fact no peerage, not so much as a knighthood. When he died in 1806, however, he was on his way to take up another onerous Imperial duty as commander-in-chief in India. He never returned to Canada, and although his new province there may have developed along lines very different from those anticipated by the staunchly authoritarian, aristocracy-biased soldier-administrator, his tremendous energy had in short time laid a firm foundation for whatever might develop.

Of Simcoe's successor, Peter Russell, it was said that 'he was more anxious to acquire lands than to make roads.'[97] However that may be, he was soon lamenting his new responsibilities and a lack of local activity in a letter to the chief justice of Upper Canada, William Osgoode: 'The withdrawing of the two Regiments from this Province and the great desertions from the Queen's Rangers have reduced our Military assistance so low, that all public & private works are at a stand.'[98] The future growth of Yonge Street would now lie with the settlers or whoever might be found to put up the money for its development.

Chapter Two

Settlement and Trade (1796-1811)

Both Simcoe and Berczy were energetic, capable men, but as they saw the problems of Upper Canada from different angles, their ideas developed along divergent lines. Simcoe was concerned above all with military requirements — the need for defence against threats or influence from the United States. This was Britannia's bulwark behind which settlers would be encouraged to shelter. Berczy was concerned with the more immediate business of land development and the prosperity and conditions that would attract more settlers and so increase the value of the settlement. Military matters were not ones to loom large in the minds of those whose main purpose was the acquisition and improvement of land.

The settlers themselves were a mixed bag of American Loyalists — German-speaking Pennsylvania 'Dutch' artisans and peasant farmers, political and religious refugees, and some few moderately well-to-do individuals. Many of them were slightingly regarded by those of an earlier exodus as 'late Loyalists'. Among the more affluent were some who belonged to what was perhaps the most privileged group of settlers — those Loyalists who had held officer rank in the British forces during the American War of Independence.

All had one ambition: to make most of the opportunity to establish themselves on the free lands in Upper Canada. They came to put down roots, to carve something of their very own from the wilderness. In this firm determination they set themselves as a breed apart from the administrators, soldiers, traders, and adventurers who passed through Upper Canada, transients on the path of empire, as had Simcoe's retinue.

If there was any support from the settlers for Simcoe's imperial ideas, it came from the Loyalists, particularly the officer class, who had little sympathy for the republican shenanigans across the border. To them grants of land in Upper

Canada were a reward for their services or a compensation for their losses in the American war. In consequence, they were not always ideal settlers, preferring on occasion to make a good cash profit by selling some of their property to later arrivals.

By 1796 the flow of Loyalists to Upper Canada had become a dribble, and the people who now came into the country for the most part had no particular loyalty one way or the other. That shrewd, stingy, Irish rascal, old Peter Russell, who was quite happy to grant land 'from Peter Russell to Peter Russell', didn't mince words in his expression of 'the futility of the Mode he [Simcoe] had espoused for the peopling of his Province, and the Justness of Our Opinion that the Applicants for Townships had no other Object in View than the raising a little Money for themselves by selling their Pretentions to others.'[99] Russell did nothing for his popularity by having the lists of United Empire Loyalists revised, restricting their claims for privileges.

Two property-dealing Loyalist ex-officers were Captain Richard Lippincott and Captain Daniel Cozens, both from New Jersey, who received the 3,000 acres apiece to which they were entitled in the mid-Yonge, Markham-Vaughan area. They then, in the words of Peter Russell, raised 'a little Money' by selling a good portion of these grants to Pennsylvanian settlers in the region.

A less adept veteran, who was gradually bogged down in financial difficulties, was Frederic, Baron de Hoen, or von Hoen, formerly an officer in a Hessian regiment during the American war. He took up and farmed the land on Lot 1 on the west side of Yonge Street at Eglinton in addition to land in the Whitchurch area. Melchior Quantz, who performed the duties of schoolmaster in Berczy's Markham settlement, had also been with the Hessian troops in America; Sommerfeldt and Boyes, from the same group, were Prussian ex-soldiers.

It would not be surprising if the latter were looked upon with some coolness by the loyalists who felt that they had sacrificed a great deal in a cause that the Hessians and others had taken up as soldiers-of-fortune or mercenaries. Opportunists they may have been, but they were not quitters; Quantz and Sommerfeldt were among those who stayed on after many of Berczy's settlers had given up the struggle and drifted away in 1796.

Perhaps of the most immediate and practical value to the new colony were those who were encouraged by Simcoe to come to his province to work as artisans on government projects. On 31 May, 1793, the lieutenant-governor wrote to Alured Clarke: 'Upon this River [the Don] the Banks of which are covered with excellent Timber I propose to construct as soon as possible a Saw Mill, principally for the benefit of the Settlement. ...'[100]

As with many of his proposals, he did not hang fire, waiting for some cautious official to come to a tardy conclusion on the wisdom of his 'enthusiasm'. Apparently, even before his letter to Clarke, Simcoe signed a document dated 29 April, 1793, granting permission to bring in free of duty from the U.S.A. the household goods, clothing, and chests of Nicholas Miller, Asa Johnson, Jacob Phillips, Abraham and Isaac Devins, and Jacob Schooner.[101] These artisans came from the Genesee area of New York State and were, for the most part, German-speaking and either known to or related to each other.

At first they lived in the area of the Humber River, about three miles from the lake, where Simcoe had decided to build his sawmill in preference to the Don River. They were soon at work under Miller's direction, and Simcoe could report to the Duke of Richmond on 23 September, 1793: 'A Saw Mill is building for the Government at a most convenient spot within three miles of the post & from which I propose to supply all such materials as may be wanted at any post on Lake Ontario at the Cheapest rate.'[102] This was the king's sawmill on the Humber, and it was followed by other mills on the Don and its tributaries, built by enterprising settlers from the Genesee area.

Their work on government jobs around York gave these settlers an opportunity to decide upon a good area in which to take up land for settlement. Nicholas Miller, for one, seems not to have been as conscientious in his job as hoped,[103] but on 25 May, 1794, he petitioned the lieutenant-governor 'to grant him a lot of land No 34 on the east side of the road that is newly opened above York.'[104] Asa Johnson also applied for a grant of land on Yonge Street at about the same time.

It is difficult at this stage to separate the facts from the legend. Some old stories suggest that Miller and his family and possibly others lived in wigwams on the untamed Yonge Street before being established definitely on their lots.[105] If the stories are any indication, their experiences were certainly no picnic; potatoes were their main crop and the staple of their diet at the time.[106] The first recorded log hut was that of Asa Johnson, who moved onto Lot 29 on the west side of Yonge Street about the time of Berczy's arrival in Upper Canada in 1794. Johnson, who with hard-headed frontier sense later married the widow of Nathan Chapman on the adjoining Lot 28, was closely followed in settlement by Nicholas Miller on Lot 34 on the east side.

Miller continued to live up to his name and set up the first gristmill in the area. It was a contraption that the settlers had devised from the Indian method of pounding corn in a hollowed-out tree stump. A heavy weight, such as a block of wood, was hung on a long pole set at right angles across the top of a notched post. The corn, which was placed in the hollow stump, was pounded by the weight either falling at the end of a rope or being swung down on the end of the pole, which acted as a lever or sweep.[107]

In those days, before the clearing of the country, the volume and waterpower of the Don River was much greater than it is now, and it obviously offered opportunities for people experienced in the milling business. John Lyons, a relative or acquaintance of Nicholas Miller (just which is unclear), followed him

"In the stump of an oak tree, he hollowed out a space in which the grain could be placed; then a high post was erected with a crotched top which held a long cross-piece; from one end of the cross-piece a heavy block of wood was hung directly over the stump; this block was pulled up with a rope, then let go crashing down on the grain to reduce it to flour." *(A History of Vaughan Township – G. Elmore Reaman, p. 214.)*

from New York State in 1794 and settled at York. From there he moved north to Lot 32 on the east side of Yonge in about 1796. He built the first sawmill on the Middle Don where it crossed Yonge Street at Thornhill in 1801.[108]

The Berczy settlers also put up sawmills and gristmills on the East Don, no doubt with assistance from Miller and his associates. A road was cut toward these mills from Yonge at Thornhill, and the settlement there came to be known as German Mills. The provincial surveyor, D. W. Smith, remarked in his *Gazeteer*, published in 1799, that the Markham area had 'good mills and a thriving settlement of Germans'.[109]

For the settlers the task of taking their grain, often on their backs, to a mill for grinding was a formidable one. It had to be carried along winding, stump-strewn paths through the forest, usually for distances of several miles, before it could be made into flour. The grinding was done on a barter system whereby the miller took an agreed amount of flour in return for the use of his mill. Sometimes the settler would stay overnight with the miller's family before starting the long trek back to his farm.

The wives of these early pioneer settlers had to be every bit as hardy as their menfolk. A favourite story was that of Mrs. Lyons' carrying close to 180 pounds of wheat on her back for almost a mile to the nearest mill, to the amazement of the three men who had made up the bag of wheat for milling.[110]

A hint of the hardships that the settlers had to accept can be found in an account by Sommerfeldt, one of Berczy's settlers: 'Then we got to York and I had the fever every other day. When I was well I made me a sled. Late in the fall, he [Berczy?] let me have a yoke of oxen. Then I got under way, and also my wife, who carried one child on the back and drove the pigs. Between Christmas and New Year I came to my land, there I had to stay in the tent till spring [1795]. In that time we three went together and chopped and brought wood together and built houses. In the spring we moved in.'[111]

Another memory of those days was related to the Reverend Isaac Fidler in 1832 by his landlady at his lodgings in Thornhill, where he had come to take up the ministry: 'Our landlady was a widow, and had come originally from New York. She was one of the United States Loyalists, and the second or third person who settled at Thornhill. This was at a time when Yonge Street was no better than a continuous forest, and a foot-path, or at most a horse-path, was their only road. At that period [1796-8], their wheat had to be carried through forests, or by water, fifty or sixty miles, before it could be converted into flour; and letters might remain for six months in the Post Office at York, before they could be forwarded to the proper persons.'[112]

Obviously the 'fifty or sixty miles' was a wild flight of the imagination and a clear example of the danger of relying on word-of-mouth information. Nevertheless, it probably *seemed* to be all of fifty miles to those who had to make the journey to the mills. Not only was the road, or what passed for one, rough trudging, but there were also bears and wolves at large in the forests. (In 1809, Lieutenant Fawcett of the 100th Regiment came upon a large bear on the south end of Yonge Street and cut its head open with his sword.) The going government bounty was ten dollars for a bear's scalp and twenty dollars for that of a wolf, although the prices seem to have varied at the whim of the bounty payer.[113] On the other hand, there was the advantage that the wild life offered a fair range of game to anyone who was a good marksman.

Old tales, too, relate that the Indians would often provide the settlers with deer meat in token of friendship or in return for presents of knives and other implements. These tales, however heart-warming, are offset by the complaints from the Indians that promises made to them by the officials with whom they made the land deals had not been kept. While declaring a friendship for Simcoe, they brought it to his attention that 'the new settlers drove them away like dogs.'[114]

A moot point, but there were the incidents already mentioned — at Cuthbertson's trading post during Jones's survey and at Bond's Lake. Bread, a precious commodity for the settler, was sometimes stolen from the outdoor ovens by Indians, who could be dangerous customers when drunk unless their women were around to prevent serious trouble.

There were still large areas of land over which no agreement of purchase had been made with the Indians. From Etobicoke to Burlington along Lake Ontario, the Indians were still in possession, as at Matchedash where Simcoe, in spite of his intentions, had never secured a clear title to the land.[115]

To the imperialistic mind such as Simcoe's, water routes with advantages for strategy and trade were perhaps of greater consequence than land itself, however great its potential for cultivation. For the settler, the rivers provided power for their mills and, in the case of the Don where it crossed Yonge Street, an abundance of fish; they were also a means of transport often superior to the crude roads of the day. Berczy's settlers used the river Rouge as their highway to the lake shore, to which it offered easier access than did Yonge Street.

Nevertheless, to help with the work on Yonge Street was almost an obligation upon which Simcoe insisted. Miller and Lyons may well have assisted in the opening of the road, perhaps by providing oxen or sleighs for the work. Isaac Devins probably worked as an axeman for Berczy in the attempts to continue work on Yonge Street in January 1795 — work that finally ground to a halt and thereby shattered Berczy's plans. Devins was listed with a small group that set out to open the 'Road till Mundshauer.'

Balthasar Mundschauer or, as he later became, Balsar Munshaw[116] was one of the pioneer axemen who followed Berczy from the Genesee and settled on Yonge Street, probably in the region of Elgin Mills. In 1796 he was persuaded by Nicholas Miller to move farther south to Lot 35 on the east side of Yonge. Here he developed a flourishing farm and holding following his relocation.

Although the land along Yonge Street in the area of Berczy's settlement had a good potential for farms, the most sought-after lots seem to have been those that were closer to York itself, York being the proposed seat of government and the hub of what activity there was in the new province.

The business of the administrators and officials at York was to govern, not farm. A number of them had farms outside the town, but these were more in the way of being an investment than a business. Although they may on occasion have chosen to putter among the cabbages like Cincinnatus, farming was neither their livelihood nor main çoncern. Naturally, and for practical reasons, those closely connected with Simcoe or involved in his administration would seek to obtain lots in the town itself.

In the grants of land patents in 1797 and 1798 at York, this group figures

Liste of the Settlers which I brought in the Province of Upper Canada in the Month of June 1794 & which I settled in the County of York in the Townships of Markham Nov: 1794.

#	Name	Conce/ Sion	Lott	#	Name	Conce/ Sion	Lott
1	Philippson	I	26	34	John Geister	III	18
2	Seiffer	I	25	35	John Rumohr	III	17
3	John Yohnetten	I	23	36	Buhrmester	III	15
4	John Boye	I	22	37	John Henry Schultz	III	14
5	Nicolaus Henry Hubner	I	21	38	Schütze	III	13
6	Stöber	I	19	39	Peter Lindemann	III	10
7	Bukendahl died march 1795 & left his widow & children which lives Since on the farm	I	18	40	Conrad Wagner	III	7
8	Dederic Banse after a residence of two years in the Settlement went abroad but intents to return Soon	I	17	41	Francis Brumstedt after two years Residence went abroad but intents to return Soon	III	8
9	Peter Philippsen	I	15	42	John Kramer	IV	24
10	Joachim Lunau	I	14	43	George Koopmann	IV	23
11	Melchior Quantz	I	13	44	Stöber	IV	20
12	Francis Dunn	I	11	45	John Stephens	IV	22
13	Peter Dining	I	10	46	Frederic Stamm	IV	19
14	John Gretmann	I	8	47	Jacob Bötger	IV	18
15	Nelson	I	7	48	Wichur	IV	17
16	John Dietzmann died in the month of Oct: 1795 and left his family on the farm	II	24	49	Marcus Rumohr	IV	16
17	Jacob Ebers in the month of June 1795 listed in the Regiment of the Royal Canadians	II	23	50	Frederic Busch	IV	14
18	Schmelter died march 1795 and left his orfan Son which is educated on acct of the Co	II	22	51	William Busch	IV	13
19	Peter Holst	II	20	52	George Sigmund Liebrich	IV	10
20	Powel Philippsen	II	19	53	Charles Vogel	IV	7
21	Mary Tempel widow & Children	II	18	54	Hageman died & left his family	IV	6
22	Peter Ernst	II	17	55	John Dubrey	V	26
23	Christian Ritter	II	16	56	George Pingel	V	25
24	Francis Schmidt	II	14	57	Frederic Sommerfeld	V	25
25	John Ulsen	II	15	58	Joachim Pingel	V	22
26	John Longenhorst	II	12	59	Stephen	V	21
27	John Machofsky	II	10	60	Christian Husing	V	19
28	Christian Schröder	II	9	61	Cornelius	V	18
29	Löcke Died June 1795 left his Children	II	7	62	Emilius Westphalen	V	17
30	Jacob Meissner	III	23	63	John Henry Bötger	V	15
31	William Neuschultz	III	22	64	Bauer	V	14
32	Wünsch	III	21	65	Spannaus	V	13
33	Henry Tiede	III	19	66	Engelhardt Helmke	V	8
				67	Philipp Ekhardt	V	7
				68	John Henry Pingel	VI	22
				69	Michel Houser died in the Settlement indebted to the Co in the month of Jan: 1795	VI	23
				70	Wm Berczy		10.11.
				71	Joachim Joson died at Newark indebted to the Co		
				72	Jacob Wintee		
				73	Bathasar Mundthausen Settled afterwards on Yonge Street		
				74	Christian Hendrichsen		
				75	George Hall Settled afterward in Whitby		

Newark 4th Nov: 1796   William Berczy prominently, and several notable names appear, headed by the lieutenant-governor himself. Others are Peter Russell, McGill, Macaulay, D. W. Smith, Robinson, Macdonnell, and Shank. Although Simcoe wished to encourage settlers 'of the right sort' in Upper Canada, his dreams for the province were to be given substance by British leaders and British government — none but the bulldog breed for Simcoe in the direction of his colony.

Something of Simcoe's attitude, then prevalent among British officers, may be seen in a letter of a contemporary, Vice-Admiral Sir Cuthbert Collingwood, who commanded Nelson's Lee Squadron at Trafalgar: 'In my ship's company I have some of all the states of Germany, Poles, Croats and Hungarians — a motley tribe.' The officers of this motley mob, however, were British, as was the 'tone' that they set. So it was with Simcoe. There would be no objection to the settlers being enrolled in the militia, or even to Berczy holding a captaincy in their organization. Berczy's 1796 lists of men suitable for the militia included Nicholas Miller, John and Thomas Lyons, the Johnsons, and, at a later date, Munshaw.[117] Baron de Hoen, the Hessian ex-officer, also held a captaincy of one of the York militia companies.

Simcoe, in common with most professional soldiers, had no great enthusiasm for the militia, counting rather on the regular troops to give drive and purpose sufficient to carry the militiamen along. The British Government was not prepared to go as far even as Simcoe in granting a militia commission to Berczy because of his 'alien' status. Their decision to withdraw Simcoe's offer was no doubt based on the rumours that Berczy was influenced by political backers in America.

If any preference was shown to Americans by the lieutenant-governor, it was to those Loyalists who had seen active service in the War of Independence or to those with undoubtedly British origins. Examples of the extensive land grants to military officers according to their rank have already been evident in the cases of Lippincott and Cozens. Several people with Loyalist or British affiliations were settled along Yonge Street on lots running north from number one at Eglinton to the north side Lot 25 at Steeles Avenue.

The Kendrick brothers — Duke, Hiram, John, and Joseph — were well known for their skill as sailors and had been pilots on the Lakes during the American war. Joseph was captain of the schooner *Peggy,* but he and his brothers also worked as contractors and house builders. They settled on Lots 6, 7, 8, and 9 on the west side of Yonge Street. Hiram, in 1797, sold his Lot 8 to Seneca Ketchum, whose family came up from New York, first to Kingston, then to York, determined to be near the seat of government.

Thomas Mercer was a Loyalist of Irish origin who made his way from Pennsylvania to York by wagon in 1794 and took up land on Lot 10, east of Yonge. Then there were, of course, the inevitable Scots. Cornelius Anderson, after serving with the British troops in America, migrated to New Brunswick;

from there, like many other Loyalists, he moved to Upper Canada. He arrived in York at about the same time as Mercer, and he settled on Lot 11, west of Yonge. Typical of the enterprising Caledonian merchant was Samuel Heron who went from New York City to Niagara and then to York, where he opened a shop in 1796. By 1797 he was on Lot 9, east of Yonge, eventually setting up sawmills and gristmills and, to the delight of his drouthy countrymen, a distillery.[118]

A notable exception to this Loyalist-British pattern, and perhaps the most enterprising of them all, was a character by the name of Abner Miles, or Mihells as he originally wrote it. He came up from the Genesee to York in 1794 and set up a store and tavern-hostel in the budding town. A shrewd and thrifty businessman, he was soon doing a comparatively roaring trade in the area. He sold cattle to Berczy, supplied him with lumber for the German Mills project, and imported meat and dairy produce to the embryo capital. As business boomed, he expanded his activities, moving in 1801 to Lot 45 east on Yonge Street, where he owned close to 1,000 acres in Markham and Vaughan townships. Here he opened the first tavern and hostel on Yonge Street. The village that later came to be called Richmond Hill was at first known as Miles's Hill, after this energetic settler.

Perhaps the most bizarre group of settlers to come to Upper Canada at this time was the colony of French Royalist émigrés headed by the comte de Puisaye. Joseph-Geneviève, comte de Puisaye, was a colourful and attractive individual, with considerable gifts for leadership, who had planned to start a rising in Brittany against the new republican rulers of France. He became friendly with the English prime minister, William Pitt, and members of his government, who had a deep-seated horror of what was taking place in France and supported the schemes that de Puisaye hatched in England for an invasion through Brittany.[119]

The proposed rebellion collapsed, and de Puisaye for some reason decided upon Canada as a place for his exile. He may have been influenced by the fact that Canada had already been considered as a place of refuge by Frenchmen threatened with the Reign of Terror. Simcoe, the stalwart, uncritical champion of those who opposed republicanism, had replied to earlier inquiries about Canada with a letter to the Abbé Desjardins at Quebec on 1 July, 1793: 'It would be an extreme pleasure for the government of Upper Canada to prove its devotion to his Majesty and its conformity with his kind intentions, by offering to the nobility and clergy from France an asylum as comfortable and as suitable as the infant state of the colony will permit. It may be good for you to know that the province of Upper Canada is inhabited principally by persons who were chased out of the United

States of America because of their attachment to their King, an attachment which characterizes at this moment, the conduct of the royal Frenchmen who suffer the horrors of exile.'[120]

While in England in the summer of 1798, de Puisaye met with Simcoe; the latter was inclined favourably toward the French ex-officer, and offered him his support and a letter of introduction to Peter Russell. One of de Puisaye's proposals, which must have sounded most attractive to the former lieutenant-governor, was that of forming a troop of soldiers to clear the land, their pay being provided by the military establishment in Canada.

Although it would seem that the British government, burdened by the cost of war with France, could not provide the expected financial backing for de Puisaye when the time came to set out for Canada, he was not leading a crew of paupers. He himself had considerable wealth, and he was accompanied by people such as the brothers René-Augustus, comte de Chalus, and Jean-Louis, vicomte de Chalus, one a major-general, the other a colonel in the Royalist army; Ambroise de Farcy, ex-captain, and de Fougères, ex-colonel; and, most memorable in Canadian history, Laurent Quetton St. George, an ex-major who had received in France a mercantile education that would stand him in good stead. The group numbered some forty in all, swelled with non-commissioned officers, privates, and servants.

With the exception of Simcoe, those officials who had some experience of life in Upper Canada were not completely convinced of the wisdom of de Puisaye's venture. They were, nevertheless, the servants of the home government. The comte's easy charm had impressed the guillible William Windham, the British secretary at war, who wrote to Peter Russell, on 30 July, 1798: 'The general purpose is to provide an asylum for as many as possible of those whose adherence to the ancient laws, religion and constitution of their Country, has rendered them sacrifices to the French Revolution. . . .It is wished that these latter should be kept as much as possible separate from any other body of French . . .considering themselves as of a purer description than the Indiscriminate class of emigrants and being in some measure known to each other they wish not to be mixed with those whose principles they are less sure of. . . .'[121]

The hard-headed Russell and his Executive Council, however, were very sceptical of such high-flown stuff, and sounded the opinions of others in the province. One of those from whom advice was asked was Mr. Robert Hamilton, a Queenston merchant of long experience. Hamilton, a Scot, was wealthy and influential and detested by Simcoe, who couldn't stand his pushy, tradesman's ways and considered him that most damnable of beings, a republican. He provided Russell with the following down-to-earth advice on the subject of de Puisaye: 'We do not want Settlers faster than we can Maintain them with ease and Comfort to ourselves. . . .The Trade of Farming in this new Country, Requires to Europeans as much an apprenticeship, as any handcraft profession. Mixed with older Settlers it may be learned by such in time, & by patient perseverance.'[122]

Russell, however, as a representative of the British government, had to abide by its wishes, and on de Puisaye's arrival at York in November 1798, arrangements were made to provide him with every assistance as well as agricultural equipment and rations. One of Russell's suggestions was that weapons could be issued to these experienced military men, and they would then form a local defence force and buffer against any possible Indian threats from the north.[123]

The Indians worried Russell at this time as a result of Chief Joseph Brant's demand to have the right to sell part of their lands and from the profits set up an annuity to provide for the Indians in the future. There had been a war scare in 1797 when it was rumoured that French agents were stirring up the Indians in the American Southwest to spread trouble into Upper Canada; thus, the loyalty of the Canadian Indians was then at a premium. Russell, in a flap, agreed to some of Brant's wishes, much to the annoyance of the Duke of Portland who told him that he should find out how much the Indians expected from their land sales and that the British government would then arrange an annuity rather than give permission for the Indians to sell their land outright.

So much for the folklore about the friendly ways of Indians and the settlers upon their lands. The trouble-making elements of fear and suspicion lurked close to York and its surroundings at that time. There would seem to have been several incidents between Indians and Europeans. These culminated in the death of Wabacine, one of the three Missisauga chiefs who had been present at the Toronto Purchase of 1787, shot by McEwen, a drunken soldier of the Queen's Rangers.[124]

Russell was very much alive to what might be sparked by the tension and he issued a proclamation in the *Upper Canada Gazette* of 30 December, 1797, promising the 'utmost severity' against anyone doing injury to the 'fisheries and burial places' of the 'Mississague Indians'.[125] His hoped-for defence force of de Puisaye's soldiers did not take form, and neither did his elaboration of Simcoe's scheme that sixty of the émigrés be used to clear roads and build bridges.

By late December 1798, some thirteen of de Puisaye's group had followed on from Kingston to join their leader at York. How different was their treatment from that accorded Berczy's artisans and peasants. There was not the delay in the survey of land for the settlement that Berczy had experienced. Twenty-two lots of two hundred acres each were granted at de Puisaye's request to form the basis for his settlement. These lots were taken up on the east and west sides of Yonge Street from 52 to 61, and 51 east and 62 west sides. This 'Puisaye Town' its founder planned to call 'Windham' after the secretary at war who had lent so much support to the undertaking.

The start was quick. By 14 February, 1799, eighteen log cabins had been built, and a church and parsonage were shortly to be added. Mr. Hamilton's fears

"In the fall of 1798 some 40 exiled French Royalists under the leadership of Joseph-Geneviève, Comte de Puisaye (1754-1827), emigrated from England to Upper Canada. The following year they were given rations and agricultural implements and settled along Yonge Street in the townships of Markham and Vaughan. However, these members of the nobility and their servants were unable to adapt themselves to a pioneer existence and by 1800 their settlement, known as Windham, was abandoned. De Puisaye lived for a time on an estate near Niagara, but returned to England in 1802."

Erected by the Ontario Archaeological and Historic Sites Board.

were soon to be realized, however, if we are to believe the description by William Harrison: 'The colonists made no advance beyond their settlement duties. Their log houses always remained the same, and their owners acted as if they were but sojourners in a foreign land. . . .It is said that it was no unusual circumstance in those days to see a gentleman of France dressed in the latest fashion of the time, outside the shanty gathering chips to cook the daily meal, and many of the ladies were costly dressed while attending to their domestic affairs.'[126] They preferred the society, such as it was, in York to the isolation of the woods beyond, and given their background the majority cannot be blamed for their preference.

Even York must have seemed a poor place to them. Mrs. Simcoe had recorded the Upper Canadian flora and fauna, the gossips, visits, and teas in the best Jane Austen fashion, but she showed a well-bred indifference to the ruder aspects of life in the small garrison outpost that was York. York may have become the official capital in 1798, but it was not much improved. Mary Breckenridge, daughter of William Baldwin, wrote an account that was not flattering, to say the least, after arriving at York in the summer of 1798 'and finding it composed of about a dozen or so houses, a dreary, dismal place, not even possessing the characteristics of a village. There was no church, schoolhouse or any of the ordinary signs of civilization, but it was, in fact, a mere settlement. . . .There was no inn, and those travellers who had no friend to go to pitched a tent and lived in that as long as they remained.'[127]

It may not have been as depressing as all that, but it was bad enough. Despite these discouraging surroundings, a social brittleness, 'Pride and Prejudice', still managed to grow. Official circles held receptions and fêtes in the little capital, at which the jewels of the vicomtesse de Chalus were reported to have caused a considerable sensation. The codes and manners of far-off Europe continued to guide the town's 'society,' even to the extent of the gentlemanly absurdities of the duel: 'Yesterday morning a duel was fought back of the Government Buildings by John White, Esq; his Majesty's Attorney General, and John Small, Esq; Clerk of the Executive Council, wherein the former received a wound above the right hip, which it is feared will prove mortal.'[128] Baron de Hoen was White's second in this affair, which resulted from some remarks made by White that cast a shadow over Mrs. Small's virtue. White and Small were neighbours, both serving the province in an official capacity, but precious honour had to be observed, although the town had few enough lives to spare as it was. For years afterward Mrs. Small was cut by the 'society' of York.

The essentials of a gentleman's paraphernalia for the duel, the pistols, were said to have been Berczy's, taken from his home during his absence in England.

The cause of the Small-White duel is given in a gossipy letter written by Peter Russell on 13 February, 1800, [128a] and would appear to have been the result of the Attorney-General's fit of pique at a slight to his wife by Mrs. Small at a soirée. In a rash moment, triggered by his annoyance with Mrs. Small, he hinted to David Smith that he had been 'great' with the lady, but broke off his connection with her because he feared injury to his health 'from the variety and piquancy of her amours with others.' Little wonder that there was a rumpus once that story got around.

Women in humbler stations of life could act more freely, and often did, if some of the advertisements in the *Gazette* are anything to go by:[129]

> Whereas my wife Sarah, refuses to go live with me on my Farm on Yonge-street, where I have for her a comfortable house, and as I am not able to support her in town, from the high price of provisions, and the heavy expence of house-rent, I therefore caution the Public not to harbour or credit her on my account, as I will pay no debt of her contracting from this date.
>
> his
ABRAHAM ✕ MATICE
mark

York, March 1, 1800.

John Matthews announced to all and sundry that his wife, Magdelina, had quit his bed and board 'without provocation'. Under the dramatic heading ELOPEMENT!, B. Haines of Yonge Street warned the public against harbouring his wife Juda 'or trusting her on my account'.

In the freer atmosphere of a frontier society, escape from domestic service or desertion from the army were more readily accomplished than they might have been in a long-established community. Peter Russell advertised that his 'Black Servant PEGGY', not having permission to absent herself from his service, was not to be employed or harboured 'without the owner's leave'.[130] Versatility rather than specialty was the asset of a good servant in the fluid society of York:[131]

> To be sold
>
> A Healthy, strong Negro WOMAN, about 30 years of age understands Cookery, Laundery, and the taking care of Poultry. N.B. She can Dress Ladies Hair — Enquire of the Printers.
>
> York, Dec. 20, 1800.

It may have been the isolation, strangeness, and unusual freedoms of this bizarre settlement, or indeed an unrequited passion such as excited the romantic affectations of the eighteenth century, or even an unhappy combination of both, which led one of de Puisaye's young followers to take this quick exit from his gloom-sodden surroundings:

> SUICIDE
>
> How powerful, and how irresistable is the influence of love! when it reigns predominantly it is too frequently productive, in many instances, of fatal consequences to the unhappy one, whom it has made subservient to its extremes! which was the case a few days since on Yonge street: One of the French emigrants, it is said, shot himself because a young lady, whom he admired in the extreme, discarded him.[132]

De Puisaye himself had cast his eye on more valuable land, but it was held by the Missisauga Indians at the western end of Lake Ontario. Seasoned in the arts of diplomacy and persuasion, he made a considerable impression on the great Indian chief, Joseph Brant, who was agreeable to de Puisaye's obtaining a tract of land, but the Executive Council thwarted any possibility of a deal. Peter Russell, to be sure, wouldn't miss the implications. He and his council reasoned that the price to be paid by de Puisaye would be relatively high, and as a result might prevent any cheap acquisitions of land by the government in the future.

The comte then removed himself to what he regarded as a more appropriate locale at Niagara in 1799, leaving much of the responsibility for his colony in the hands of the comte de Chalus. 1799 was also the year in which Peter Russell was succeeded by Lieutenant-General Peter Hunter, who assumed the position and title of lieutenant-governor. Hunter was often absent from York on military duties and much of the running of affairs was left to a commission of the Executive Council.

The question of granting land patents and rights of possession to de Puisaye's settlers now became an exercise in procrastination. Like Berczy's group they were regarded as aliens by the British government, and various devices to get around this difficulty had still come to nothing as late as 1805. Patents could be issued after a residence of seven years in Upper Canada, but de Puisaye would seem to have felt that he and his followers were an exception to this rule. The whole business remained bogged down in a clutter of correspondence until 1806 when Francis Gore became lieutenant-governor and granted the patents, apparently unaware of all the ins-and-outs of the matter.

As soon as they had a clear title to their lands in 1807 and 1808, most of the Frenchmen disposed of their holdings. De Puisaye himself had withdrawn from the enterprise in 1802 when he took up residence in England and there married his housekeeper who had been with him throughout the years at Niagara. The finale was described by William Harrison: 'With the glad news that La Belle France had again become a monarchy in 1814, they gave away their farms or left them as they were, and with all the eagerness of children long away from home, they hastened away to their native land. Their little clearings were soon overrun with second-growth pine or were squatted on by neighbours and strangers.'[133] And a fine hullabaloo in litigation that would cause.

Although there may be a temporary equality in austerity and co-operation in adversity, it would have been odd had there not been some distrust and suspicion of de Puisaye's band. The background and way of life for many of them was utterly removed from the ken of their neighbours in Upper Canada. In spite of Harrison's remarks — and they seem to have been prejudiced against something that he could never understand — a scant half-dozen did stay on to persevere in their new surroundings. The majority, however, lacked the peasant's advantage in the struggle to survive: a glum obstinacy to endure such conditions as first existed on Yonge Street.

The only real success story on record from among de Puisaye's followers was that of Mr. Quetton St. George, Wau-be-way-quon or 'White Hat' as the Indians came to call him. He had a store in York and set up trading posts near the present Atherley in the Narrows between Lake Simcoe and Lake Couchiching and at Amherstburg below Detroit. Although he returned to France with the profits from his enterprises,[134] his son returned to Upper Canada and took up residence on the family property, wistfully named 'Glen Lonely' by his wife, located on Lake St. George, which is now known as George Lake.

De Puisaye's people seem for the most part to have flitted like satin butterflies across the bleak setting of early York and Yonge Street. Their place was taken by less flamboyant, homespun creatures with an immense capacity for work and a proven competence in farming. These people were also in a sense refugees, but refugees because of the moral attitudes fostered by their particular society. Totally self-sufficient, they did not seek assistance or favours in the formidable task of breaking and cultivating frontier land.

By the time of their arrival in Upper Canada, they were already a close-knit community, less colourful than the fortune seekers who gambled on the accidents of trade and war, but industrious, sober, and thrifty, the types needed for success in settlement and farming. The pragmatic Simcoe was well aware of the value of such people in developing unbroken territory. As early as the spring of 1792 he was writing to Phineas Bond, the British consul in Philadelphia: '[His Majesty's] interests will be essentially promoted by the speedy condensation of a numerous, virtuous, agricultural people in Upper Canada, and such, I have experience, are the inhabitants of Pennsylvania. I have only to add, that should any Society wish to emigrate, I should be happy to see those persons who should be authorized under mutual confidence for that purpose, and to give my best assistance to promote their views and establishment.'[135]

The specific 'Society' that Simcoe had in mind was the Society of Friends, or Quakers, who did not make the move from Pennsylvania until after his departure from Upper Canada. The appeal to them had been in Simcoe's statement that they would have 'a just right to . . .exemptions from bearing arms.' This policy had a like attraction for the Mennonites, the Swiss-German members of the Brethren in Christ, also from Pennsylvania and sharing the Quakers' dislike of violence.

Several factors combined to make the new republic of the United States less acceptable to people of their persuasion. Following the American Revolution there were several local petty squabbles and fights, and in 1794 political differences spilled over in the Whisky Rebellion that flared out through the western part of Pennsylvania. Simcoe was delighted by this evidence of the disorder that, in his opinion, was inherent in the American system. More alarming than any of these minor disputes were the Indian wars that burst like brush fires as the frontier was pushed westward.

The Quakers in particular had a long history of friendship with the Indians since William Penn had made a pledge of peace with the sachems of the Leni Lenapes and neighbouring tribes on the banks of the Delaware at the close of 1682. The rumbustious exuberance of an emancipated America was not much to the liking of the 'plain folk' with their quiet ways.

Timothy Rogers, a Quaker from Vermont, was attracted by the prospects in Upper Canada, and made the long journey to York on foot and horseback in April 1800. From York he travelled north along the line of Yonge Street where he saw land suited to his shrewd farmer's instincts, some twenty-five miles north from the capital. He applied for a grant of 40 farms, 200 acres each, on the undertaking that he would be able to supply sufficient settlers for them.

He returned to Vermont, and in February 1801 he set out with his family and seven sleighs on the snow-tedious trudge back to the Yonge Street settlement site — a trek that took almost three months to accomplish. During the next two years, several other Quakers from his community followed to settle the land along Yonge Street in the townships of King and Whitchurch.

The state of Yonge Street at this time may be imagined from a report submitted by the provincial surveyor, John Stegmann, in 1801: '. . . From the Town of York to the three-mile post on the Poplar Plains [at the hill on Yonge Street just north of where the present CPR track crosses] the road is cut, and that as yet the greater part of the said distance is not passable for any carriage whatever, on account of logs which lie in the street. From thence to lot 1 on Yonge Street the road is very difficult to pass at any time, agreeable to the present situation in which the said part of the street is.'[136]

Stegmann reported to Surveyor D. W. Smith the condition in which he found the frontage of each lot along Yonge Street as far north as Newmarket, where the Quakers had established themselves. For the most part the settlers had done their job of clearing away the trees cut down in front of their lots, although on occasion the clearing was done only to the middle of the road, the settler on one side having failed to carry out his obligations. Progress had been slow but steady. On the lots on both sides along the length of Yonge, Stegmann counted eighteen houses and eighty-nine clearings. He found the best section of the road to be that part between Aurora and Newmarket where Timothy Rogers had so recently started his Quaker settlement.

An interesting contrast to the efforts of the settlers was the lower part of Yonge Street, in York, where improvements had to be made by private subscriptions at the urging of Justice Elmsley; his lot on Yonge lay just north of Queen Street, or Lot Street as it was then called. The *Upper Canada Gazette* of 20 December, 1800, carried a notice that Chief Justice Elmsley had chaired a meeting in one of the government buildings in which a number of 'the principal inhabitants' of York had gathered, and where '[a subscription] by which something more than two hundred dollars in money and labour had been promised, and that other sums were to be expected from several respectable inhabitants who were well-wishers to the undertaking [of opening the road to Yonge Street, and enabling the farmers there to bring their provisions to market with more ease than is practicable at present].'[137]

Matters obviously did not proceed speedily enough for some impatient individuals. An irate resident who cloaked himself in the alias of VORAZ wrote in overworked dudgeon to the *Upper Canada Gazette* on 12 March, 1804: 'Will any one ascribe to virtuous motives, the refusal of a mite towards effecting so

desirable a purpose as rendering the beginning of Yonge Street passable? No —
little will be expected from mediocrity, but something from all.'[138]

The Queen's Rangers had been employed again at the beginning of 1799 to cut
trees along Yonge Street. Desertions were becoming a frequent feature of the
corps, and they can't have been too happy in their work in light of a letter from
Castle Frank Creek on 27 February, 1799, in which Stegmann informed Smith
that 'the party of Rangers now on this road begged of me to inform you that they
have not received any pay for the work since they have been out with Mr.
Jones.'[139]

To keep the roads in order and to check that the settlers cleared away the
debris left in front of their lots by the soldiers, pathmasters were appointed by the
authorities at York. The pathmaster was empowered to call upon a householder to
put in a number of days or hours of work upon Yonge Street. The appointments
were made at the town meetings that were often held in the smoke-hazed,
booze-fumed dimness of Abner Miles's tavern. Nicholas Miller was one of those

"In 1800 an extensive grant of land in this vicinity was
made to Timothy Rogers and Samuel Lundy who, with
other members of the Society of Friends (Quakers),
settled here in 1801–03. Originally under the religious
jurisdiction of Philadelphia and New York Yearly Meetings
the settlers were organized in 1806 as the Yonge Street
Monthly Meeting of Friends. In 1807 Asa Rogers deeded
two acres of land for the erection of a meeting house,
and construction began in 1810. By 1812 the building had
been completed and was the first church in the area
north of Toronto."

Erected by the Ontario Archaeological and Historic Sites Board.

appointed as 'Fence-viewer and Overseer for Highway' in 1797 and 1798, and in 1799 John Lyons was made one of the first pathmasters. If taken seriously, the jobs could never have been sinecures.

Beyond a doubt the Quakers seem to have been the most industrious in carrying out the job of road clearing. Even so, they still ran into problems with delays and lethargy in the creaky process of official business. They made several representations to the lieutenant-governor that despite the timely discharge of their required duties, the patents for title to their lands were still not forthcoming. Lieutenant-General Hunter, irritated by this delay to people whose efforts were worthy of better recognition, questioned the secretary, William Jarvis, who trotted out the sorry old excuse about the load of work and pressing business. Hunter was not impressed. If the patents were not forthcoming in the space of a day, he thundered at the tardy secretary, 'Then, by God, I'll un-Jarvis you!'

On 29 December, 1803, the lieutenant-governor gave Timothy Rogers the coveted certificate 'These are to certify that Mr. Timothy Rogers has completed the settlement he undertook in this Province, much to my satisfaction, and has, in all respects, conducted and demeaned himself as a good moral character and faithful subject.'[140] These 'faithful subjects' presented a loyal address to his Excellency Lieutenant-Governor Gore on 30 September, 1806, from a meeting of the Yonge Street Society of Friends. Timothy Rogers and Amos Armitage were appointed to 'attend on the Governor therewith.'[141]

The Yonge Street Society of Friends, in conformity with Quaker practices, established a meeting house, the first of which seems to have been built before 1806. Little, if any, of its history is known, but a second building was agreed upon by the Friends in 1808, after Asa Rogers had deeded two acres of land for the use of the congregation at Lot 92 on the west side of Yonge at Newmarket. Work on this second meeting house began in 1810 and it was finished in 1812, a structure in keeping with the character of its builders: plain, strong, and dependable. It is still standing today with few modifications beyond the normal requirements of upkeep.

The Quaker colony on Yonge Street at that time was hard hit by the plague of 1809. Timothy Rogers recorded in his *Journal* that 'a great death has gone through this Upper Canada — first it was call Typhus Fever, but latterly we have had the Measles, by which some has departed this life; but mostly it has been such an uncommon Disorder that it seems to baffle the skill of the wisest and best Physicians.'[142] Some thirty of Timothy's friends died in the settlement from this sickness.

The settlers persevered, however, and in time received passing praise from that inquisitive Scots laird, Robert Gourlay, whose detailed *Statistical Account*, compiled after a visit to Upper Canada in 1817, caused a great furor in the York 'establishment': '[For five miles around York] the need for firewood has stolen from the forest its chief ornaments, and left a parcel of scorched and decaying pine trees to frown over the seat of rapacity. The only connected settlement

"These wagons came to be called "Conestoga Wagons." It was common for the more robust persons to walk since the wagons were heavily loaded. Each family usually brought a cow with them. The cows were shod and driven after the wagons. The milk that remained from the daily needs was put into the churn, which was suspended from the wagon. Usually at the end of the day's journey the butter was ready for use. The tar bucket, used for lubricating the axle, was hung under the wagon. Frequently the wagons had to be dismantled, and everything was carried piece by piece, across the mire or over the mountain. The wagon-box was sometimes used as a boat to cross the streams." (*A Brief History of the Mennonites in Ontario:* L.J. Burkholder, p. 25.)

commences about five miles to the north, on Yonge Street. ...Where Yonge Street is compactly settled, it is well cultivated and thriving, particularly beyond what is called the Oak Hills or Ridges. ...In this quarter the land is excellent, and it is well occupied by industrious people, mostly Quakers. In other quarters, simple and unsuspecting Germans, — Tunkers, and Menonists, have been thinly stuck in by the knowing ones among their precious blocks and reserves, by whose plodding labours the value of this sinecure property may be increased.'[143]

Gourlay, like more than a few of his fellow countrymen when they found a point to argue, tended to belabour his case. The Mennonites and Tunkers deserved better than a description as 'simple and unsuspecting' dupes of the scheming English administrators in York. Peter Reesor, who was the forerunner of the Mennonite colony on Yonge, was a man to drive a shrewd bargain if the tales of him are true, and if his portrait is anything to go by.[144]

The Swiss-German Mennonites in Pennsylvania were attracted to Upper Canada for much the same reasons as were the quakers. Setting the pattern for the legend of the lone rider who would venture into the unknown to chart its features for his people, Peter Reesor rode from Pennsylvania to York in 1796 and sized up the surrounding land for good farming areas. On the way back, so the story goes, he happened to meet Baron de Hoen in York. Peter's horse was typical of the fine specimens raised by his people and it appealed to the cavalry eye of the ex-Hessian officer, who wasted no time in making an offer. In return for the horse and its saddle, the baron would exchange the script for 400 acres of land which he held in the region of Whitchurch, north of Markham. Only script could be given, because no need of ownership could be issued until the settlement duties were completed. Peter accepted the deal, but, so the legend goes, he kept the bridle, which was of a special design, in spite of the protests of the bargain-driving baron.

The move to Upper Canada was not immediately made because of family reasons, and it was not until 1804 that Christian Reesor, Peter's father, set out with his family for the lands in Markham and Whitchurch. Other Mennonite families had already preceded them to the province, but headed for the Grand River where a settlement had been established in the region of Waterloo. There seem to have been problems with the mortgage on the lands at Grand River, and one group of Mennonites, hearing of this sometime in 1803, diverted their course to Markham instead.

Like Berczy's settlers before them, they piled their belongings in the robust 'Conestoga' wagons, which could be dismantled and used as boats if necessary to float across small bodies of water, ferrying people, furniture and equipment. John Ross Robertson described how the Yonge Street track that they followed was so rough that 'when, in 1797 Balser Munshaw, one of the founders of the village of Richmond Hill, sought a wilderness home along this thoroughfare, it was found necessary to take his canvas-top wagon apart, and drag the wheels and axles and other equipment up the steep hills by means of strong ropes.'[145]

Like Munshaw and the other Pennsylvania Germans, the Mennonites came totally prepared for life in the forests of Upper Canada. It is doubtful that anyone without their experience in the United States and of the ways of frontier life could have coped equally well, if at all, with their new surroundings. This was a fact of which Simcoe, hardened by forest campaigns, had been well aware when he sought to attract these 'Societies' to his province.

It is probable that the Quakers were as successful in their relations with the Indians in their district as they had been with those in Pennsylvania. This being the case, they would have made a far better 'defence force' than would any formation of Peter Russell's armed and suspicious ex-soldiery.

Suspicion and novelty no doubt did much to colour the average settlers' views of the Indians, all the way from 'noble savage' to drunken pest. An account by Nicholas Miller's grandson, Simon, describes the Indians as 'magnificent specimens of manhood, their heads decorated with eagle plumes and war spears in their hands, when they came down Yonge Street to collect their yearly bounty.

Jesse Ketchum's Tannery at the s.w. corner of Yonge and Adelaide Sts., 1834.

When Jesse Ketchum started his tannery business in 1812, it was the first major industry in the town of York, where a blacksmith, cobbler, hat-maker, clock maker, candle maker and waggon maker were already practising their trades.

Frequently by the time they reached Thornhill on the way home they were as poor as when they started, having spent money and supplies for whiskey. It became such a scandal that the Government finally adopted the plan of paying them at the reserve.'[146,147]

Apparently, when they came down on this annual junket to York, a favourite camping spot along the way was on the farm of the younger Jacob Munshaw, Lot 17 west on Yonge at the rise just south of the village of Thornhill. The feathers and war spears were an imaginative touch more appropriate to a troupe from Buffalo Bill's circus. Yonge Street was not exactly an Indian warpath, regardless of Peter Russell's panics.

By the early 1800s the Indians continued quiet, and the evacuation by the British from the disputed western posts by the fall of 1796 had brought less strained relations with the United States. There appeared to be less need for a military presence in Upper Canada, and toward the end of 1802 the Queen's Rangers were disbanded. Home governments always pruned military expenses whenever possible, leaving the militia in the provinces to hold the fort.

A Yonge Street company of the York County Militia existed, but military drills and duties never loomed large in the mind of the settler, whose exclusive concerns at that time were surviving and farming. C. W. Jefferys' drawings of the occasion and contemporary accounts leave little doubt that the annual militia muster on the king's birthday, 4 July, was little more than a chance for a drinking

Upper Canada Gazette, 21 Dec.1799.

ASHES, ASHES, ASHES,
THE subscriber begs leave to inform
the public, that he is about to erect
a POT-ASH upon lot No. 7, West side
of Yong-street; where he will give a ge-
nerous price for ASHES; for House-
ashes NINE-PENCE per bushel, for field-
ashes SIX-PENCE, delivered at his Potash.
He conceives it his duty to inform those
who may have ashes to dispose of, that
it will not be in his power to pay cash,
but merchandize at cash price.
York, Dec. 7, '99   DUKE W. KENDRICK.

"When potash was made on a large scale it was most convenient to erect the
equipment on a hillside along a running stream. Above were the wedge-shaped
leaches of double-thick planks, from which the raw lye ran into a reservoir
trough or tank. Still lower down was the large potash kettle, perhaps five feet in
diameter, into which the lye was dipped by ladles or ran directly through a
faucet. Large stones were built around the kettle to hold it in place. ......
Potash was usually shipped eastward to Montreal in large oak-stave barrels
holding 560 lbs., which were valued at from $80 to $120 each. The early
settler frequently found that cash could be more readily obtained for potash
or black salts than for wheat."

(*The Pioneer Farmer and Backwoodsman*; E.C. Guillet, Vol. II, p.212).

binge. Few would rely on the ill-assorted mob with umbrellas and sticks who
shambled out to the muster.

As the number of settlers along Yonge Street increased at a steady but
painfully slow rate during the early 1800s, individuals began to branch into
activities other than farming and land clearing. Gristmills and sawmills had been
developed almost concurrently with the first settlements and soon were followed
by potasheries and distilleries. The *Upper Canada Gazette* carried advertisements
for a growing variety of businesses.[148]

Duke Kendrick set up a 'Pot Ashery' on his property, Lot 7 on the west side of

Yonge, as did Abijah Jones in Markham. 'Potasheries' were a popular business until the 1830s when scientific progress made the hot, heavy, and sometimes dangerous work of producing soap and potash no longer worthwhile. Jesse Ketchum, closer to York, started a tannery. Samuel Jackson announced the establishment of 'a Hat Manufactory' on Yonge Street in the vicinity of York at the end of 1807. William Bond of Bond's Lake had earlier tried to get a hat business going, but his venture was premature and, 'missing the current,' did not get off to any sort of a start.

There were, of course, the inevitable taverns to ease the traumas of travelling in those days. That of Abner Miles at Richmond Hill has already been mentioned, and David Bridgford, who had come with his parents from New York in 1796 to settle on Lot 41 east on Yonge, started an inn close by in 1806, the year of Miles' death. William Cowan, the grandson of Trader Cowan of Matchedash Bay, was brought up by his maternal grandmother who for some years kept a wayside hostelry at Hogg's Hollow (York Mills) during the early 1800s.

For those who indulged too freely or fell victim to the harshness of their surroundings, there was soon to be assistance other than native herbs and remedies. In *The York Gazette* of 6 June, 1807:

> Doctor Tolman presents his respects to the inhabitants of Yonge Street, and informs them, that he has taken a Room in the house of Mr. Elisha Dexter in the Township of Vaughan. . . .He will likewise attend to the Vaccine Innoculation when required thereto by those who reside near him.

Oscar Wilde once commented in his brittle fashion that 'it is only by not paying one's bills that one can hope to live in the memory of the commercial classes' — in which case there must have been many well-remembered citizens around York and Yonge Street. If payments could not be made in cash, then grain would do — anything rather than nothing. In *The York Gazette* of 20 January, 1808, John Lyon of Lyon and Walker's Mill on Yonge Street was desperately pressing for cash or grain from his debtors whom he asked to pay up 'without his being obliged to apply for payment in a legal way.' In the previous week's paper:

> Doctor E. Tolman having appointed the subscriber his attorney to collect his debts in the town and county of York, now calls upon his debtors of every description for immediate payment.
> — John Cameron
> Grain of good quality will be taken in payment.

With such reluctance to pay for what were necessary services, it must have been a considerably risky undertaking for Thomas Humberstone, from Staffordshire in England, to start a pottery on his farm at Lot 14, on the west side of Yonge.

Simcoe had hoped that by encouraging the fur-trade business to use the route along Yonge Street the settlers would profit by supplying necessary goods, especially corn, to the traders. Simcoe's attitude toward the fur trade is given by Robert Gourlay in his *Statistical Account of Upper Canada* in which he quotes the opinions formed by the duc de la Rochefoucauld on his visit to America: 'Although the fur trade, in General Simcoe's opinion, is not so profitable to England as many Englishmen imagine, yet he will not divide its profits with the Americans; who, by the surrender of the forts, acquire a share in the navigation of the lakes, and excellent harbours on their coast; and of consequence are possessed of every means to participate in this branch of commerce.'[149] Simcoe was interested only in profits for Upper Canada, and damn the rest.

After his return from what he considered to be his very successful journey from York to Matchedash Bay, Simcoe received the following letter from Colonel R. G. England of the 24th Regiment, commanding the British garrison that was then in the post at Detroit: 'I congratulate you on your return from Matchedash Bay, and rejoice at the account you give of the harbour and the easy communication. Whenever you establish it you will ruin this miserable place [Detroit] and defeat the purpose for which I have taken much pains these twelve months past to form settlements in its neighbourhood, but this I will not much regret if a better purpose is answered.'[150]

The better purpose was not answered. Although the North West Fur Company partners would eventually present a complaint that the United States' officials had been interfering with their trade since 1796,[151] they were not at first perturbed by the threat of competition and so saw no reason to divert their trade along Yonge Street.

The North West Company had been formed in 1779 by a group of enterprising Montreal fur merchants. During the period from 1794 to 1798, steady and impressive progress was made with the launching of ships on the Great Lakes, the building of a canal at Sault Ste. Marie, and roads on the portages along the Ottawa River.

There were three routes available to the fur traders for their annual expeditions from Montreal to the rich fur lands of the Canadian Northwest. The fur brigades would set out from Lachine as soon as the ice began to leave the upper St. Lawrence. The most expensive but quickest route was that of the Ottawa and French rivers, along the north shore of Manitoulin Island to Michilimackinac or Mackinac Island — 900 miles from Montreal. It was a tough, gruelling canoe trip, made by the pick of the voyageurs, but it became increasingly popular as the westward expansion of the trade made speed a crucial factor in the year's profits.

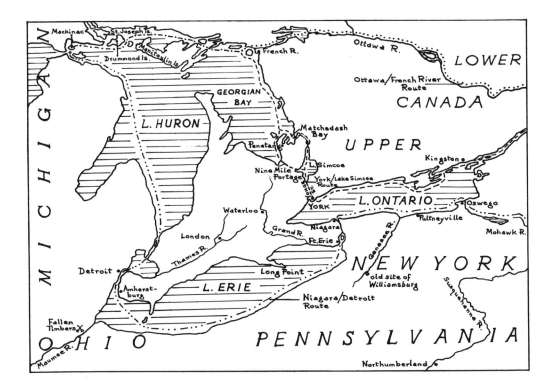

The cheapest route was to go by sailing schooner or barge to Kingston, across Lake Ontario and the Niagara portage to Lake Erie, then past Detroit to Mackinac. It was also slow and risky. In between the two extremes came the York-Lake Simcoe route. This followed the north shore of Lake Ontario from Kingston to York. Boats could make their way up the West Don as far as Yonge Street at the present York Mills where they would be lifted out of the water and carried on flat wagons as far as the Holland River.[152] From there the route could go by Lake Simcoe to Matchedash Bay and on to Mackinac, or it could cross the Nine-Mile Portage from Kempenfeldt Bay in Lake Simcoe to Nottawasaga Bay, and from there follow the shore line north past Manitoulin to Mackinac.

Near the top of the hill at Poplar Plains on Yonge Street there is supposed to have been an old capstan-style device, turned by oxen to winch the flat wagons with their load of boats and goods up the slope.[153] It could as easily have been set there by seamen of the Royal Navy transporting supplies north during the War of 1812 as by North West Company traders. For whoever undertook it, the journey was arduous, unpleasant, and back breaking, but D. W. Smith in his *Gazetteer* of 1799 was prepared to promote the route with the detached ease of the map-student: 'This communication affords many advantages. Merchandise from Montreal to Michilimackinac may be sent this way at ten or fifteen pounds less expense per ton than by the route of the Grand or Ottawa Rivers, and the merchandise from New York to be sent up the North and Mohawk Rivers for the North-West trade, finding its way into Lake Ontario at Oswego, the advantage will certainly be felt of transporting goods from Oswego to York, and from thence across Yonge Street, and down the waters of Lake Simcoe into Lake Huron, in preference to sending it by Lake Erie.'[154]

The *Upper Canada Gazette* of 9 March, 1799, reported: 'We hear, that the N. W. Company, has given TWELVE THOUSAND POUNDS towards making YONGE STREET a good road, and that the N.W. commerce will be communicated through this place. An event which must, inevitably, benefit this country materially; as it will not only tend to augment the population, but will also enhance the present value of landed property.' That certainly had not been Simcoe's intention, but the last line expressses the hopes of those who held land as an investment, a source of easy financial profit.

The hopes pinned on the North West Company died hard in legend although they never amounted to much in reality.[155] The Montreal traders, content with things as they were, preferred the Ottawa River and Detroit routes, even if Detroit was in the hands of the Americans. The hard facts of business easily surmounted any other emotions or loyalties.

The merchants at York were equally determined to promote their own interests. The following contribution to the *Upper Canada Gazette* of 7 March, 1801, was sent by someone who signed himself 'CITIZEN' and was in all probability a merchant in the town: 'The citizens and inhabitants of this town and part of the country, have the strongest imaginable inducements to open roads to the interior, and in particular to Lake Simcoe, as well as from views of local convenience, as the certain and extensive advantages which will arise, from having the rout of the North West traders transferred to this quarter. . . .and when it is considered, that this place will be a depot to the exports and immense imports (the fruits of the North West trade) every one in the least interested, will contribute something to put us in possession of advantages, which we now enjoy but in prospect.'

Far from putting up money for Yonge Street, the Nor'Westers would have been only too happy to bargain over the amount that the citizens of York might have been prepared to invest in a road in return for the prosperity that the company could bring to York by using the route to Lake Simcoe.

In *The Town of York, 1793-1815,* Edith Firth effectively scotched the rumour that the North West Company had contributed £12,000 toward improving Yonge Street as being 'unfortunately not true': 'Before 1810 a few consignments for the fur trade passed through York; Joel Beaman was in town with ''a load of Goods

" 22nd (August 1809) Joel B(eman) call'd & took Breakfast on his way to town with a load of Goods from North West — a large Canoe and a Number of Men......"

(*Ely Playter's Diary* in *The Town of York, 1793-1815* ; ed. *Edith G. Firth*, p. 251).

from North-West — a large Canoe and a Number of Men'' on August 22, 1809. The usual route, however, was through Lake Erie and the Detroit River. The powerful merchants of the Niagara and Detroit areas had no intention of losing this lucrative business.'[156] It must be remembered that the North West Company was less of a business organization as it would be understood today, and more of a loose association of merchant-traders with a common interest in the fur trade west of Lake Superior, or as they called it, the upper country.

They were a hard-driving, hard-headed lot, ready to take any risk in the pursuit of adventure and fortune in the fur business. Their names read like a roll call at the Gathering of the Clans: McTavish, McGillivray, McGill, Mackenzie, McLeod, Fraser. They had about them nothing of the 'schmaltz' of the

German-background settlers, nor of the cloying family sentiment of the Lowland-Scots farmer. Instead, there was a stubbornness, nepotism, porridge-sticky clannish loyalties, and intemperate Highland pride. It would need another Sir Walter Scott, who put romance into the hooligan habits of the Highlanders, to give glamour to the great fur game.

Such qualities do not make for co-operation, and despite its great surge of enterprise in the late 1790s and financial success, the being of the North West Company was rent by internal strife among its members. In 1798 a group headed by the Richardsons and Forsyths broke away to form The New North West Company (or X.Y. Company as it became more popularly known), and they were joined in 1799 by that forceful, independent maverick, Alexander Mackenzie. If any thought had been given to the use of a route along Yonge Street, it would not have received much attention while other issues of more critical moment were being resolved.

A reconciliation took place in 1804, no doubt from the very practical realization that a house divided could not stand against the competition from the Hudson's Bay Company and later from the ambitions of John Jacob Astor in the United States. Seeing the near-monopoly of the Nor'Westers, the Americans had no compunction about creating irritations and delays for them. In 1805, when two North West Company canoes were held up by winds at Mackinac, no longer garrisoned by the British, the U.S. Customs there impounded the cargo.

In keeping with Jay's Treaty, Mackinac had been evacuated by the British in August 1796 and the garrison transferred to St. Joseph Island where the North West Company had had a post since 1792. The military reasons for the choice of St. Joseph are evident in a letter written by Lieutenant John Humfrey of the Engineers to Simcoe on 18 February, 1792: 'Should it ever be thought an object to establish a settlement at the head of the Lake or change the present Post at Michillimackinac, the Island of St. Joseph appears to be the best situation for that purpose, it is in the direct route of the canoes from the French River, and on the north side the ship channel to St. Mary's, which passes thro' Lake George, the narrows leading into which are not more than 200 yards wide. A Battery at these narrows dependent on a Post at St. Joseph's would effectually command this communication. . . .'[157]

St. Joseph Island was purchased from the Indians for £1200 in blankets, guns, flints, silver medals for the chiefs, and fifty gallons of strong wine. The Indians became so drunk and rowdy from the latter during the land deal that the British agents negotiating the sale panicked and hid themselves from the scene. John Johnston, a trader for the South West Fur Company at Sault Ste. Marie, left a none-too-flattering account of the new purchase: '[Fort St. Joseph] is certainly one of the bleakest spots in His Majesty's dominions, though at present the seat of justice, honour, politeness and of the most liberal hospitality. Although the position of St. Joseph is far from being the most judicious that might have been chosen for a permanent post, yet, as a great deal of money has been already laid out upon it, all that is now left to the wisdom of government is to improve to the best advantage what can no longer be conveniently changed.'[158]

In spite of its eventual transfer to total American control, Mackinac itself remained the established rendezvous for those engaged in the North West trade, the great entrepôt that many of the voyageurs, so indispensable to the trade, made their base. Even after 1796, 'the burr in the voice of the traders was still primarily Scotch, the talk of the workers in French, and the loyalty of the Indians totally toward England.'[159]

It was a state of affairs that could not last for long in the face of hostility from the merchants and officials in the United States who resented the dominance of the fur trade by British interests. Governor Wilkinson of Louisiana roundly denounced Mackinac to Secretary of War Dearborn in 1805 as 'the Den from which this description of Persons annually issue forth.'[160] As can be imagined, his description of the fur-trading 'Persons' was a long way from complimentary.

The associates of the North West Company now began to consider the route that they had previously ignored. An additional encouragement was the annual mail communication that had been organized between York and St. Joseph via the Yonge Street, Lake Simcoe, and Matchedash route. This scheme had resulted from a minute to Peter Russell from Chief Justice Elmsley on 1 February, 1799: 'The Board takes the liberty of recommending to your Honor, the propriety of opening a Correspondence with the Officer Commanding at Fort St. Joseph for the purpose of obtaining from him the earliest information of every step that may be taken, and every Report that may be circulated in that quarter — this correspondence may we apprehend be very easily conducted through the intervention of Mr. Cown at Matchadash —'[161]

The local merchants of York found a sympathetic ally in Lieutenant-Governor Gore and they played up the advantages of the route north from York with greater insistence as time and opportunity slipped by: 'To such of our Yonge Street friends, as feel themselves interested in its improvement, and who can foresee the advantages of turning the North-West communication into this channel, we recommend industry and alacrity. We beg leave to remind them, that as next year will provide a general Election, the ensuing session will be the proper time to petition for a Turn-Pike. . . .'[162] Money, not good will, was what was needed to improve Yonge Street, and in March 1808 a bill was passed in the Assembly granting to the Crown 'a certain sum of Money out of the Funds applicable to the uses of this Province to defray the expenses of amending and repairing the Public Highways and Roads. . . .'[163]

There was also a need to make a road connecting Lake Simcoe with an outlet on Matchedash Bay. Simcoe, as a result of his journey there, had arranged for a purchase of the title to land around Penetanguishene, but this was not completed until 1798, after his departure from Upper Canada. This purchase, however, did not include the lands for a right of way from Kempenfeldt Bay where it was proposed that the new road should start.

An agreement to purchase the land, but not a final treaty, was drawn up in March 1808, and the surveyor, Samuel Wilmot, was sent on an inspection of the area to decide upon a suitable route for connecting the head of Kempenfeldt Bay with Penetanguishene. Wilmot was a Loyalist who had settled on Lot 47 on the east side of Yonge and married the daughter of the surveyor, John Stegmann. When the latter was lost in the schooner *Speedy* at the end of 1804, Wilmot got his job.[164]

In 1810 the surveyor general, Thomas Ridout, ordered that a road from Kempenfeldt Bay to Lake Huron be laid off in lots. Again the surveyor on this task was Wilmot, who was accompanied on this occasion by Angus Shaw of the North West Company.[165]

Archibald Norman McLeod, an associate in the company, travelled to its annual 'clan gathering' at Fort William on Lake Superior in 1810, going by the Yonge Street, Lake Simcoe, and Penetanguishene route so that he might be able to give a first-hand account of it. His impressions must have been favourable, because the result was a long memorial to His Excellency Francis Gore from Messrs. McGillivray, Hallowell, and Shaw, and 'their associates the North West Company', dated 5 November, 1810: 'That your Memorialists have been given to understand that it is in the contemplation of your Excellency to open a Road and establishment from Kempenfeldt Bay to Petinguishingue Bay on Lake Huron the establishment of that Road and Settlement would be more safe and eligible for the Transport of Goods and Provisions to the Upper Country than the Route now followed as it will conduct your Memorialists and others His Majesty's Subjects by a Road which will supercede the necessity of their following the Frontier of the Americans and from passing under their Forts and Guns, and free them also from the very vexatious and arbitrary impositions of the American Government: . . .the Country adjoining the said Road settled by His Majesty's Subjects is susceptible of raising the Corn and Provisions which is wanted for your Memorialists Trade, to the North West Country —'[166] People had been saying this sort of thing for long enough, God knows, but Yonge Street as a trade highway was still very much a blow-hot, blow-cold affair.[167]

The Nor'Westers were now perturbed by the need to obtain the corn and other staples for the North West trade from settlers in American territories, and they hoped for a source within Canadian borders. Like good Scots merchants, however, they were mightily careful of their pennies and were not about to disburse any great sums to pay for the opening of the road.

In return for the benefits that their trade would bring to the country through

which the proposed road would run, the Nor'Westers asked the
lieutenant-governor for a grant of 2,000 acres of the 'Waste Land' on the north
side of Kempenfeldt Bay and 2,000 acres on the south side of Penetanguishene
Bay. At the 'Landing Place at Gwilliamsbury' they requested 200 acres for a store
house and other buildings.

The only official reservation was that the land should not be a monopoly of the
company, but should be made available to settlers in the normal fashion. The fees
for the grants of land for which it had asked were paid by the company at the end
of February 1812, in York, but the deeds of title were not issued at that time and
probably nothing was really resolved until the final Land Purchase Treaty with the
Indians on 17 November, 1815.

It seemed that at last Yonge Street, as part of a great trade artery running north
from York, would come into its own, much as Simcoe had hoped. John Askin,
Jr., who ran the North West Company's store on St. Joseph Island, wrote to his
brother from there on 11 August, 1811: 'Should the NW Gentlemen establish the
road as is proposed from York to Matchedash it will be the making of that Country
and will injure Mr McIntosh very much which I'm sorry for, he having a large
family and a Worthy man. His son, Alex left this about 4 o'Clock PM on the
Nancy loaded with Packs for Fort Erie.[168,169]

T. G. Ridout, the son of Thomas, while on a visit to England in April 1812,
met Governor Gore there and wrote back to Upper Canada to say that the latter
was assured of the North West Company carrying its trade through
Penetanguishene.[170]

The year 1812, however, would be critical for Yonge Street and its trade in a
way very different from what had been anticipated by the planners for the future.
As is so often the case, the eddies in the tide of events upset their schemes and
ventures, and it was war, not trade, that marched up Yonge Street to the tunes of
1812.

Chapter Three

War and Settlement (1812-35)

Aye, — war; it will whistle up a wind for any sort of a change, for good or for bad, depending upon your opinion; but guaranteed to alter things, be it win, lose or draw. And so it was with Yonge Street.

It was the urgent drumming of war, the War of 1812, that forced along the development of Yonge Street, despite those glamorous myths from an association with the rough-and-tumble of the fur trade, which would have it that the North West Company was the spur. The war completed Simcoe's vision of a road that would run from York to Penetanguishene, with the establishment there of a base for Georgian Bay–Lake Huron. The entire length of this route would in time become known as Yonge Street, as noted by F. H. Armstrong in his edition of the Reverend Henry Scadding's *Toronto of Old*.[171]

Ely Playter, who had a farm on Yonge Street, mentioned in the daily monotone of his diary that on 6 July, 1812, he went to town where he 'heard that War was Declared by the Americans.'[172] *The York Gazette* of 11 July, 1812 carried the proclamation issued on the sixth that 'on the seventeenth day of June last, the Congress of the United States of America declared that War then existed between those States and their Territories, and the United Kingdom of Great Britain and Ireland and the dependencies thereof. . . .'

The causes seemed very remote from Upper Canadian concerns and interests. In his war message to Congress, President Madison gave the main reason for the clash between Britain and America to be England's policy on the high seas and her claim to a virtual monopoly of navigation and commerce thereon. Driven to desperate measures by the protracted Napoleonic Wars and their tangled alliances, England deployed her navy to full effect. Her men-o'-war blockaded ports, searched ships of other nations for deserters from the Royal Navy, and sailed close off American ports, harassing inbound and outbound traffic.

The ironic note, so often struck by History, was that the confrontation came at a time when England was prepared to moderate some of her more high-handed actions; by then, however, national emotions in America had been too thoroughly aroused. There had been rumours of British and Canadian agents stirring up the Indians of the western territories to go on tomahawk rampages against American settlements. These territories did not as yet have a vote to influence decisions in Congresss, but such stories were one more irritation to add to the fundamental grievances on maritime matters.

From the American point of view, Upper Canada was merely an area that could be attacked to strain England's already war-stretched resources even further, and perhaps become a hostage to be held to ransom at the postwar bargaining table.

The governor-in-chief of the Canadas at the time was Lieutenant-General Sir George Prevost, of Swiss descent and a somewhat bland, indecisive personality. Dr. William 'Tiger' Dunlop, the strong-opinioned army surgeon who would work on the opening of the road to Penetanguishene, stated flatly that 'a more incompetent Viceroy could hardly have been selected for such trying times. Timid at all times, despairing of his resources, he was afraid to venture anything. . . .'[175] Pneumonia killed him very shortly before he was due to stand court-martial for his actions at the end of the war.

In complete contrast to this uninspiring individual was Major-General Isaac Brock, appointed Administrator of Upper Canada in October 1811 during the absence in England on leave of Lieutenant-Governor Gore. Brock had been Commander of the Troops in Upper Canada since July 1810, and had vastly more experience of the Canadas than Prevost, who had arrived as governor-in-chief as recently as September 1811 after having been lieutenant-governor of Nova Scotia since 1808.

Brock had first come to Canada in the spring of 1802 as commanding officer of the 49th Regiment of Foot, and spent his time thereafter in Canada except for a period of leave in 1805 and 1806. He was indeed the beau ideal of the British army officer in background, personality, and ability — a man whom Simcoe might at heart have envied and wished to be like.

Isaac Brock came from an old-established aristocratic family of soldiers and statesmen from the Isle of Guernsey. Like many of his forebears he was noted for his height and qualities of leadership; he was a handsome, athletic figure, very popular with his men, although one suspects that he may at times have been short in his manner to those civilians with whom he had to deal. He was a good disciplinarian, relying as much upon example as upon regulations. His reputation has stood the test of time better, perhaps, than any other officer of his rank and position in the Canadas and has certainly overshadowed that of Prevost.

Almost immediately after taking up his duties as administrator, Brock wrote to Lord Liverpool on 23 November, 1811, in an abrupt military style, the antithesis of Simcoe's wordy prose: 'I have directed a survey of a tract of land on Lake Simcoe belonging to the Indians to meet your views. The merchants are particularly anxious to obtain a route for their goods unconnected with American territory. It is proposed to purchase 428 acres of land and erect grist mills for the convenience of a populous neighbourhood.'[174] With this letter he enclosed the 1810 memorial from William McGillivray and his associates in the North West Company. It would be the last time that he would pay any attention to proposals for Yonge Street.

Here in Brock, however, is evident much of the pattern of thinking developed in the professional soldier. The construction of gristmills to encourage the growth of settlement he doubtless regarded as a necessary official policy, but he would take no great personal interest in the progress of settlement, nor show any warmth or concern for the settlers themselves. Brock was a soldier first and last, and hang the rest.

As early as 1803 he had shown a prejudice against American settlers coming into Upper Canada, believing that they might undermine British authority there. Like Simcoe, Brock wanted to see a settlement of military veterans in the province to give it a nucleus of steadfast loyalty. Very few of the military profession, however, shared Brock's devotion to his calling whereby he could tolerate whatever conditions the service put upon him.

Upper Canada had few attractions at that time for the officers of its garrisons. That old curmudgeon of Fleet Street, Dr. Johnson, had declared the principal amusement of officers in country quarters to be spitting over a bridge. So it must have been for those at York, or in even remoter posts. For the soldiers there was little more than alcohol to keep them in a state of chronic numbness sufficient to allow them to endure their surroundings. *The York Gazette* carried the particulars and descriptions of deserters, for the harbouring of whom the fine was £20.[175]

Still, these regulars were the men upon whom Brock would have to rely, his expectations of Upper Canada being almost nil. As president of the Executive Council, he had hoped to put some teeth into measures for the defence of the province, but much to his disgust his efforts were unsuccessful: 'The many doubtful characters in the Militia made me anxious to introduce the oath of abjuration into the bill . . .this highly important measure was lost by the casting voice of the Chairman. — The great influence which the vast number of settlers from the United States possess over the decisions of the Lower House, is truly alarming, and ought by every practical means to be diminished.'[176]

Even a century later the memory of this situation would arouse intense rancour in those citizens of Toronto whose forebears had been loyal to the Crown: 'A large proportion of [Upper Canada's] population . . .were long known as "Proclamation men," Yankee settlers, who had taken advantage of Governor Simcoe's liberal system of land grants, and had come to Canada from purely mercenary motives, bringing with them their republican sentiments and

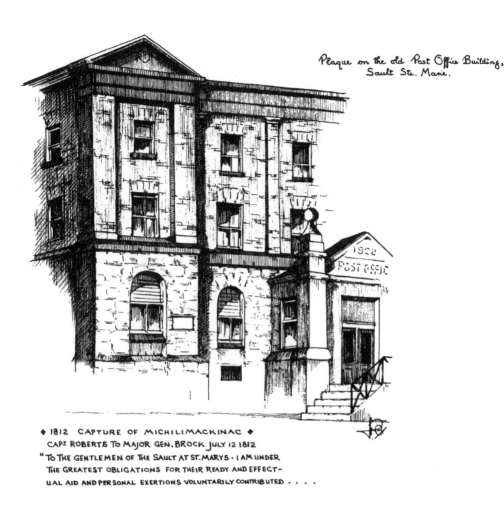

Plaque on the old Post Office Building,
Sault Ste. Marie.

♦ 1812 CAPTURE OF MICHILIMACKINAC ♦
CAPᵗ ROBERTS TO MAJOR GEN. BROCK JULY 12 1812
"TO THE GENTLEMEN OF THE SAULT AT ST. MARYS - I AM UNDER
THE GREATEST OBLIGATIONS FOR THEIR READY AND EFFECT-
UAL AID AND PERSONAL EXERTIONS VOLUNTARILY CONTRIBUTED . . . .

anti-British proclivities, amounting in many instances to hatred. This disloyal element was much more extensive than is now generally known or supposed, and came nigh to the undoing of the country.'[177]

Brock was well aware that those with undecided loyalties are quick to cast their lot with a winning cause. In December 1811, he had pointed out to the unimaginative Prevost that even before war had become a reality, 'before we can expect an active co-operation on the part of the Indians, the reduction of Detroit and Michilimackinac must convince that people, who conceive themselves to have been sacrificed in 1794 [by Jay's Treaty], to our policy, that we are earnestly engaged in the war.'[178] And the same would apply to the citizens in and around York.

Amherstburg would be the base from which he intended to carry out his strike, and in Brock's opinion the main American attack would come along the frontier between Niagara and Fort Erie. In such event a naval force would be needed on Lake Erie to guard the line from Amherstburg to Fort Erie; Brock, however, like

Simcoe, considered the state of the Provincial Marine on the Lakes to be a shambles. Its commander, benign old 'Commodore' Grant, was eighty-five years old, twice the age of Brock.

When the war came, Brock was left much to his own devices by the lackadaisical Prevost, and he took full advantage of his opportunity. Express instructions were sent via Yonge Street on 26 June, 1812, advising Captain Charles Roberts, the commanding officer at St. Joseph, to attack the American garrison on Mackinac Island. There was then some uncharacteristic shilly-shallying as these orders were suspended on the twenty-seventh and renewed again on the twenty-eighth; then by a despatch of the fourth of July that reached Robers on the fifteenth he was finally instructed to use his discretion to attack Mackinac or concentrate on the defence of St. Joseph.

Roberts attacked. He descended on Mackinac with 45 officers and men, seasoned grizzlies of his 10th Royal Veterans, plus about 180 voyageurs and almost 400 Indians organized by Toussaint Pothier. The entire force was convoyed by the North West Company's schooner *Caledonia,* commandeered by Roberts on its way down from the Sault. So isolated were these posts that even by that date, 17 July, 1812, the Americans at Mackinac were as yet unaware of the declaration of war. The 'Gibraltar of the West' fell without any resistance. Lieutenant Porter Hanks, its American commander, while awaiting court-martial at Detroit for his surrender of Mackinac, was killed on 15 August by a cannon shot that crashed through his room from the Britsh battery on the opposite bank of the Detroit River.

Brock still remained pessimistic about the attitudes in Upper Canada as he wrote in a letter on 29 July, 1812 that 'the population, believe me is essentially bad. — A full belief possess them all that this Province must inevitably succumb. — Legislators, Magistrates, Militia Officers, all, have imbibed the idea, and are so sluggish and indifferent in all their respective offices that the artful and active scoundrel is allowed to parade the Country without interruption, and commit all imaginable mischief. —'[179]

He was sure, however, that many 'cool calculators' would rally to his support 'were the regular troops encreased.'[180] The sequel to Mackinac encouraged in some degree that support. General Hull, 'a short, corpulent, good natured old gentleman', in command of the U.S. Army at Detroit, was completely rattled by the sudden British success at Mackinac, and on 16 August, 1812, the British took Detroit in what was almost a walkover. Poor old Hull was court-martialled for cowardice and sentenced to be shot, but was pardoned because of his services in the War of Independence.

All sorts of strange rumours were now abroad. One such rumour ran that 'a Mr. Wilmot [Wilson?], Surveyor General of Upper Canada, who lived near York for many years, has collected a respectable number of men (about 60 in number), attached to the American cause and proceeded on his march through the wilderness to join General Hull. Wilmot, they say, is much exasperated against the Government of Canada and his followers not unlike their leader.'[181] A fine tangle of a tale: the surveyor general was Thomas Ridout, Wilmot was still surveying for the government; and the former surveyor general, C. B. Wyatt, who had cause for grievance after being at odds with Gore, had gone to England in 1806 to start a libel suit.

The victory against Detroit was a tremendous lift for Upper Canada and did much to prevent the disaffection rife in rumours from spreading. The 'glorious year' for British arms in the province was indeed 1812. The defeat of the Americans at the battle of Queenston Heights, however, proved disastrous for the British; there they lost General Brock, shot while leading his troops in what was little more than a glorified rally in an apple orchard, on 13 October, 1812. His was a dashing gesture of leadership that ended in costly waste, his death.

Brock's successor was Lieutenant-General Roger Sheaffe, a most unpopular, harsh-mannered martinet. That renegade Presbyterian, Bishop Strachan of York,

"Miss Russell, loaded her phaeton with all sorts of necessaries, so that the whole party had to walk. My poor old grandfather (Mr. Baldwin) by long persuasion at length consented to give up fighting, and accompany the ladies. Aunt Baldwin (Mrs. Dr. Baldwin) and her four sons, Major Fuller, who was an invalid under Dr. Baldwin's care, Miss Russell, Miss Wilcox, and the whole cavalcade sallied forth: the youngest boy St. George, a mere baby, my mother (Miss Baldwin - later Mrs. Breakenridge) carried on her back nearly the whole way."

(Miss Mary Warren Baldwin's (Mrs. Breakenridge) story as related by her daughter, Mrs. Murray in <u>Toronto of Old</u>; Henry Scadding, D.D., p.434)

who held about as many opinions on military matters as on the Church, could never find enough bad things to say about Sheaffe and his military competence, or lack of it.

The inhabitants of York and its vicinity were for the most part uninterested in the play of politics and maintained a general indifference to the pitch and toss of events. They watched and waited, and in 1813 saw a reversal of fortune for the British, when they then found themselves threatened directly by the Americans.

On the evening of 26 April, 1813, a fleet of fourteen ships under Commodore Chauncey, U.S.N., flying his flag in the 24-gun corvette *President Madison*, appeared off York. In this force were embarked 1,700 troops commanded by Major-General Henry Dearborn. They landed on the morning of the twenty-seventh to be met by Sheaffe's totally inadequate force of regulars, militia, and Indians.

The brunt of the attack was taken by the Grenadier Company — the heaviest, most powerful men for use in close combat — of the 8th, or the King's Regiment. They had only Indians for support, because the Glengarry Light Infantry Fencibles, led by Major-General Aeneas Shaw, senior militia officer, followed the wrong track and got themselves hopelessly lost in the woods. With such fumbling and floundering at the outset, defeat was a foregone conclusion; even the British talent for making defeats sound like victories couldn't retrieve this mess.

The regulars of the 8th made a desperate bayonet charge, but were forced back with heavy casualties. The Indians and the militia, who were late in arriving, were totally flummoxed by this fierce fighting and the noise and confusion from the naval bombardment covering the landing. No attempt was made to rally them, and they remained more or less disengaged for the duration of the brief action. Sheaffe, who has been criticized for even attempting to offer resistance, decided to withdraw what was left of his force to Kingston and let the local citizens and militia make what terms they could with the victorious Americans. Bishop Strachan worked himself into a fine froth of disgust at this lack of leadership, as he saw it, by Sheaffe.

Mrs. Strachan was not around to watch the proceedings. She had been packed off for safety to the home of Captain James Fulton on Lot 43 on the east side of Yonge Street, which he had purchased from Captain Richard Lippincott. Captain James was an Irishman, educated in the United States for an intended career as a Presbyterian divine; the War of Independence, however channelled his Celtic instincts into the fight on the British side, and so led to his eventual departure for Upper Canada.[182]

Those citizens who could clear out of town had done so along Yonge Street, the line of rural retreat from the presence of the Americans. Miss Mary Warren Baldwin, Dr. William Warren Baldwin's youngest sister who later married John Breakenridge, left this record of her departure: 'The ladies settled to go out to

Baron de Hoen's farm. ....He had at this time a farm about four miles up Yonge Street and on a lot called No. 1. Yonge Street was then a corduroy road immediately after leaving King Street and passing through a dense forest. Miss Russell [sister of Peter Russell] loaded her phaeton with all sorts of necessaries so that the whole party had to walk. ...When they had reached about half way out, they heard a most frightful concussion, and all sat down on logs and stumps, frightened terribly. They learned afterwards that this terrific sound was occasioned by the blowing up of the magazine of York Garrison when five hundred Americans were killed. ...The family at length reached Baron de Hoen's log house consisting of two rooms, one above and one below. After three days Miss Russell and [Miss Baldwin] walked into town just in time to prevent Miss Russell's house from being ransacked by the soldiers. ...[Miss Baldwin] saw the poor 8th Grenadiers come into town on the Saturday, and in church on Sunday, with the handsome Captain McNeil at their head, and the next day they were cut to pieces to a man.'[183]

Opinions and attitudes in York were varied, but the keynote seems to have been one of indifference. Isaac Willson, who served in the militia and witnessed the blowing up of the magazine, was one of the five sons of a staunch old Loyalist captain from New Jersey who had settled on Yonge Street, probably on Lot 30 west, about the time of Simcoe or shortly thereafter. There is no fervent Loyalist rancour evident, however, in the account that he wrote from 'Young Street' to his brother in England, describing the events of April 1813: 'But the Americans were greatly praised for their good conduct. There was a large quantity of farming utensils which were sent for the use of settlers in this country. The authorities would not allow these to be given out except to favorites. The Americans distributed these generally to all settlers so their visit to York was very useful in this respect. Many Americans like the country very much and said they would come and settle in it if the war was over. It struck my mind very forcibly the evening after the battle was over to see men who two hours before were doing their utmost to kill one another now conversing together with the greatest familiarity.'[184]

Governments have long been notorious for their wasteful and inefficient handling of stores, and in 1812 there seems to have been no exception. It was probably due more to incompetence than favouritism that the farming equipment had not been effectively distributed. Mrs. John Beikie, whose loyalty was beyond question, complained in a perfectly practical way to her brother that 'quantities of stores, farming utensils, etc., sent from England in the time of General Simeon, [Simcoe] were allowed to remain in the King's stores, and nothing of them did they [the settlers] ever get.'[185]

After some indiscriminate looting and the burning of the Parliament buildings, which seems to have resulted from emotions over-excited by the supposed discovery of a scruffy old scalp hanging there, the Americans left York on 1 May,

1813. Judge William Drummer Powell warned Prevost that 'in the Event of any serious disaster to his Majesty's Arms little reliance is to be had on the power of the well disposed to repress and keep down the Turbulence of the disaffected who are very numerous.'[186]

Which perhaps was overstating it more than a bit. Powell was very much on the lookout for himself, and wanted no part in anything that might jeopardize his ambitions. He was originally from Boston and came to Canada in 1779, his adherence to the Loyalist, anti-American establishment in York bringing him the appointment of chief justice in 1816.

In spite of what he thought, it was unlikely that there would be any great rioting to support the Americans actively. 'Wait and see' was the attitude most probably to be expected from the majority of citizens in and around York. The Yonge Street farmers would understandably be more concerned at the time by their spring planting. Brock had remarked with some exasperation on the militia's 'clamour to return and attend to their farms.'[187] The most that might be realized if the Americans were successful was the hope of the 'have-nots' that they would become 'haves' at the expense of the established administration and its social circle in York; hence 'windy' Powell's panic.

The Americans paid another brief visit to York from 31 July to 1 August, 1813. Ely Playter, who with his brother James had been in partnership with Abner Miles in running the latter's hotel-cum-tavern before removing to a farm on Yonge Street, recorded a hodge-podge of events in his diary. He had been present during the April attack on York as an lieutenant in the 3rd Regiment of the York Militia, witnessing the explosion of the magazine. On the evening of the twenty-seventh, he had hidden in the bushes north of the town, near the Don River, and watched the Americans loot his home. His wife, Sophie, and their children had been sent up Yonge Street to Newmarket for safety during this time.

He left the following account of the second visit:

> 31st. [July, 1813] The Yankie Fleet came into York Geo [his brother] was in town, came out in the evening told me of two Boats he had conducted up the Don one with 3 Dragons & Stores he had got up but the other lay by the Park, he went to town at Dark the Yankies had landed — opened Major Allen's & St. Georges Store Houses & were taken away the flour & c. . . .1st. August 1813. — Geo. Hanh. & me went to town they rode — I went into the Park — see the Am. fleet — one of which was coming up the bay & set of from her 5 boats up the Don. I then hastened home Geo. & Hanh. was out before me The Dragoons had gone down to the boat, we had word that the Yankies were coming up after the Stores & c. Captn. J.B. Robinson was out to help us, S. Sinclair & J. Kendrick also — we got the Ammunition all out of the boat & secreted the Arms & some Boxes of shot we sunk scuttled the boat & let her go —.[188]

Definite sides were obviously being taken in this incident: Playter and his associates were determined to outwit the Americans, but other pro-American individuals had clearly informed that Playter and the rest had hidden some government stores and ammunition up the Don River.

Those who were sympathetic to the Americans were perhaps not so much anti-British as 'anti' the town establishment figures in York. Along Yonge Street and among many of the farmers was the traditional distrust of the 'townie.' This had shown in their support for Judge Thorpe in the 1806 elections when he opposed the government candidate and what he called the aristocracy of shopkeepers in York. The barring of Thorpe from the Assembly by the autocratic Lieutenant-Governor Gore in 1807 had created undercurrents of ill-feeling that no doubt surfaced in some of the behaviour during the events at York in 1813.

Joseph Shepard (1766-1837), a Yonge Street old-timer whose colourful past seems to have been badly smudged in History's ledger, was perhaps typical of many of those who worked and farmed along that road when politics were an issue. The story is that he came up from the States some time in 1774, and long before the arrival of Simcoe in Upper Canada he was a roving Indian trader in the vicinity of York, maybe something after the fashion of Cowan at Matchedash, until in the 1790s he finally settled on Lot 16 west on the northwest corner of what are now Yonge Street and Sheppard Avenue.

He was against some of the measures that Brock had wished to introduce through the Assembly on the eve of the war, but crotchety, independent old fighter that he probably was, it is very likely that he was the Joseph Shepard serving as a private in the 3rd York Militia during the battle for York. He suffered three broken ribs and a badly crushed left thigh when the magazine blew up on that hectic twenty-seventh of April.

He would have no particular opinions on Americans one way or the other, provided that they left him alone, but he and his family would in later years be active in their support of motions against the government in the agitation for political reform. His attitudes, like those of many of his Yonge Street contemporaries, were probably due more to irritation with York officialdom than to anything else.

Realistic opportunism more than patriotic or political emotions has been the course throughout history of those practical bodies who have had to make a livelihood from the land. War to them is a soldier's business, and as such best left to those who are trained for it.

John Lyon, or Lyons, of Yonge Street was no exception to this rule when the breeze of war stirred York. In a deposition to Justice of the Peace Thomas Ridout on 17 August, 1813, one William Knott declared that 'on Sunday the first day of August last; while the Enemys forces were in York he saw John Lyon of the Township of Vaughan distiller drawing with his waggon Public Stores down to the Water Side for the Enemy, he saw no appearance of Compulsion, and for all that appeared Lyon did it voluntarily.'[189]

One of the tales of those days tells of the distribution of agricultural tools to the Yonge settlers by the Americans after they had looted the government stores in York — a fine Robin Hood touch by the settlers' way of it. When the Americans left, a search for these stores was soon under way by the officials from York. Some of this largesse is supposed to have been found in the pond on Lyons' property at Lot 36 west on Yonge, where it had been dumped to avoid detection.[190]

The Quakers of Newmarket and Gwillimbury did not, obviously, bear arms during the war, but several of their horses, being known for high quality, were commandeered by the military authorities. These horses were used to pull field guns and ammunition and stores wagons, and their drivers would be hired or conscripted civilians, into which category came the Quakers and Mennonites. Even if not so pressed, the Yonge Street Quakers would often go with their horses into York to be sure that these valuable animals were looked after properly, the military not being known for its care of other people's property.

'One of the People Called Quaker', Samuel 'the Hatter' Jackson of Yonge Street and formerly of Pennsylvania, had too much to say that was critical of the way things were being done in York and showed such American sympathies that he had to get out of town, so high did feelings run as the war progressed.[191]

A Yonge Street settler who landed inadvertently in the States at this time was Thomas Humberstone the Potter from Lot 14 west. He was an officer in the York Militia but the business of weapons was alien to him. A local story relates that an old musket dug up on his farm on Yonge Street was for long used to poke and stir the logs in his fireplace; one day while his daughter was doing this the musket, which must have been loaded all that time, blew up and killed the unfortunate girl. One of Thomas's duties during the war was to take a group of American prisoners by batteau to Kingston for confinement. Thomas's control of the situation seems to have been somewhat shaky because in the course of the journey, the Americans took over his batteau, made him their prisoner, and put in to the American shore; there he remained until the end of the war.[192]

In the general way of events in 1813, Upper Canada was exposed to serious threat by Commodore Perry's victory over the British fleet on Lake Erie in September, at the battle of Put-In Bay. This achieved what Brock had dreaded: the control by the Americans of Lake Erie; with the British retreat from Detroit, this gave the Americans ready access to Lake Huron and Mackinac. There was a great flap and flurry of letters, plans, and proposals now to improve the communication north from Yonge Street and Lake Simcoe.

Robert Dickson, an experienced trader and the commissary for stores at Mackinac and St. Joseph, wrote to Noah Freer, the military secretary, at the end of September, 1813: 'Should our fleet be totally destroyed on Lake Erie, as we have reason to believe, the bay at Machedash or Penetanguishene are both good harbours, and there is plenty of excellent wood in the vicinity for constructing a vessel of any dimensions.'[193] And on 23 October he forwarded to Freer 'a map of Lake Simcoe on a large scale. I think that if a road is to be cut the best route is from Kempenfeldt to Penetanguishene.'[194]

The case for Penetanguishene, which Simcoe had once proposed, would now be advocated with increasing urgency in the alarm following the British disaster on Lake Erie. Lord Bathurst, secretary of state, instructed Prevost in a despatch of 3 December, 1913, to proceed with the defences necessary to combat the American threat to Lake Huron.

Even Prevost seems to have been pricked into an awareness that things were looking pretty grim, and must have been somewhat relieved when Lieutenant-General Drummond reported back to him on 19 January, 1814: 'I beg to assure you that I have lost no time in giving ample instructions relating to the supply of troops and provisions to be forwarded to Michilimackinac by Lakes Simcoe and Huron, as also with regard to the building of gunboats and bateaux at Panatanguishene for their conveyance thither.'[195]

A little more than a week later and Drummond provided further details hedged about with reservations 'from the authority of several credible persons, and likewise from Mr Wilmot, the Surveyor, who had been employed in running the line, from Lake Simcoe, to Penitanguishan Bay, that it is impracticable to transport anything by that route, previous to a road being cut upwards of thirty miles in length; and that it was calculated to take 200 men for at least 3 weeks, before it could be made passable; and, in case of deep snow, it could not be done at all. In consequence of the delay, and difficulty, attending such a measure, Mr Crookshank has made arrangements for forwarding the supplies to Nottawasaga Bay, on Lake Huron, a distance of only 20 Miles from Penitanguishan. . . .The opening of the road to the river, leading to Nottawasaga Bay, will take but 12 Men for about 10 days; and, in the course of a few days, as soon as a shed can be erected, on the other side of Lake Simcoe, he will commence sending the Stores across it, should a thaw not prevent. This mode of proceeding would undoubtedly prove somewhat expensive; but I see no alternative.'[196] Some sort of extension had to be pushed through from Yonge Street, but it was not going to be easy, and time had run out.

The man chosen to lead the expedition to bolster the defence of Mackinac was Lieutenant-Colonel Robert McDouall of the Glengarry Light Infantry Fencibles. He had served as A.D.C. to Prevost in 1812, had recently distinguished himself at the battle of Stoney Creek in June 1813, and had subsequently become commandant of a company of Glengarries stationed at Three Rivers.

Madelaine Askin, the wife of John, Jr., would say of McDouall when he was at St. Joseph in 1815 that [he] makes the service so hard that scarcely anyone can stand it. He has driven Mr. Monck, the commissary, crazy.'[197] This was probably something of an overstatement, but the task for which he was chosen would need a hard man, a man who could drive when the wiles of leadership were exhausted.

He set out from Kingston sometime at the end of February, 1814, with a party of thirty carpenters and shipwrights, twenty-one seamen of the Royal Navy, eleven artillerymen in charge of four field guns, and two companies of the Royal Newfoundland Regiment whose men were probably more expert in the ways of boats and the sea than in those of the army. With this group went the urgently needed supplies for Mackinac and trade goods and presents for the Indians there whose loyalty was now more necessary than ever.

They disembarked at York, which with its charred legacy from the events of April 1813 must have been a more than usually dismal sight in the cold, slushy misery of winter. From York the contingent ploughed and plodded and marched as best it could up Yonge Street, hauling the equipment and supplies to the frozen Lake Simcoe. And here the road ended.

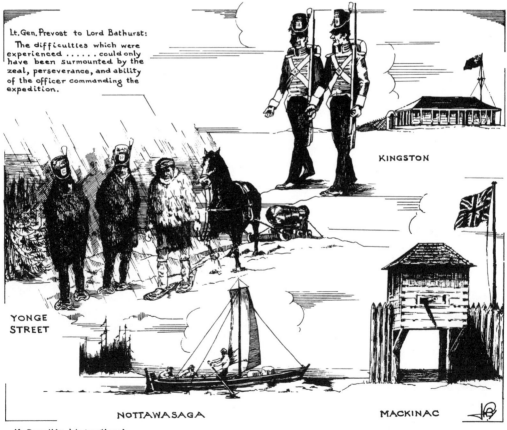

Lt. Gen. Prevost to Lord Bathurst:

The difficulties which were experienced . . . . . . could only have been surmounted by the zeal, perseverance, and ability of the officer commanding the expedition.

KINGSTON

YONGE STREET

NOTTAWASAGA

MACKINAC

McDouall's Winter March

Dr. Johnson, who in his dictioneering way could whistle up an opinion on any subject, declared roundly that 'no man will be a sailor, who has contrivance enough to get himself into a jail; for being in a ship is being in jail, with the chance of being drowned.' To the shipwrights of the naval yard at Kingston, and to the Royal Navy men who had replaced the Provincial Marine on the Lakes, a voyage on a leaky ship would probably have been a welcome alternative to the journey that they were embarked upon.

McDouall must have been glad to have the Royal Newfoundlanders along: they were men of a breed long known for an ability to improvise in the bleak harshness of their island home's outports. Dr. William 'Tiger' Dunlop left an interesting observation that the regulars of the line regiments were helpless in adapting to unusual conditions, whereas provincial troops were adept at putting up shanties for shelter and at woodcraft.[198] And, by God, they had to adapt this time.

McDouall's force tracked across the frozen lake to the head of Kempenfeldt Bay; from there they followed the old Indian trail, the Nine-Mile Portage, to Willow Creek. Where the creek joined the Nottawasaga River they built temporary huts and the shipwrights set to building thirty bateaux to transport the stores across Lake Huron. These bateaux, hastily shaped and joined from the timber cut by the soldiers, were really double-ended, flat-bottomed barges that were pushed along by poles, oars, and sometimes sails. They must have been put together at the rate of about one a day.

On the nineteenth of April they started down the length of the Nottawasaga River, the soldiers filing along the banks and hacking at the branches and brush as the bateaux veered clumsily at the twists in its winding course. The journey to the mouth of the Nottawasaga took six days, in what turned out to be unusually mild weather for the season, until the unpredictable winter wastes, the slush and floes of Georgian Bay and Lake Huron were reached.

After a rough and hazardous voyage, with the loss of only one bateau — its crew and cargo saved — McDouall arrived at Mackinac on 18 May, 1814. As if his difficulties were not enough, he had to put up with the nonsense of Lieutenant Poyntz of the navy, who believed that when they were on Lake Huron he should be in charge of the fleet and therefore the whole expedition. McDouall later expressed his exasperation with the 'pertinacious' Poyntz in a letter to Drummond.[199]

Prevost was loud in his praises to Bathurst of McDouall's success in getting 'open and deeply laden batteaux across so great an extent of water as Lake Huron, covered with immense fields of ice and agitated by violent gales of wind.' It was no doubt with a feeling of considerable relief, because he also wrote to His Lordship on 10 July, 1814, that 'the Island and Fort of Michilimackinac is the first importance, as tending to promote our Indian connexion and secure them in our interest: its geographical position is admirable; its influence extends . . .among the Indian tribes to New Orleans and the Pacific Ocean . . . .it gives security to the

"The want of oxen produced another enormous source of expenditure; when a log was cut it had to be drawn by drag ropes out of the way, and thirty men could not perform, in the deep snow, what a yoke of oxen could easily have performed in light snow or none at all."

(*Recollections of the American War; 1812-14: Dr. Dunlop.*)

great trading establishments of the North-West and Hudson's Bay Companies.'[200]   Yonge Street played an important part in the lifeline to the 'Gibraltar of the West' where McDouall successfully beat off an American attack on 4 August, 1814. It was, however, a precarious lifeline. Yonge Street ended at Holland Landing, and if Penetanguishene was to be established and reliably supplied as a base, then something more than the round-about routes by the Nottawasaga or Severn rivers was needed. In recommending such a base, Lieutenant-Colonel Robert Nichol, quarter-master general of militia, advised that 'the road, however, to the north of Lake Simcoe which is, I understand, about twenty-four miles, should be previously opened.'[201] And, as Drummond had pointed out, it would be expensive.

The road was put through from the north shore of Kempenfeldt Bay as had been proposed, and the man in charge of the cutting party was the colourful and eccentric Dr. Dunlop, the massive, uncouth, carroty-headed Scots army surgeon, chosen perhaps because of the lack of any other suitable volunteers. He started in December 1814. The description is best left to the doctor's own sharp style:

> At this time, it was proposed to build a large ship on Lake Huron — we having then so many on Lake Erie — that would be able, from her size, and the weight of her metal, to cope with the small vessels that composed the American flotilla on Lake Erie. As there is a channel through Lake Saint Clair, and the Rivers Detroit and Saint Clair, by which she could pass from the one lake into the other, an inlet, called Penetanguishene, was selected as the proper site of a new dockyard unluckily, at this time, Penetanguishene was in the woods, thirty miles from Lake Simcoe; and before a ship of the line could be built, a road must be cut, and stones broke along it . . . .a company of the Canadian Fencibles, with about the same number of militia, under the direction of Colonel Cockburn, of the Quarter Master General's Department, was despatched up to the north, with instructions to have the road cut at all hazards . . . .The labour of cutting the road in deep snow was great, and the expense proportionately enormous. Our provisions had to be carried in on men's backs for the snow had not been broken in time enough to admit of horses or even oxen, so that one half of our men were employed in carrying, or, as it is technically termed, *packing* provisions for the other. The want of oxen produced another enormous source of expenditure; when a log was cut it had to be drawn by drag ropes out of the way, and thirty men could not perform, in the deep snow, what a yoke of oxen could easily have performed in light snow or none at all. When the snow got very deep, too, we had, before felling a tree, to dig a pit round it of sufficient diameter to allow a man to stand in it and swing his axe.[202]

Dunlop, of course, with all the Scots disdain for the bumbling ways of the English when it came to doing something practical, could not resist a dig at the manner of the performance: 'I would undertake tomorrow to cut a better road than we could possibly do, for forty pounds a mile, and make money by it, — give me timely warning and a proper season of the year, whereas I am convinced that £2,500 to £3,000 did not pay for the one we cut.' He also, however, had the annoying Scots habit of being right. For all the effort that went into its hurried, last-minute creation, the road was a sorry extension of Yonge Street with which it still was only connected by water traffic between Kempenfeldt Bay and Holland Landing.

Potholed, narrow, and ill-marked, it was barely passable by individual travellers, let alone supply-encumbered convoys, heading from York to Penetanguishene. George Head, travelling that way in 1815, left what perhaps has been the most-quoted account of the conditions that existed after 'Tiger' Dunlop and his gang had hacked out a pathway:

> On the 25th of February [1815] I left York with Mr. C——, in a two-horse sleigh, on our way to Lake Huron. The snow was soft and the draft heavy; however, the horses were good, and we travelled thirty miles to the village of Newmarket (which lies about a mile out of the road on the right hand), and arrived a little after dark. We were hospitably entertained by Mr. Peter Robinson, who provided us with a good supper and comfortable beds. Our host, as well as being a contractor with Government, was an agent of the North West Company, and held, moreover, sundry provincial appointments. Added to this, he kept a shop in the house where we now were, which was plentifully stocked with all manner of commodities, particularly such as were suited to the wants and tastes of the Indians: it was in fact, the great mart to which all those in this part of the community resorted, to furnish themselves with the different articles of which they stood in need, — flour, cheese, blue cloth, cottons, hardware, & c; besides guns, powder and shot, for the men, and all sorts of millinery and ornament for the squaws, such as flaring gown patterns, beads, and rings for their noses.
>
> February 26th.— . . .we had what might be called an agreeable drive along a very good road to Holland River, . . .a distance of eleven miles. There was a sort of public house established at the spot where we had arrived, and which was called the Landing, being the point from whence the river was considered navigable in the summer Our sleigh was soon brought out, and, being launched down the sedgy bank, the horses were put to; . . .We had overtaken a party of English shipwrights at the public house we had just left, who were on their way to join the new station at Penetanguishene Bay . . . .These men finding we were going thither also, followed in our train, and, as we travelled

slow, they were enabled to keep up with us on foot . . . .We bore about three or four miles up [Kempenfeldt] bay, and put up at a log-house, which had been newly erected on the north bank . . . .This log-house had been built for the purpose of the communication to Penetanguishene . . . .We made a roaring fire, and roasted some potatoes, which we eat with cold meat, with which we had taken care to provide ourselves; and this repast occupying but little time, the whole party, shipwrights and all, each measured his length on the floor before the fire. I now began to think I had enough of all this . . . .
February 27th. — We had already advanced thirty-six miles from the house on the banks of Holland River, which was the nearest human habitation worthy of bearing the name between the spot we were and the town of York; and the road we were now about to travel had been newly cut through the forest, so that it was as bad as it could well be. To assist the communication, however, a hut at the distance of twenty miles had been erected, where we intended to pass the night . . . .When we reached the hut, we found it nothing more than a few boughs raised up; of an oblong form, and having one of the long sides quite open to the weather . . . .
February 28th. — The road was still miserably bad, but with the assistance of the shipwrights we were enabled to reach Yeo [Wye] River, a distance of ten miles. We were frequently obliged to take the horses out of the sleigh for two or three hundred yards together, while the men drew it over trees which had fallen across the road . . . .When we reached the ice of Yeo River, we got on a great deal better . . . .We pursued our course till we came upon Gloucester Bay, and from thence we reached that of Penetanguishene.[203]

By the time Head had struggled through to take up his duties as commissary at Penetanguishene, where a warship was to be built for a British presence on Lake Huron, it was all an anti-climax anyway. The war with the States had ended more or less in a draw with the signing of the Treaty of Ghent on Christmas Eve of 1814, although to the amazement of the Indians, Mackinac, on which so much effort had been spent, was returned to the Americans. McDouall and the British garrison were then transferred to nearby Drummond Island, a place that seems to have been loathed by all who had the bad luck to be sent there.

Tradition has it that a party of troops proceeding up Yonge Street with stores for Penetanguishene, including a heavy anchor — for the warship — that was being laboriously dragged by oxen, heard the news of the war's end as they reached Holland Landing. In the general jubilation that followed, the anchor seems to have been forgotten, and has remained to this day at the Landing. The ship was never completed.

At this stage, then, Yonge Street offered a fair highway from Eglinton to Holland Landing, although it made a sorry bog in the rainy season of spring and early summer when the corduroy sections would be awash, and horses could break a leg on the slippery, rolling logs. Below Eglinton, in York itself, it had at last been extended below Queen (Lot) Street to the bay by the energies of some of the town's more active citizens.[204] Northward from Queen to the present Yorkville, the soil made the road atrocious in spite of attempts to lay a log surface over it — this was the corduroy road described by Miss Baldwin (Mrs. Breakenridge) in her retreat from the invasion of York.

The necessities of war had finally persuaded the North West Company to use the Yonge Street route over which they had dithered for so many years, and so at last the fur trade made its full impact on the road — for good or bad depended upon the occupations affected by it. This use continued from 1812 to 1821, when

Robinson's Store, Newmarket.

"He kept a shop in the house where we now were, which was plentifully stocked with all manner of commodities, particularly such as were suited to the wants and tastes of the Indians : it was in fact, the great mart to which all those in this part of the country resorted, to furnish themselves with the different articles of which they stood in need, —— flour, cheese, blue cloth, cottons, hardware, & c; besides guns, powder and shot, for the men, and all sorts of millinery and ornament for the squaws, such as flaring gown patterns, beads, and rings for their noses."

(*Forest Scenes and Incidents in the Wilds of North America*; George Head, Esq., pp. 178-185).

the North West Company was finally swallowed up by its arch-rival, the Hudson's Bay Company.

Isaac Willson, again writing to his brother Jonathan from 'Young Street', complained on 20 August, 1815 that 'the Government is carrying out a great many expensive undertakings at York such as building barracks storehouses wharfes and a house for the Governor. [Sir Frederick Philipse Robinson was then provisional Lieutenant-Governor until Gore's return in September, 1815.] This makes labor very high and hands very hard to get $1.50 per day being the common price with victuals and grog. There is very little done in the farming line on that account and the high wages that are given for people with waggons to carry goods through the country to the Lakes for the North West Company to trade with the Indians and bringing stores back for Government which were conveyed up at an immense expense during the war. They pay no regard to economy.'[205] Although the high cost of labour and the expenses of the unpopular Lieutenant-Governor Gore may have been a sore point with Yonge Street farmers such as Isaac Willson, the trading business would benefit the merchants who could take advantage of it.

Old associations would slowly dissolve as other patterns of partnership emerged among those who were making a name for themselves in the changing society of Yonge Street. Ely Playter, in the haphazard scratchings of his diary that record the daily social trivia, makes frequent mention of the Bemans, St. George, Samuel Heron, and Abner Miles in entries such as the following unexceptional selections:

> Thursday 9 Novr 1804 ....fell in with Doctr Tallman lent him my spare horse & we rode together to the Town, stopp'd at Miles's & Dined.
> Tuesday 24th Sept 1805 ....call'd at Mr Miles & took Dinr — drank some Whiskey at Wilsons Inn, and at Herons came to Father full of glee —.

And after the War of 1812:

> 2nd [March 1815] — ....Had a party out to Bond's in the evening Danced all night, got home by Day-break.
> 30 [April 1815] — ....Sunday — Sophie-self rode up Y[onge] S[treet] Dined at J Arnolds, I went up to Langstaffs & we returned by evening.[206]

Bond, Arnold, and Langstaff — probably John who, about 1809, had married Lucy, the daughter of the late Abner Miles — all were names well known on Yonge Street throughout the 1800s. Playter's other old associate of earlier years, Elisha Beman, had emigrated in 1803 from New York to Upper Canada, where he settled on Lot 92 on the east side of Yonge Street. By now, however, he had graduated to a more successful, privileged circle; his social rise was helped by his second marriage in 1805 to the widow of Christopher Robinson. Christopher Robinson, United Empire Loyalist, descendant of Virginian tobacco aristocrats, had been with the first Queen's Rangers in the War of Independence and had worked with Simcoe in 1793. Thus his name was well established in the society of York before his early death in 1798.

It was Elisha Beman's store and mills that became the nucleus for the town of Newmarket — a business that boomed during the immediate post war years when it was taken over by his stepson, Peter Robinson.

From the Reverend Henry Scadding's statement in his *Toronto of Old*, it was quite possibly around the wartime period — when Yonge Street became, willy-nilly, the route of the North West trade — that the name New Market was coined: 'Here is an additional *mart* for the convenience of an increased population: a place where farmers and others may purchase and exchange commodities without being at the trouble of a journey to York or elsewhere.'[207] Ely Playter noted in the confusion of York's occupation during 28 April, 1813: 'Joel Beman knock'd us up he had come down with the waggon hearing I was killed, & Sophie with the children & some of the things I sent out with him to New Market, George & me went with them to Ridouts . . . .'[208]

Elisha's two sons, Eli and Joel, were associated with Peter Robinson in his merchant venture at Newmarket, which prospered considerably as he purchased property on Yonge Street during the period from 1814 to 1832: Lots (or parts of lots) 103 to 105, 109 and 118 on the west side, and 106 to 108 on the east side. In 1821 Peter Robinson built the successful Red Mill on Lot 106.[209]

With the further addition of stores run by Cawthra and by Roe in the 1820s, a fairly extensive market centre was developed for the Indian trade that reached a peak around 1825. Peter Robinson was not slow in setting up a tavern, always a very profitable adjunct to the trading game, south of the Red Mill at Holland Landing in about 1822. This was near the southern Upper Landing, also known for obvious reasons as Canoe Landing, a favourite Indian rendezvous. North from here was the Lower Landing, in frequent use during the War of 1812 because it was the farthest point up the east branch of the Holland River that could be reached with heavily laden bateaux.

Sometime in the 1820s the Upper Landing became known as Johnson's Landing after Joseph Johnson and his family; they had originally settled on Yonge Street between Thornhill and York Mills. Johnson made a shrewd move in this shift to the Landing where he, too, began a tavern shortly after the 1812 war. The North West Company had established a storehouse there, and by the end of the 1820s, Newmarket had replaced York as the centre for the annual distribution of 'presents' to the Indians.

A description of this yearly junket to the Lower Landing was given by the

Methodist missionary, Peter Jones, a son of the old Welsh surveyor of Yonge Street, Augustus Jones, who had married an Indian woman, Tuhbenahneequay, the daughter of a Missisauga chief: 'Col. Givins had already arrived and appeared quite friendly until a drunken Frenchman made a complaint to him about the Methodist preachers . . . .It took the Commissary all day to divide the goods, which consist of blankets, cloths, calicoes, shirting, hats, guns, rifles, powder, shot, balls, tin and brass kettles, pots, axes, silk handkerchiefs, ribbons, thread, brooches & c. The amount of their payments is £1,200 currency per annum, besides the King's presents, which perhaps are nearly as much more; . . . .The men were seated in rows on the ground by themselves, the women and children in the same order . . . .they finished dividing the presents about five o'clock.'[210]

It would obviously be good business for any merchant who could supply the variety of articles that made up the 'presents'. Peter Robinson's home-based emporium has already been described by George Head on his way to Penetanguishene. John Cawthra of Newmarket 'employed a man and several women making women's and children's slippers, hats, (as an offshoot of the fur trade), and other small wares that his brother, William, sold through the Quaker settlement on Yonge Street.'[211]

A description of the state of road along Yonge Street from York to Holland Landing at this time has been left by one of those typically enthusiastic, record-keeping, travelling Englishmen then becoming so common about the globe. John Goldie, in *The Tramp of a Botanist Through Upper Canada in 1819,* had this to say of the road north to Lake Simcoe: '27 June, 1819 — It was about six o'clock in the morning when I started, [from York] and in a short time it became so hot that travelling was very oppressive. At 9 a.m. the thermometer stood 84. The roads were now again become remarkably dry and dusty, so that when any wheeled carriage passed I was involved in a cloud of dust which was extremely disagreeable. This is the best road that I have seen in Upper Canada, and since I left York there have been more waggons travelling this road than all those that I have seen since I left Montreal. Having gone on slowly I arrived in the evening at what is called the Upper Landing Place, which is about nine miles by water from Lake Simcoe. I stopped at the farthest house upon this road and have bespoken a week's lodging here, as I expect that it is a spot very interesting to the botanist.

July 3rd. This evening a Company of the 70th Regiment from Drummond Island in Lake Huron arrived here. They have been up the country for two years, and have been exchanged for two companies of the 68th. Lake Simcoe is between thirty and forty miles long and of considerable breadth . . . .On the south side there is what is called a river, which although of no great breadth, has yet sufficient depth to allow schooners to come to the Upper Landing Place, which is nine miles from the Lake and thirty-six from York . . . .After crossing the Lake there is nine miles of a portage and then there is water carriage all the way to Lake

Huron. It is very probable that at no very distant period this will become the most frequented of all the routes to the north-west. At the present time there are no houses or stores on the north side of Simcoe at the portage, which makes it very inconvenient and renders the goods transported liable to be injured by the weather. Since a steamboat has commenced to sail on Lake Erie the cheapest and most expeditious mode of sending down the furs from the interior is by that route, although it is four hundred miles longer than by Simcoe. There is only one steamer upon the Lake, which is sufficient for all the trade at present.'[212]

The fur-trade boom for Newmarket and the Yonge Street route would be of brief duration; it lasted only until better alternatives of transport were developed, but while it did last, those who could take advantage of the fleeting moment prospered, and the road itself was improved by the steady to-and-fro of the increased traffic.

On the other side of the swamp, however, northwest from Holland Landing, it was a vastly different story, although the tale had some similarity to that of Yonge Street's early years. The trail through the woods north of Kempenfeldt Bay had been cut hastily by 'Tiger' Dunlop and his soldiers, and soon settlers, government-inspired by the free grants of land to 'U.E. Loyalists, or such persons as have served His Majesty in the Navy or Regular Army,' moved in at infrequent intervals along its length.

They were for the most part military veterans, and they appear in general to have been from the non-commissioned ranks with a sprinkling of half-pay officers who had neither prospects, nor connections, nor future beyond what offered in a gamble in Upper Canada. Although in theory the Penetanguishene Road was an extension of Yonge Street, the people who settled along it had very little in common with those who were now firmly established on the stretch between York and Holland Landing.

Sorrier yet was the lot of those people who came into the area around the western head of Kempenfeldt Bay, between the Holland River's west branch and the start of the Penetanguishene Road. They were alien to the veterans and to the Yonge Street settlers alike. Poor Scots artisans and labourers and 'shanty' Irish, they had nothing left to lose in life, and in what little they could find in Upper Canada lay a last hope for renewed pride and opportunity.

In Britain after the wars against Napoleon had come the rumbles of social and political discontent, the usual twin offspring from any large-scale, long-drawn-out war. To the government of the day, reform carried an ugly republican taint and smacked of those 'Jacobin' notions that had led to the excesses of the French Revolution and the upheaval of its aftermath. It has been said that 'every time France caught a cold, Europe sneezed', and to prevent the spread of the virus in England repression became the order of the day. In 1819 the Peterloo Massacre went down in infamy when a detachment of enthusiastic but ill-controlled mounted militia used excessive violence to break up a crowd gathered out of doors to hear 'Orator' Hunt deliver a political speech. Glasgow saw the angry, frustrated fury of the 'radical' weavers' strike in 1820.

George Eliot in her novel *Middlemarch* portrayed the opposite ends of English society; she contrasted 'those poor Dagleys, in their tumbledown farmhouse, where they live in the back kitchen and leave the other rooms to the rats' with the editor of the Tory *Trumpet* who is against those reformers who 'get up and speechify by the hour against institutions which had existed when he was in his cradle.' The benefits from these institutions, however, were by no means universal.

"The usual dimensions of a house are eighteen feet by sixteen. The roof is covered with bark or shingles, and the floor with rough hewn planks, and the interstices between the logs that compose the walls being filled up with pieces of wood or clay."
(John Howison, *Letters from Upper Canada* -1820)

Even before the bloody clashes and bitterness that the peace ushered in and the sorry state of things described by George Eliot, the philanthropic but muddled schemes of Lord Selkirk in 1811 and 1812 had brought some of the excess population of Highland Scotland, Glasgow, and Ireland to Canada. The Irish at this time were in their perpetual bog of disaster, relieved only by their spirited and continuous rebellion against their conditions.

The journey undertaken by the impoverished emigrants was worse than any trek that the Pennsylvania 'Dutch' or the Loyalists had endured. Cramped and confined in the pens of whatever might float and shown less consideration than any thrifty Highland laird would give to his shorthorn cattle, they hazarded the North Atlantic.

There were as many reasons for emigrating as there were individuals, but poverty and despair more than the attraction of land grants drove these Scots and Irish to take whatever out was offered from their fate in Britain.

The first settlers to cross the Holland River in 1819 are said to have been three Irishmen: Wallace, Armstrong, and Algeo (the last is an un-Celtic name of Italian origin).[213] At about the same time a group of some seventeen men and their families, disillusioned with Selkirk's Red River scheme, settled in West Gwillimbury. They had left the Red River during 1816, made their way somehow from the area of Fort William on Lake Superior to the mouth of the Nottawasaga River, and then traversed the Nine-Mile Portage to Kempenfeldt Bay and Lake Simcoe. Their extreme poverty forced many of them, men and women, to hire themselves out to work in the settlements already on Yonge Street, until in 1819 they were able to move up the Holland River to Gwillimbury.[214]

Some of the Yonge Street originals were prepared to try their hands at whatever might offer in the new areas of the Kempenfeldt-Penetanguishene extension of Yonge. David Soules, a member of the pioneer family that had 'prayed permission' to 'locate Lot No 31 — west side of Yonge Street for *immediate* settlement' in 1798,[215] moved to the shore of Kempenfeldt Bay in 1823. He is supposed to have been with McDouall at the Nine-Mile Portage and later with 'Tiger' Dunlop on the Penetanguishene Road.

Eli Beman, at some time early in the 1820s, built a log shelter between present-day Barrie and Shanty Bay to cater to the traffic passing on to Penetanguishene from Yonge Street and Holland Landing. This astute entrepreneur had a further stake in this early travelling trade: he was the owner of a schooner that he ran on Lake Simcoe. It was described by Mary O'Brien as 'little, dirty and worse-managed ....chiefly manned and occupied by Indians.'[216] Obviously Beman had no great degree of competition in this business.

As in the earliest days along Yonge Street, there was now plenty of opportunity at its Lake Simcoe end for those enterprising enough to seize their chance. Samuel Lount, who had been born in Pennsylvania, came to Upper

Canada just before the 1812 war and finally settled with his brother George on Lot 103 on the west side of Yonge at Holland Landing where he prospered as farmer, blacksmith, and surveyor. Their father, Gabriel, with whom they had come to Upper Canada, originally settled on Lot 84 on the east side of Yonge.

The attitudes to the settlers and immigrants arriving after the war are evident in a long editorial in the *Upper Canada Gazette* of 17 July, 1817. Although cast in the precise prose of its time, it has a remarkably up-to-date ring in what it says about these new arrivals: 'Many of the soldiers serving during the first American War, at its conclusion, received grants of land, but from the habits of intemperance and idleness too frequently predominant amongst soldiers, they with some few exceptions, merely prolonged a miserable existence; and an idea thence prevailed that Europeans were utterly unfit for settlers, and that none but Americans could succeed; the children of those loyalists and soldiers are now grown up, and have proved themselves to be as fine a race of brave, hardy and loyal men, as any in the British Empire; . . .The late European settlers arrived here are of a different character to the first settlers; being for the most part, men early inured to patient and persevering industry, what they want in skill they will make up by assiduity; accordingly wherever they have settled they have astonished the old inhabitants with the unexpected progress made by them in a short time, and from their acquaintance with many modes of lessening human labor, have introduced some valuable knowledge to the country: even of those arrived this season, we are informed that some have already cleared and planted 2 or 3 acres of land each. 420 with passports from our Consul at New York, have already arrived at this place, and several hundreds more are expected; — indeed there are many thousands of British Emigrants who have been decoyed to the back States, that would most gladly join their countrymen here if it was in their power, but they are entirely at the mercy of the unprincipled wretches by whom they have been duped! many have come in without passports and a great number have found employment on the road; we are sorry however, to observe, that having heard reports of the very high price of labour in this country, they very much weaken the interest excited in their favor, when, upon their arrival in a large number, there is not immediate employment for them all in this town, and although they acknowledge themselves completely destitute, yet they ask even more exorbitant wages than have hitherto been given, and too many of them when disappointed in their unjust demands, turn their abuse most ungratefully upon the Government, that has been at so very great an expense to prevent their starvation in a foreign country and has offered to give them lands that would sell in the States, for at least from 12 to 20 dollars per acre.' The postwar influx clearly had its fair share of 'Micks-on-the-make.'

For some of the earliest settlers on Yonge Street, even those newcomers with means were not particularly welcome. In his detailed 'Observations' upon life in North America, the Reverend Isaac Fidler had this to note from his residence in

Thornhill during 1832: 'Our landlady sometimes alluded to the changes she had witnessed in the removal of forests, the cultivation of lands, and in conveniences of all kinds. But she deplored these changes; since people from England of some capital, who generally prefer to purchase farms partially cleared rather than seclude themselves within almost impervious forests, were hereby induced to take up their residence along the road, [Yonge Street] and to buy out the original settlers. She had witnessed the departure or death of most of her co-temporary settlers; and began to feel herself among a strange people of another generation, with whom she had little intercourse and less sympathy. The former husband of our landlady had left her with a family of sons and daughters, with a highly improved farm, with flocks of sheep and herds of cattle, with five hundred pounds in money. American republicans have been frequently found prowling up and down Canada, in search of something which they might be able to convert into their own profit, regardless of the character or welfare of their dupes. Our landlady, a handsome widow with a handsome fortune, was not likely to continue undiscovered. One of them, a physician by profession, learned her history, was introduced, gained her heart, and married her. He obtained possession also of her cattle and her money; but not of her land, for this was a grant from government originally conveyed to herself, and she would never part with it. This American, after living with her for some time, and obtaining all she possessed but her farm, found his way back into the States, where he had another wife. The cattle and money obtained by our landlady had previously disappeared.'[217]

The differences in background and outlook among those who now came to settle, aggravated by the reciprocal dislike between the majority of English and Americans, were too great to be easily reconciled and absorbed into the fabric of Upper Canada. Emigrants were regarded by some of the politely condescending observers among their countrymen as being the 'brown bread' of humanity, coarse of figure, mind, and feature; they seemed to be disorderly, illiterate, and slovenly scum. To others, mainly their descendants, they were full of the virtues of honesty and hard work.

The general advice to gentlemen was that unless they had an 'army of daughters' to provide for, it was sheer folly to emigrate until unfortunate circumstances made it a necessity. The Englishman with an assured place in society exhibited abroad the peculiar characteristic of being totally immune to any dislike and criticism that he might incur from those around him. Thus armoured, his favourite sport was baiting Americans, and they, less assured, reacted to this contempt by kicking like colts flicked on a raw sore.

In spite of their happy illusions to the contrary, the English without means did not in general make good pioneers, lacking as they did the endurance of the Scot, the shrewdness of the Irish, or the woodcraft of the North American frontiersman. The half-pay officer who was unlucky enough to have no capital usually found the life of the bush too hard for him. That ranting laird o' Fifie-oh, Robert Gourlay, was perhaps overdoing it a bit in the Rumpelstiltskin wrath of his Scots righteousness when he declared with would-be heavy sarcasm: 'Simcoe's settlers and contractors may growl; but what are they? a handful of poor, insulated farmers and land-jobbers . . . .but — we [the British Government] can populate it [Upper Canada] with all sorts of drones, — half-pay officers; legislative councillors. — direct the wild lands to be given away to everyone except those of enterprising spirit.'[218]

True, the half-pay officer was not often the most enterprising individual, nor had years of army life suited him for pioneer hardships; it didn't need a Robert Gourlay to tell people that much. Universally, he seems to have cut a rather sorry figure, but one which excited sympathy as opposed to the distemper of Gourlay's huffings and puffings. The *Upper Canada Gazette* of 17 July, 1817, repeated a long poem from the *Morning Chronicle* that began:

> The Half-Pay Officer
> Mark well that haggard eye, that brow of care
> Where pride seems nobly struggling with despair;
> That sullen look that dignity of mein,
> Which e'en those faded garments cannot screen . . . .

When pride did not have to struggle with despair, however, but was allied to sufficient means to allow expression, then many of the earliest Yonge Street settlers, such as the Reverend Isaac Fidler's landlady, took a strong dislike to the postwar arrivals from England.

If the money was there, then so also was the land, cleared or partially cleared, sometimes in a substantial way. Gentleman John Mills Jackson was an old Oxonian who had come to Upper Canda in 1806 and settled on a farm that he called 'Springfield' on Yonge Street at Newtonbrook. He was called 'Jacobin' Jackson on account of his criticism of the council and to distinguish him from Samuel 'the Hatter'. He advertised his property for sale as follows:

> 240 acres of LAND on Yonge Street, Lot No. 19, commonly called Springfield; with about 60 acres of improvement. This lot contains advantages that must be obvious; it has two excellent Dwelling-houses, Still house, Barn, Stables & c. with a never failing creek running through the front, sufficient for a Grist or Saw Mill. Its vicinity to the metropolis of the Province, combined with these advantages, must make it a valuable acquisition to the Merchant or Farmer.[219]

Just before the 1812 war, lots had been sold at public auction, advertised in the *Upper Canada Gazette*[220] as 'several Building Lots divided into half one acre Lots; being the North part of Lot No 68, 1st concession Township of Whitchurch.

(On Yonge Street). Each Lot will be put up at one Dollar.' By the time that he arrived, the Reverend Isaac Fidler could say that 'the value of land in Canada is increasing regularly and rapidly. For instance, Yonge Street was first settled thirty-seven years ago. At that time land on it was given to any person who applied. A few years after, a lot was worth from fifty to a hundred dollars. A lot now is worth from one to two thousand pounds on many parts of Yonge Street.'[221]

And for those who had the money and the capital for development, Yonge Street had a good deal to offer. Families such as the Gappers and O'Briens who had more than just the miserable prospects of half pay could make something of it when they chose to settle in the area of Thornhill in the 1820s. Richard Gapper was a former army officer and his brother Southby had been in the Royal Navy; so had Edward O'Brien before switching to the army from which he resigned in 1824. Richard Gapper took up Lot 41 east on Yonge, and Southby Lot 38 west. Edward O'Brien, who married their sister Mary, the journalist, soon struck out farther and built a home at Shanty Bay near Kempenfeldt. They were fortunate in having sufficient means to employ labour to carry out the settlement duties of land clearing for them.

Thornhill itself took its name from one of these moderately well-to-do Englishmen who arrived at this time: Mr. Benjamin Thorne, who settled on Lot 32 west on Yonge Street. Thorne went into business partnership with his brother-in-law Parsons, and in time came to own the largest mills in the area. A disastrous financial loss in 1847, however, ruined him, and he was left with the only possible out — suicide — in that callous, smugly complacent age of *Vanity Fair* that saw divine justice in others' misfortune.

Dr. Paget was a medical man from England who took up residence on Yonge Street in Thornhill after the war. His profession now offered more chance of financial security than it had to the debt-chasing Dr. Tolman. 'The English medical gentleman near us, was often sent for to the above distance [15 or 20 miles to his patients]. His charge for an ordinary journey was a dollar a mile. He was making a rapid fortune, and becoming one of the wealthiest gentlemen in the neighbourhood. There were many places upon Yonge Street, and in every district of the country, which are very populous, and where any respectable medical practitioner might settle his family in certain affluence.'[222]

Yonge Street, then, had prospered directly and indirectly from the war. The Reverend Henry Scadding, who was favourably inclined to the English influx, wrote in his history, *Toronto of Old*: 'At a certain period in the history of Yonge Street, as indeed of all the leading thoroughfares of Upper Canada, about 1830-33, a frequent sign that property had changed hands, and that a second wave of population was rolling in, was the springing up, at intervals, of houses of an improved style, with surroundings, lawns . . .winding drives . . .indicating an appreciation of the elegant and the comfortable.'[223] Simcoe would have approved of newcomers of this type, but they did not sit easy with those who had arrived to settle before them.

A more local and less favourable view of this 'second wave' was expressed at a much later date by a historian of Vaughan Township, who no doubt accurately reflected the thoughts and biases of many who had been on Yonge Street for some time before 1812: 'The coming of such well-to-do British families as the Thornes, Parsons, Gappers and O'Briens [who left diaries] and the Pagets created an entirely new class of settler. They were friends of the ruling families such as the Strachans and built imposing houses and looked down their noses at the original settlers whom they called "Americans".'[224] The fact was that the happy myth of frontier democracy and equality so beloved by the Americans was fast disappearing with the advance of civilization on Yonge Street.

The group of earlier settlers with whom the new type might associate would be the definitely pro-British, military-oriented element such as Captain David Bridgford of Richmond Hill, the Robinsons of Newmarket (Peter was said to have been at the attacks on Detroit and Mackinac and for a brief period a

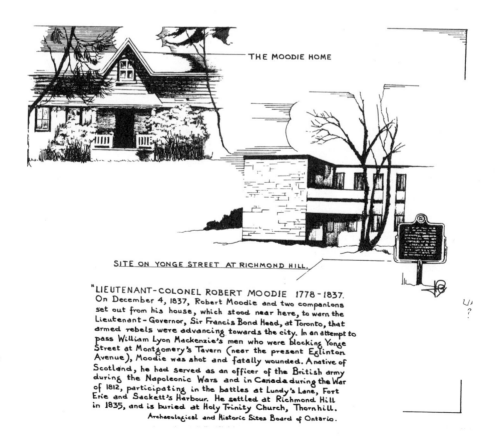

THE MOODIE HOME

SITE ON YONGE STREET AT RICHMOND HILL.

"LIEUTENANT-COLONEL ROBERT MOODIE 1778-1837. On December 4, 1837, Robert Moodie and two companions set out from his house, which stood near here, to warn the Lieutenant-Governor, Sir Francis Bond Head, at Toronto, that armed rebels were advancing towards the city. In an attempt to pass William Lyon Mackenzie's men who were blocking Yonge Street at Montgomery's Tavern (near the present Eglinton Avenue), Moodie was shot and fatally wounded. A native of Scotland, he had served as an officer of the British army during the Napoleonic Wars and in Canada during the War of 1812, participating in the battles at Lundy's Lane, Fort Erie and Sackett's Harbour. He settled at Richmond Hill in 1835, and is buried at Holy Trinity Church, Thornhill. Archaeological and Historic Sites Board of Ontario.

prisoner-of-war), and Loyalist families like that of van Nostrand. Cornelius van Nostrand had fought as an officer in the British army during the American War of Independence: he came to Upper Canada in 1797 and settled on Yonge Street in the region of York Mills in 1805. His grandson, also Cornelius, served throughout the 1812 war after enlisting as a private in Colonel Chewett's division of the militia.[225]

Of the others whom she found settled about her, Mary O'Brien takes a somewhat detached, annoyingly English attitude of mildly pleasant indifference, as though making a record of specimens: 'The labourers will address their masters with a tone of perfect equality but do not seem to be a whit less docile. Of the farmers I have not seen anything, but it seems that formal visiting is quite out of their way. At all events they do not expect it from us. Even Squire Miles [Abner's son James on Lot 45 east, called 'Squire' because of his duties as a Justice of the Peace] is like that. He is a very good and civil man . . . .He is so far from liking to show off his magisterial capacity that when he the other day surprised a man in the act of stealing his apples, he helped him down from the tree in which, in his haste to escape, he had entangled himself. Then, taking the bag in which the stolen fruit had been deposited, he gave it to the man, desiring him the next time he wanted apples to come to him and ask for them.'[226]

The new British tone on Yonge Street received strong reinforcement in the late 1830s with the arrival of distinguished veterans of the Napoleonic and 1812 wars. Two of them were of that tough, uncompromising breed of the Scottish military officer; Lieutenant-Colonel Duncan Cameron, C.B. and Lieutenant-Colonel Robert Moodie.[227]

Colonel Cameron had been second-in-command of the old 79th Regiment, or Cameron Highlanders, and was wounded at Quatre Bras just before the decisive struggle at Waterloo. He came to Upper Canada in 1835 and in the following year settled at York Mills, on Lot 12 on the east side of Yonge Street.

Colonel Moodie, a native of Fifeshire, spent his career in regiments much less prestigious than the Cameron Highlanders, but he saw a lot of active service and earned advancement in his career through the hard school of experience. He was with the New Brunswick Fencibles, which was raised in 1803 and incorporated into the British army as a regular unit, the 104th Foot Regiment, and accompanied them on the famous winter march from Fredericton to Kingston between February and April, 1813. Moodie had temporary command of that regiment from May to December, 1813, and when it was disbanded in 1817 he returned with his family to Scotland.

The 104th, or New Brunswick Fencibles, like the Glengarry Light Infantry Fencibles and the Newfoundland Regiment of Fencibles, was raised in Canda for local service so that the regular line regiments of the British army could be kept available for the European war against Napoleon. It was made up of tough, competent backwoodsmen, as handy with the rifle as with the axe, so that Moodie was no stranger to the ways and temperaments of Canada; he served during the War of 1812 and is said by some to have taken part in the action at Queenston Heights. Colonel Moodie returned to Upper Canada in 1835 and settled with his family on property that he bought from the Reids on Yonge Street, Lot 49 east. Thereafter, a flag flew from the staff set up in front of his house, denoting the residence of a British officer. The *Liberal*, 16 October, 1890, records the blowing down of the flagstaff in front of the Moodie property during a gale on 13 October. The paper relates that the first settler on this property was Col. S. Wilmot, the provincial surveyor, who set up a flagstaff from which flew the Union Jack. The actual house that Moodie occupied was built by Dr. Reid in 1820.

A much later arrival, who does not quite belong to this chapter of events, was the dashing Hon. Aemilius Irving. Formerly an officer in the elite 13th Dragoons, he possessed the romantic cachet of a wound from Waterloo. He did not settle in the area until 1839 when he established an estate, 'Bonshaw', on Lot 98 on the west side of Yonge.

As might be expected, of course, there were some grandly nonsensical, eccentric notions, such as only the English could produce, that arrived with some of this postwar group. What effect these must have had on the practical, steady descendants of the pioneers is best left to the imagination. They seem to have found much of it to be even beyond the realm of rational comment.

The greatest bit of foolery, perhaps, took place in the mid-1830s with the building of what was to be a grandiose hotel on Lot 50 west in the locality of Elgin Mills. This exotic edifice was to be trimmed and titivated by imported craftsmen for the social set and the gentry whom it was intended to attract, an indication of the new era that had been thrust upon Yonge Street. It was a flop.

The scheme, as might be expected, was started by an army officer, but it was never finished. Its originator committed suicide, as did the first owner. In the absence of occupation and doing no business, wind and rain and finally fire did for the building. In the end, according to William Harrison, 'all that remained of the huge folly was a pile of rubbish.'[228]

The stopping place for the new 'ton' of York and Yonge Street would be the Bond Lake Hotel built in 1834 on the opposite side of Yonge Street from Bond Lake. It provided a residence superior to the noisy straggle of taverns and inns that littered Yonge Street northward from York, and lasted the better part of sixty-six years before fire destroyed it at the turn of the century.

What pretentious nonsense a lot of it must have seemed to some of the head-shaking locals who watched these newfangled goings-on. Even amongst the recent immigrants there would be some to whom the new way of things was just so much tomfoolery. James Hogg, or Hogg the Miller, who arrived from Scotland in 1824 and bought Thomas Arnold's mill, expanding in 1832 with the purchase of forty acres on Thomas Mercer's Lot 10, was one who had little patience with frills, practical-minded, dour Caledonian that he was.

There was one other, too, from Scotland, who would make an unforgettable impact on Yonge Street, although he never settled upon it: William Lyon Mackenzie. The waspish shopboy from Dundee arrived in Canada in 1820, bringing with him many of the new political and social ideas that had surfaced in Britain in the wake of the wars. With all the infernal contumacy of the Scot passionate upon a cause, he would be forever at odds with those who hewed to established ways, although at no time did he claim to be against tradition if he felt it to be worthy.

He started out in Canada, however, in his accustomed trade by shopkeeping in Dundas, where in March 1823 he 'respectfully' informed the public that having dissolved his partnership with Mr. John Lesslie, also from Dundee, he would carry on business in a part of their premises, 'but . . . .declined to retail Spirituous liquors.'[229] Politics would be a heady enough brew for wee Willie Mackenzie, and never far from his thoughts.

He took the sensible but officially unpopular attitude that it was ridiculous for American and Canadian farmers on opposite sides of the frontier to waste precious farming time in shooting at each other as in the recent 1812 war; not that he was a pacifist, but shooting was a business for soldiers. There was also support enough from the farmers along Yonge Street for his opinion that there was overmuch control of affairs by an entrenched oligarchy composed of the privileged adherents of church and state establishments, who incurred needless expense with little return to the public.

An example of these grievances may be found in Mackenzie's newspaper, the *Colonial Advocate*, which reported twenty-three resolutions from a political meeting in Markham.[230] Three of these are sufficient to underline the main complaints: the land set aside for the established church should be sold and the money used for schools and roads; there should be no single established church in the province; salaries to officials in York were often being increased without any consent from the legislature of the province.

The Reverend Isaac Fidler soon noticed this feeling when making a journey from York to Newmarket in 1832. When he was about half way along Yonge Street, 'at a house on the roadside I called at, to make inquiries and to quench my thirst, there was an elderly man seated, who eyed me for some time with a keen and steady look. At last he began questioning me; ''You are lately from the old country, I suppose . . . .I thought by your appearance you were one of those who come into the country and get grants of land. You have obtained five hundred acres, I suppose.'' . . .I told him [that] I left England a downright radical, and am certainly without the smallest claim to partiality, and without any expectation of such a favour. ''You tell us so,'' said he, ''but we know things better. We gave them a sample last winter [1831-2] of what they may expect. We want nothing with governors and bishops, and archdeacons.'' He left the place soon after; and I was given to understand, that he was a republican, an adherent of Mr. Mackenzie.'[231]

At Newmarket itself, the Quakers would in time also follow the general trend and add their particular grumbles to the list: 'Public notice is hereby given, that the Religious Congregations or Societies of Menonists, Tunkers, Quakers, and Moravians, intend petitioning the legislature at their next Session, for an Act in their behalf, to afford them relief from the payment of fines now imposed on them as exemption from Militia Services.'[232]

There were, to be sure, grumbles enough at almost everything and anything. Although the Reverend Isaac Fidler pronounced that 'the business of farming is becoming better every year.' the farmers themselves were not so convinced, and at the end of the 1820s they were complaining of the low prices for farm produce.

Settlers from the United States and many of the Scots brought with them their national obsessions and enthusiasms for education, the key, for them, to democratic opportunity. The only trouble they found in Upper Canada was that there was no door. Such education as existed was in a large degree a private matter.

An early school on Yonge Street was the one set up by the American settlers on land given by Balser Munshaw on Lot 35 west side. This was in about 1796 when Munshaw built a new home and his old log house then became the school; one of the first teachers was John Langstaff, who left for the militia in 1812. During the war a new schoolhouse was built, known as the Cober schoolhouse after a family that came from Germany to Pennsylvania and on to Upper Canada in 1796. Nicholas Cober donated half an acre of his Lot 34 for the location of this school, which was also to double as a church.

After the war some improvement was made upon this system of purely private endeavour, and in 1829 Mary O'Brien described a little schoolhouse on the east side of Yonge Street, just north of Thornhill: 'These schools are built by public authority and placed under the superintendence of trustees who appoint the masters, etc. They are supported by the regular half-yearly payments from the children of a dollar and a half per quarter. Besides this the parents are bound to find the master in board, lodging, and washing. But how they manage this matter I don't understand.'[233]

After 1812 there was a good deal of carping at the employment of 'American' teachers who might contaminate the youth of Upper Canada with republican, un-English notions. One Englishman who was sufficiently detached in outlook to be free from these xenophobic shakes was able to write in appreciation of a young American 'seated near us [on Yonge Street] as a schoolmaster, whose system of education in my opinion does him credit.'[234] This was by no means the general view, however.

The status of teachers in the province was very low, and the standard of education consequently poor, and so they remained throughout the nineteenth century. For those who could afford it, the classical pattern of English education was provided in the school opened by William Warren Baldwin at York in 1802, and at Upper Canada College, begun by Sir John Colborne in 1829 to preserve

British traditions against the nonsense of American democracy. Colborne, like Brock and Simcoe, was an advocate of bringing more loyal British subjects into Upper Canada to bolster its institutions.

The English tone of gentility was upheld in such places as:[235]

York House Seminary

for

Young Ladies

To Parents and Guardians

Mr. and Mrs. ROBERTS (from England) will open a Boarding and Day School at York, on Monday 23 of June, where every polite and useful branch of Education will be taught.

The strictest attention will be paid to the Morals and Health of the Young Ladies.

N.B. Mr. & Mrs. ROBERTS have brought a Piano Forte, Globes, & c. with them.

York, 18 June, 1817.

In a later issue of the *Gazette*, Mr. and Mrs. Roberts had to reassure parents that there was no truth in a rumour that they were planning to make off with the linen and silver that some of the 'Young Ladies' in boarding had brought with them.

The much more dignified York Boarding School for young ladies was founded in 1828 under the patronage of the Rt. Hon. Lady Sarah Maitland, wife of the Lieutenant-governor, with the added nota bene, 'A Professor of Dancing is engaged to attend.'[236]

The greater part of the prosperous and genteel sections of English society as well as the church and the Army reacted vigorously against any hint of 'Jacobin,' democratic theories, and their attitude was shared by those in Upper Canada who dreaded the taint from American ideas of liberty, which were considered to be crude, egalitarian bluster. The lieutenant-governor at this time (1818-1828) was Sir Peregrine Maitland, a handsome, mannered gentleman who loathed the very mention of reform. In the end his attitude became so harsh that he was removed from his position and replaced by Sir John Colborne. It was not so much the result of arrogance, or of stupidity, but a blissful ignorance of life as it was lived beyond his small circle of society.

The officers who came to Canada after the Napoleonic Wars had done their service in any army patterned by the leadership of the Duke of Wellington, where both Maitland and Colborne were prominent figures and exemplars of its rigid creed. Sir Peregrine had been in one of the 'blood' regiments, the Foot Guards, and commanded the First Brigade of the First Division at Waterloo. He was an upright soldier, brave, and with a firm sense of duty, but without the remotest idea

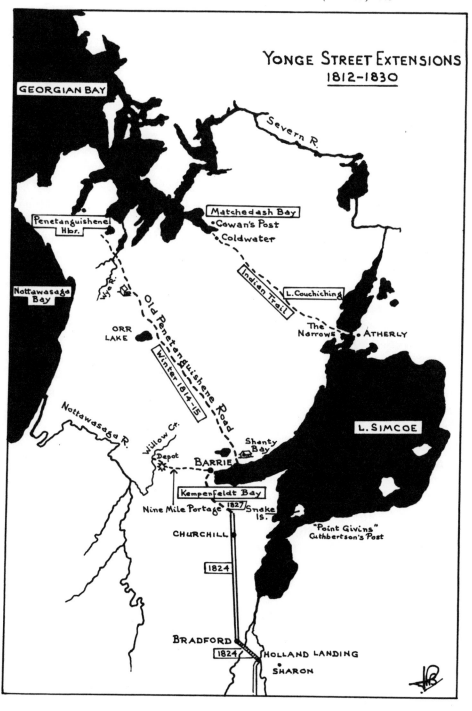

YONGE STREET EXTENSIONS
1812-1830

of what hopes and aspirations meant to those who did not have his advantages.

Sir John Colborne was also a most able soldier, who had commanded the 52nd Light Infantry at Waterloo in the final, desperate tangle with the veterans of Napoleon's old guard. He was more prepared to listen than was Maitland, but his attitude to reform was still of a piece with that expected from Wellington's officers. Courage for them was found on the field of sport or battle, not in the fight for political and social recognition, as it was for Mackenzie.

Old Beaky's approach to reform was notorious. In what was probably one of the many apocryphal pronouncements attributed to him, he is rumoured to have declared that if you 'once give the English lower classes one foot upon the ladder of social ascendancy, then the race of English gentlemen is dead, sir.' And whatever you might care to think about his views, there could be no denying that the old duke was a gentleman, steady, well mannered, and with a strong sense of duty. The gentleman was required to act in accordance with a code of conduct that seemed quaint at the least to those whose life called for hard-headed sense.

Another of the stories about Old Beaky tells how he met another gentleman to settle a question of honour in a duel. Facing each other early on a typically dewy, English morning, they could not get their damp-powdered pistols to fire. Two farmers, watching these capers, remarked with down-to-earth wisdom, 'Why doan' 'ee settle it wi' fists?' But that was not the gentleman's way.

These ways were still copied in York, and on 12 July, 1817, young John Ridout met Samuel Jarvis for a duel in a meadow northwest from the corner of what are now Yonge and College streets. This dispute, aggravated by bad blood between the Ridout and Jarvis families, ended in the death of seventeen-year-old John Ridout. Probably twitched by nerves, fear, and excitement, he fired before the starting signal; his pistol was then taken away from him, so that Jarvis, unharmed, was free to fire at will. The immediate cause for the duel seems to have been the question of a debt. Not something over which gentlemen were supposed to quarrel — cheating, or perhaps a fancied slight to honour, but not money. 'Poor, sir, very poor,' the duke might have said.

Mary O'Brien set some store by the station of gentleman. She found 'Mr. G. Ridout, a very gentlemanlike man though he has never seen the world,' and Abner Mile's son James, 'a very respectable man but not within the pale of society.'[236] For her there was a fine shade of difference between being called a gentleman and gentleman*like*.

The farmers on Yonge Street had enough to bother them without pondering these subtle nuances. To them, Sheriff Jarvis, the Ridouts, and their ilk represented the interests of the officials in York, whom they saw as controlling public matters in the province to suit themselves. Scarcity of schools, poor farm prices, and rotten roads were at the core of their own discontent, and in this much the recent arrivals from England such as O'Brien and the Gapper brothers of Thornhill were prepared to push for the farming interests. With the replacement of

THE MAIL STAGE will start from Joseph Bloor's Hotel, York, on Mondays and Thursdays, at 12 o'clock, noon and arrive at nine o'clock, the same evening in Newmarket; —and will leave Mr. Barber's Tavern, Newmarket, for York on Wednesdays and Saturdays, at 6 in the morning, and arrive in York at 2 P.M. on the same day.

the unpopular Maitland by Sir John Colborne as lieutenant-governor in 1828, it seemed that matters might improve. Mary O'Brien noted in her journal that: 'The new governor is said to be making himself very popular. He is ashamed of the state of the roads and I hope he will forward some arrangement for mending them. The last parliament after long debate, voted that they were bad, but could get no further. . . . .The church is getting on so that it will perhaps be usable shortly, though it will not be finished till spring.'[237]

Sir John was quick to act. After viewing the Yonge Street extension from Kempenfeldt Bay to Penetanguishene in 1829, 'Colborne . . .urged immediate expenditures of   1400 currency in the completion of the road between Gwillimbury and the termination of Yonge Street on Lake Simcoe and Penetanguishine, a measure which has also been recommended by Mr. Commissary General Routh. Yonge Street from York to Gwillimbury, a distance of about 40 miles is practicable for the waggons of the country: from thence to Penetanguishene through [67 miles] the route is a narrow path passable with difficulty for horses.'[238]

As early as 1810, commissioners had been appointed in York to lay out money for the repair of roads,[239] but the war had provided a convenient distraction. Following the peace, the flow of new emigrants made available a source of labour

The Second Toll Gate, Yonge Street at Hogg's Hollow.

John Ross Robertson–Landmarks– from a sketch in
Richmond Hill Library.

"That hill (Hogg's Hollow) was the terror of all travellers. Teams hauling grain had to rest
three or four times before the straining horses reached the top; and then with a face of
pleasant jocularity out popped the toll-keeper, his breath freezing in the frosty air, and
made the driver pay for the privilege of climbing that awful hill. He felt that he had been
made the victim of a practical joke."

(Palatine Settlements in York County, –Mabel Burkholder – in Ontario Historical Society, Vol. XXXVII, p.89).

for work on the roads, although the matter of wages was a sore point with the employers. It was not until 1824, however, that recent settlers in the west part of Gwillimbury, unhappy at their isolation across the Holland swamp from the thriving settlements on Yonge Street, asked for assistance from the Upper Canada legislature.

The result was a corduroy bridge of logs reaching across the west Holland River to the site of Bradford. A road was then pushed through to the present-day Churchill, and in 1825 it was supposed to continue the last four miles to the western end of Kempenfeldt Bay, a job that was done by 1827.

Extract from the *Colonial Advocate*, 12 March, 1829:

ROADS IN THE HOME DISTRICT.

Mr. Ketchum, from the Committee of Members for York and Simcoe presented the following scale of appropriations of road money, agreed upon by the members for the Home District, viz:
For arching and filling up the Blue Hill on Yonge Street £250. — Commissioners, John Elmsley, Esq. James Hogg and Joseph Turton, all of York Township.

. . . .

To repair Yonge Street, between Bond's Lake and McAdam's Tavern, £50. — Commissioners, John Hartman of Whitchurch, Thomas McAdam of Vaughan, and James Pearson of Whitchurch.

. . . .

In the aid of the road and bridge leading across the West branch of the Holland River to the Hon. P. Robinson's Mills, £50. — Commissioners, Joseph Hodgeson, William Armson and Hugh Stodders, all of W. Gwillimbury.

The Colonial Advocate, 25 March, 1830, carries a notice under the heading of YONGE STREET ROAD that James Hogg and his fellow Commissioners will receive 'plans and estimates for arching and levelling the Blue Hill.'

There was also a growing pressure for expansion at the Lake Simcoe end of Yonge Street. In 1832, notice was given that an application would be made to the Parliament of Upper Canada to form the county of Simcoe into a separate district to include the townships of East Gwillimbury, North Gwillimbury, Georgina, Scott, and Brock, with the district town being placed 'at the head of Yonge Street, near the Mills of the Hon. P. Robinson.'[240] Two years later an application was

The old Toll Gate House on Yonge Street at Langstaff.

proposed for a canal or railroad from York to Lake Simcoe.[241]

The wagon road of Yonge Street at this time was fast becoming 'practicable' for more than just the transport of stores, trade goods, and the occasional spare anchor. The following notice was carried in the *Upper Canada Gazette* on the twenty-fifth of August, 1825:

NOTICE TO TRAVELLERS

The Subscriber begs leave to inform Travellers, and the Public in general, that he has commenced running a Light Covered Waggon for the accommodation of Travellers, between York and the Holland Landing, on Monday, Tuesday, Friday and Saturday, in each week, regulated as follows:

To start from the Landing at 8 o'clock on Monday and Friday, and stop at the Newmarket Hotel half an hour; will also stop at B. Van De Burg's Tavern one hour, and will put up at the Mansion House Hotel, York; which place he will leave at 10 o'clock on Tuesday and Saturday, and hopes from careful attention on his part, to merit a share of Public Patronage.

York, 1st Aug. 1825   LEWIS BAPP

Shortly before this, the Arctic explorer Sir John Franklin had passed along this route on his expedition to the mouth of the Mackenzie River. In April 1825, after travelling from New York to Niagara, Franklin's party 'crossed Lake Ontario in a sailing boat, and came to York, the capital of Upper Canada, where we were kindly received by the Lieutenant-Governor Sir Peregrine Maitland. . . .From York we passed on to Lake Simcoe, in carts and other conveyances, halting for a night at the hospitable house of Mr. Robinson of Newmarket. We crossed Lake Simcoe in canoes and boats, and landed near the upper part of Kempenfeldt Bay, but not without being obliged to break our way through the ice for a short distance. A journey of nine miles, performed on foot, brought us to the River Nattawassaga, which we descended in a boat; and passing through a part of Lake Huron, arrived at Penetanguishene.'[242]

To drive the distance from York to Thornhill in 'a small waggon with one horse' took two-and-a-half hours if the road was dry, according to Mary O'Brien, writing in 1828.[243] In this year, apparently, George Playter and Sons of Newmarket started a stage service between York and Holland Landing, which by 1833 had become a daily run after the line was bought by William Weller of Cobourg in 1832.

The business obviously gave scope for competition; the *Colonial Advocate* of 9 April, 1829, ran this advertisement:

NEWMARKET
MAIL STAGE

WILLIAM GARBUTT, having taken the contract for carrying His Majesty's Mails between York and Newmarket, for the next four years, respectfully informs the public that THE MAIL STAGE will start from Joseph Bloor's Hotel, York, on Mondays and Thursdays, at 12 o'clock, noon, and arrive at nine o'clock, the same evening in Newmarket; — and will leave Mr. Barber's Tavern, Newmarket, for York on Wednesdays and Saturdays, at 6 in the morning, and arrive in York at 2 P.M. on the same day.

Price for passengers conveyed between York and Newmarket, six shillings and three pence currency, and in proportion for shorter distances, — Packages carried on this route at moderate rates.
York, March 30th, 1829.

The Golden Lion, S.W. Corner Yonge and Sheppard.

Newmarket during this period was described by Mary O'Brien as being 'a post town consisting of about fourteen houses, three of which are stores. It boasts a comfortable Inn, a doctor's house, a blacksmith, a hatter, a shoemaker, with a mill near at hand ....'[244] Her Englishwoman's accolade went to the nearby Quaker settlement on Yonge Street, where 'farms are cleared of stubs and stumps and are as neat as an English farm.'

Although it might have been scenic in spots, the journey was no jaunt; the coach would bog down in wet weather and have to be heaved out by log levers, shoves, and curses, or else in dry weather it would jerk viciously over potholes,

Yonge and Dundas (Queen) Streets "Rebels' Corner."

Sun Hotel,
CORNER OF DUNDAS AND YONGE STREETS

THOMAS ELLIOT,
RESPECTFULLY informs his friends and the public, that he has opened Mr. *Charles Thompson's* old established Hotel, at the corner of Dundas and Yonge Streets, with a choice assortment of WINES AND LIQUORS, of every description. His TABLE will be well furnished, and the STABLING extensive and convenient.

(The Colonial Advocate, 19 August, 1830).

stones, and corduroy logs. To take the force of such continuous jarring and bumping the stages were slung on great leather straps — how welcome winter must have been when the coach could be mounted on sleigh runners. On a very optimistic schedule the stage would leave York at noon and arrive at Holland Landing at eight in the evening. Unless spattered in mud on a bad day, Weller's bright yellow coaches must have made a colourful splash as they rolled, or in winter sledded, along Yonge Street, drawn by a team of four horses.

William Garbutt in his 1831 advertisements naturally promoted Yonge Street with an almost travelogue bounce as 'the great road leading from York to Newmarket, which now renders it one of the most pleasant Stage Routes in the Canadas.'[245] During the 1830s, however, in York itself the stages still had to detour east to Parliament Street and then north to where the cemetery stood; from there they followed a farm lane to the head of Jarvis Street at Bloor, along which they went as far as Yorkville and then up Yonge Street.

The rainy season made such a sorry pottage of Yonge Street that the O'Briens felt that the only way to raise the money for a necessary improvement would be by a turnpike or toll, that would cover the cost. Mary O'Brien commented in her journal on 13 April, 1831, that the state of Yonge Street was so deplorable in wet weather that 'I think it is such as ought to convince everybody of the insufficiency of an earth road to support the immense travelling to which it is subject.'[246] In this they were strongly supported by people such as Hogg the miller and Seneca Ketchum, who signed a petition to the government for the formation of a turnpike company. Following this, the *Upper Canada Gazette* carried a notice on 6 October, 1831:

> Application will be made to the House of Assembly in the next Session of Parliament, for a Turnpike Road on Yonge Street, on the following plan: —
> A Company to be chartered for the purpose of raising the necessary funds and constructing a permanently good Road; the Company to be repaid by Tolls, and to be either limited in the amount of its profit, or be obliged to deliver up the road in thorough good repair at the end of a certain period, the road then becoming public property. The Statute labour on this road to be commuted, and the money thus raised to be laid out on the side lines.
> Vaughan, 21st July, 1831.

As a result, Yonge Street was established as a toll road under the control of a company that agreed to maintain the road in return for the authority to charge a toll. During the period from 1831 to 1833, tollgates were set up on Yonge at Bloor Street and at Hogg's Hollow, York Mills. Eventually, four additional tollgates were brought in; at Langstaff on the north half of Lot 35 west; at Elgin Mills; at the Aurora Gate on the north half of Lot 75 west; and at Cady's Corners, about one-and-a-quarter miles north of the line between Whitchurch and East Gwillimbury.

Like everything that costs money, the tollgates enjoyed great unpopularity, and cheating the tolls became something in the way of a favourite Upper Canadian winter sport. So common was it that Cornelius Krieghoff made it the subject of two of his paintings. Both were called 'Running the Tollgate,' and the scene, a one-horse sleigh with three characters jeering wildly as they dash through the gate, is much the same in both. In one they are waving whip and bottle and

Old Presbyterian Church, Yonge Street, Thornhill.

thumbing nose at the keeper who is frantically pegging along on a crutch as though in some freak race for charity.

The tolls did, however, help in the 'macadamization,' or laying of a crushed stone surface, on Yonge Street between 1833 and 1835 when some twelve miles of the road were finished in this fashion north from York. Mary O'Brien was enthusiastic: 'The stone road, however, is going on successfully and will now, I believe, be carried on, on the risk of paying itself.' And two years later: 'The part of Yonge Street that is already done [macadamized] has paid so well by a very moderate toll that it is impossible even to seem blind to the advantage of continuing it.'[247]

Parting with money for Yonge Street brought a quicker loss of vision than could even be achieved on the road to Damascus. When Bond's farm was put up for sale in 1834, the imminent improvement of the road was listed as a selling point, but it was anticipated too early by far, as the stone surface did not reach there until some twenty years later.

The Reverend Newton Bosworth, writing on 8 January, 1835, from Toronto (the old name had been reverted to upon York's incorporation as a city in March of the previous year) said this of Yonge Street: 'Near Toronto, on this road, is a grand Turnpike gate, the only one in Canada . . . .The traffic along Yonge Street is amazingly great, and almost resembles that of some of the roads leading to London, so that the Tolls pay well . . . .This said street is in reality a great public road leading from Toronto to Lake Simcoe, more than 40 miles . . . .the former arboreous appearance of "the bush" itself, is broken at intervals by numerous settlements, occupied by "a bold peasantry" as Goldsmith terms the pristine English small farmers.'[248]

The 'bold peasantry' on Yonge Street, however, were also as shrewd as Goldsmith's Tony Lumpkin; they were not about to be as enthusiastic over fancy 'city' schemes for tolls as the Reverend Newton Bosworth. Even less enthusiastic about the state of things in general, including the state of the Yonge Street road on which he ill-humouredly blamed the failure of his rebellion, was William Lyon Mackenzie.

The old Red Lion Inn, N.E. Corner Yonge and Bloor.

Chapter Four

Politics, Rebellion, and Change
(1830-60)

Malt does more than Milton can, to justify God's ways to man,' chirruped Housman, and if the number of taverns along Yonge Street in the 1800s was anything to go by, then the cosmic revelations to the patrons must have been on a staggering scale. By the middle of the nineteenth century there were close to eighty hotels, inns, taverns, and grog-shops on Yonge Street between Barrie and Toronto, an average of at least one to each mile of the road.

They ranged from 'well known and liberally patronized' houses — Daniel Tiers's Red Lion at Bloor, Shephard's Golden Lion at Lansing, Charles Thompson's (later Elliot's) Sun at Dundas, John Montgomery's rebellion-famed tavern just north of Eglinton Avenue — through lesser taverns — Morrison's Golden Ball above Queen Street, J. Abraham's Green Bush Inn (originally at Lot 26 east), Paul Pry's Inn close south and east of Montgomery's Tavern, and Mrs. O'Hearne's at Richmond Hill — down to canteens as kept at Hogg's Hollow by Vallières, a remnant from de Puisaye's settlement and husband of William Cowan's maternal grandmother, or the casual boozing den unsuccessfully run by an ex-sergeant in the area of Oak Ridges.

The Red Lion was perhaps the most prominent, being the polling place for the Home District at election time and a stopping spot for the farmers' wagons that had been pulled through the breath-breaking Blue Hill Ravine. By staying there and going into town the farmers also avoided paying a double toll at the Bloor Street Turnpike. Its ballroom provided a popular centre for many of the prominent social gatherings of York.

Thomas Elliot's Sun Hotel, 'located in a central situation for business,'[249] was on the northwest corner of Yonge and Dundas (Queen); it had became known as 'Rebels' Corner' because it was a popular meeting place for Mackenzie's party followers, the John McIntosh who built it in 1825 being a brother-in-law of Mackenzie.

W. L. Mackenzie.

Bishop Strachan.

Chief Justice J. B. Robinson.

As a source of divine revelation, the Golden Lion was somewhat redeemed by a later owner of the property, the Reverend T. W. Pickett, who held a Bible class in the bar-room, a starting point for the congregation that was to become Lansing United Church.

Overall, however, the record of Yonge Street's hostelries was sufficient to satisfy the most grim-minded, retribution-bent Calvinist:[250]

The number of liquor sellers on Yonge Street in the first fifty years of this century [19th] was 100.
In these one hundred families there were: —

Drunkards	214
Sudden Deaths	44
Suicides known to the Public	13
Premature deaths by drunkenness	203
Widows	45
Orphans	235
Murderers	4
Executions	3

The redemptive balance to this gloom and doom was for long in short supply. Robert Gourlay, in his 1817 fact-finding tour found only two such places on Yonge Street north of York: the Quaker meeting house at Newmarket and a small, wooden building overlooking the swamp at Hogg's Hollow at York Mills. In *The Banished Briton*, Gourlay described the latter as being '. . . seventeen paces by nine, and out of the roof shot a little stove chimney of brick. A person standing near informed me that it was a Church, and one of the Church of England. I forthwith inquired who was the Clergyman: there was none, specially appointed for this place of worship; but Dr. Strachan did duty in it, once a month. What! said I, has this building been erected for so little benefit to the country! Are there no Presbyterians, Methodists, or Baptists who could occupy it the three vacant Sundays of the month? — "The doctor, Sir," replied my informant, "will let nobody preach here but himself".[251] Gourlay, who was at odds with Strachan, called him 'a monstrous little fool of a parson.'[252]

The land for this little church was two and three-quarter acres of Lot 11 offered by Joseph Shepard in 1816, and Seneca Ketchum and John Wilson were

Residence and Wagon-Maker's Shop near the Corner of King and Yonge Streets, 1815.

from painting in John Ross Robertson Collection.

New Saddlery and Harness MANUFACTORY
ALEXANDER DIXON, SADDLER, & c. —
most respectfully informs the Gentry of York and Upper Canada, that from the liberal encouragement he has experienced, it has induced him to commence business in the above line in one of his New Houses, situated on the South side of King Street, a few doors East of Yonge Street.
(The Courier of Upper Canada, 24 March, 1832)

made joint trustees with him. A church of some description was felt by them to be important, although they may not have been too happy with the idea of a church being so dominated by the personality of Dr. Strachan of the Church of England.

The strong-willed Doctor, however, was quite set upon having no encroachments upon the Church of England in Upper Canada. This was clearly evident in a meeting that the Methodist missionary, the Reverend Peter Jones, described in his journal: 'John and I called this morning on Dr. Strachan; he was very friendly, and made some enquiries about the general state of the Indians. . . . At 11, A.M., we again appeared at the Government House, but waited till 1 o'clock before any communications were made to us, when we were summoned into the presence of Major Hillier — the Governor's Secretary, Dr. Strachan, the Attorney General, and Col. Givins. To our astonishment, we were now informed by Dr. Strachan, that the (Governor Sir Peregrine Maitland) did not feel disposed to assist the Indians so long as they remained under the instruction of their present teachers (Methodists) who were not responsible to Government for any of their proceedings and instructions, he was therefore unwilling to give them any encouragement. But should the Natives come under the superintendence of the Established Church, then the Government would assist them as far as laid in their power. When stating their reasons for wishing us to come under the teaching of the Church of England, the Dr. and Attorney General said, that the Indians were considered by the Government to be under the war department, and therefore it was necessary that they should be under their instruction; and that another reason was, that it would make the missionary establishments more permanent; whereas at present they were liable to fluctuation, the only resource of the Methodists being that of subscriptions. It was also proposed to my brother and me, that if we would assist them in this undertaking, and come under their direction, our salaries should be increased, and we should have access to the contemplated college. We told them that their request would cause much dissatisfaction to the Methodists, as they claimed the Indians for their spiritual children, having been the first who taught them the christian religion.'[253]

Even for the granite-jawed Strachan it was a losing battle to hold back the denominational tide. Methodism, which was looked upon as being closely linked to the United States, made little progress during the War of 1812 and the years immediately following, but it picked up again after 1820.

In 1821, a small church was built at Richmond Hill on a site donated by James Miles, to be used by all denominations except the Roman Catholics and the Children of Peace. Like the Scotsman, the Englishman, and the Irishman in the tale, one of James sisters was Presbyterian, one was Episcopalian (Anglican) and one was Methodist.

The Yonge Street circuit of the Methodist church was expanded from York to Lake Simcoe by 1824, the services being held in settlers' homes at selected preaching places along the way. In 1825 the first ministers at Newmarket were the

Reverend Egerton Ryerson and the salty, one-armed, ex-Naval veteran, the Reverend James Richardson. In his diary for November 1825, Ely Playter mentions that 'Mr. Richardson preached,' and 'Mr. Ryerson Preached a good Sermon.' Egerton's brother William followed him in the next year, and in 1827 a Methodist church was built at Garbutt Hill in Newmarket.

As religion in a variety of forms and feuds mushroomed along Yonge Street in the 1830s, Mary O'Brien recorded in February of that year the first service in the new Trinity Church on Lot 33 west at Thornhill. In 1832 a small Baptist church was started at York Mills, and in 1836 in the same area a Scottish Presbyterian church was built on what is now called Old Yonge Street at Ivor Road. At Newmarket, St. Paul's Anglican Church was established in 1834, and what could only be a Presbyterian Scots-inspired old kirk appeared there two years later.

Among the Quaker community at Newmarket a split had occurred in 1828 when those who followed the ideas of Elias Hicks of the U.S.A. quarrelled with their orthodox friends and broke away to set up their own Hicksite meeting house, a structure that stood until 1940 on Lot 98 on the west side of Yonge Street. David Willson, who had broken from the Quakers in 1812 to organize what he called the Children of Peace but who were naturally dubbed the Davidites, built a temple at Sharon just east of Holland Landing in 1825.

Come weal, come woe, religion was dragged into the roughhouse of politics. Mackenzie — who couldn't abide his fellow Scot Strachan in any pinch and detested John Beverley Robinson, attorney-general at twenty-one, younger brother of Peter and former pupil of Strachan — ran a mock dialogue between the pair to the strain of Burns, *John Anderson, my Jo* in the *Colonial Advocate* of 10 January, 1828:

Parson Strachan — John Robinson, my joe, John, our credit's cheaply
         sold.
         Experiments are hazardous and mine was quite too
         bold.
         And then I miss'd it sorely, John, my bungling
         work I trow,
         When I slander'd all the Methodists John Robinson,
         my Joe.

Some years later, the *Advocate*, in describing a fire that had broken out on Yonge Street, added that 'The most dreadful circumstance connected with the conflagration is the burning of a fine boy of ten or eleven years of age whose father had left him in bed to go to discuss the abstruse question of transubstantiation which Strachan and Macdonnell have started to set the catholics and protestants a quarelling about previous to the general election ....'[254] Bishop Macdonnell, a thundering great highland Scot and Tory, shared about an equal popularity with Strachan in Mackenzie's book.

The fire had occurred on the east side of Yonge Street, somewhere between the present-day Richmond and Adelaide streets, two years after the 1832 Act for Preventing and Extinguishing of Fires.[255] It destroyed businesses whose variety alone gives an indication of the rapid changes taking place in York and its surrounding districts: Rae and McTurk, cabinetmakers; Kesson and Struthers, upholsterers and paperhangers; Bowman's, the grocer; Lackie's, the baker; Mrs. Bell's, the tallow chandler.

The butcher, the baker, the candle stick maker were now a part of the growing town, but farther out, north along Yonge Street, the businesses were those very practical necessities in a farming community: blacksmith, tanner, wagon and harness maker, millers, shoemakers, and the manufacturers of agricultural implements.

The changes of the thirties came perhaps too fast and too soon upon the Yonge Street community, which was not yet sufficiently settled to adapt to what was being thrust upon it. Steam had arrived to change totally the old ways of wind, horse, and oxen. When Robert Fulton's side-wheeler steamship *Clermont* successfully made the trip up the Hudson River from New York to Albany in 1807 and George Stephenson's locomotive, the *Rocket,* triumphed in England in 1829, a new era in industry had been rung in. With it came the need for a new and skilled labouring class.

In 1832 the York Steam Engine Works advertised the manufacture of 'Steam Engines and other Hydraulic machines' by Charles Perry; and with a fanciful blend of old and new, the sign of the gilt plough opposite the Sun Tavern on Yonge Street marked the Union Foundry where the furnace was enlarged 'to be able to make CASTINGS of any SIZE up to TWO TONS WEIGHT,' and where the latest in plough patterns were advertised.[256] Enterprising progressives would soon begin to consider the railroad and steamship for travel upon Yonge Street and its Lake Simcoe terminus.

On Tuesday, 7 July, 1829, the Reverend Peter Jones had put in his *Journal* that 'we sailed from the Island [Snake] this morning in Mr. Beeman's schooner for Yellowhead's Island, on a little lake called Koochecheeng.' And during a nostalgic visit to Yonge Street in the summer of 1844, old Ely Playter, after spending an evening at Eli Beman's, 'concluded to go with Henry a trip in the schooner' on Lake Simcoe to Barrie and the Narrows.[257]

Eli Beman's jib-flopping, scruffy schooner, however, had by then been swept aside by the wash from the new industrial wave that brought the steamboat and eventually the railroad to the Yonge Street travel route. And with them came the new breed of industrial artisans and the 'navvies' who were often as noisy and cantankerous as the new machinery that they served.

These novelties came too swiftly to a frontier society to be absorbed easily into its way of life. The trades along Yonge Street were geared to the world of agriculture and the steady, wind-watching ways of its practitioners.

By October 1832 the steamboat *Colborne*, powered with an engine purchased in Buffalo, had been built at the Upper Holland Landing for service on Lake Simcoe; the river was so shallow that the vessel had to be laboriously winched down its muddy flats to the lake before it could be floated. Its advent was duly announced by the *Courier of Upper Canada:*[258]

NOTICE

THE Steam Boat COLBORNE, has commenced her regular trips around Lake Simcoe, on Monday last — Leaving Holland Landing for the Narrows, every Monday and Thursday morning, at 8 o'clock

A. Boland, Master

Holland Landing, 4th Oct. 1832.

And two years later:

Lake Simcoe. — The new and splendid steamboat PETER ROBINSON, Will leave the Holland Landing on Mondays, Wednesdays and Fridays, at 8 o'clock, A.M.

...... Charles Thompson, Proprietor.

As a relief from Eli Beman's rickety craft, Mary O'Brien was 'much rejoiced at the sound of the steamboat's bugle.'[260] She might have been less enthusiastic about such progress had she realized that it was the herald of an age of more noise and dispute than had yet been heard anywhere on the length of Yonge Street.

And into this new industrial melting pot was poured the scaff and raff of Europe, the horde of emigrants that reached a peak around 1833. What to do with this gaggle was no small problem for the administrators at York, and the *Upper Canada Gazette* of 26 April, 1832, announced an attempt to come to grips with the unpleasant novelty:

York Emigrant Committee

His Excellency the Lieutenant-Governor has appointed as Committee, consisting of a Chairman and nine Members, in this Town, for the purpose of assisting Emigrants who may arrive this season with information as to the places where they may settle or obtain employment, as well also as for taking a certain measure of Superintendence over the sick and destitute of the Emigrants in co-operation with the Society for the relief of the sick and destitute of York . . . .

. . . . . .

But as few of that class of Emigrants for whose benefit the Committee are acting can be expected to board themselves at . . .houses, it has appeared to the Committee that Tavern-keepers who have large yards might at a small expense, and with a fair prospect of remuneration to themselves, prepare sheds for the shelter and accommodation of Emigrants, and their families and luggage . . . .

. . . . . .

The Committee will also be happy to hear from Gentlemen in any part of the Province contiguous to York, of any mart that may exist of laborers, servants or mechanics, for the information of Emigrants . . . .

About this time the advantages of emigration to Canada were expounded in two lectures given in England by a William Cattermole, but his picture was hardly one designated for 'laborers, servants or mechanics': 'Yonge-street road leading from York to Lake Simcoe, is 36 miles, upon which large sums of money have been recently expended, and great alterations are still in progress.
From Newmarket to York, a distance of upwards of 30 miles, the bulk of the inhabitants are from the United States — they came out poor 20 years ago; and in Newmarket, now, there are many as fine farms as in some Suffolk villages, and few stumps to be seen. These are principally Dutch, Pennsylvanians, and friends from the same state.'[261]

Cattermole noted among the efforts to develop the farming interests of Upper Canada that Mr. P. Robinson had introduced the Leicester breed of sheep, and that 'an agricultural society has been formed in the Home District.' A director of this society, Mary's husband, Edward O'Brien, provided Cattermole with a letter that commented upon 'the ease with which the poor man raises himself to independence, and the independent man to wealth. . . .' He didn't, however, say what he considered to be poor, nor what wealth, in Upper Canada.

The impression was now one of the influential English moving confidently upon the stage, from which the Pennsylvania 'Dutch' and the 'inhabitants from the United States' who had settled on Yonge Street were being pushed quietly and firmly into the backdrop.

The Home District Agricultural Society, which was duly formed on 15 May, 1830, had more than passing political interest, and some of the features that Cattermole lists among its regulations are worth repeating:

> 2. - That annual subscription of 5s, constitute a member of the society.
> 3. - That the business of the society be transacted by a president, twelve directors, a secretary, and treasurer.
> 5. - That the Hon. George Crookshank, be president. The Hon.

William Allan, Peter Robinson, Alexander Wood, J. Elmsley, D. Boulton, E. O'Brien, Jun., J. W. Gamble, C. C. Small, R. Stanton, R. Gapper, J. Fitz-gibbon, and R. Anderson, Esquires, be directors.
W. B. Jarvis, Esq. treasurer.
J. Elmsley, Esq. secretary.

Any one of the 'old' York names represented there — Jarvis, Robinson, Elmsley, and Small — would be enough to set a light under the democratic bonfire that was William Lyon Mackenzie and send sparks through his red wig. Sure enough, he turned up at the meeting on 6 July, 1830, in one of the favourite Yonge Street taverns, and demanded to speak although he had refused to pay his subscription to the society. He was kicked out.[262]

There was a sense now of a near-vicious rowdiness abroad in York that spread its bitterness along Yonge Street. As if the turmoil in the taverns would not be enough from liquor alone, the heady brew of politics and religion was spilled into these places, which were the centres for the exchange of ideas, news, and opinions, like gasoline into a fireworks factory. In general the politics do not seem to have been conducted by any group on a particularly high level of knowledge or intelligence. The impression left by the behaviour of those who would shape the destiny of the frog-marsh that was York was like that of the Athenian Pnyx when the glory that was Greece had deteriorated from the drama of democracy to the slapstick of a rabble chorus.

Loyalties and stands, as in most political exercises not tidied up for textbook analysis and ease of classification, were taken up less from high principles and meritorious ideals than from pride, prejudice, ignorance, and greed; all were overhung by suspicion. It is a common tale of History's circus that once set up a pole with some sort of a coloured bunting upon it, then many of mankind's clowns will come out to caper around it, whether or no they understand what it is all in aid of. And a great caper York and Yonge Street made of it in the 1830s.

The British military governors were men who had been trained in a system modelled upon that of the Romans, not the Greeks. They tended to want things done with efficiency, despatch, and little discussion, whereas the ways of democracy are notoriously slow and often clumsy. Sparked by the behaviour of Sir John Colborne, the *Gore Gazette* made an astute summary of the situation in an article on military governors: 'They are too impatient of control — too tenacious of their opinions — accustomed to be obeyed, and exercise severe discipline in the field, they too frequently are apt to bring that preponderance of thought and action, into territories over which they are appointed to preside.'[263] Well put.

Among the legislators in York, much experience had yet to be gained in the craft of government, thus confirming the governor's feeling that if necessary he should ignore them. Those who might have a bent for administration such as Dr. Strachan, John Beverley Robinson, and very competent merchants, such as William Allan, were denounced by Mackenzie as being part of a 'Family Compact' set upon keeping political and social power within their own circle.

Many of those families whom Mackenzie reviled, however — the Jarvises, Macaulays, Shaws, Robinsons, Ridouts, and Smalls — had been long established in the official circles at York, and many of them were descended from former Queen's Rangers and associates of Simcoe. In fairness it must be said that they took a not unnatural view that they had put York on the map and were not much impressed when, after the bitter anti-Yankee years of 1812, this Scots upstart got off the Greenock boat in 1820 with his portmanteau of political notions and began telling them what to do. Little wonder that feelings became violent. Neither were these people the lackeys Mackenzie liked to imagine. When a lieutenant-governor went as they thought too far, as Bond Head did in 1836, then George Ridout and J. E. Small were not afraid to speak out even if it did mean their dismissal from government appointments.[264]

No matter; Mackenzie was all for the farmers having a say in the direction of affairs on account of their importance to the development of the province. In the pinch, however, when it came to the improvement of Yonge Street over which so much fuss had been made in 1833, the farmers were quick enough to push up costs themselves by asking a very high price for the stone that they could supply for macadamization. The cost for a mile of road improvement rose above £3,000, thanks in part to this.[265]

Whatever the attempts by men like Colborne to get things done, they would be deeply suspect to men who, by and large, were not accustomed to being ordered about like a drill company of private soldiers. Shortly before the *Gore Gazette's* article on governors, Sir John was taken to task by Mackenzie's *Colonial Advocate* for his actions on 'Schools and Roads. — It is plain enough to every one that Sir John Colborne sees the necessity of good roads and good schools — yet if he were to make the former in an unconstitutional manner, the effect of the latter would only be to expose his mismanagement the more to the public. For instance, to take the money of the country and build a bridge over a river in a necessary place, by entering into a private contract with a supposed favourite, instead of throwing the job open to public competition and afterwards applying to parliament for an act to cover the outlay. Has Sir John done this?'[266] The suspicion that public money was being mismanaged was no doubt more of a spark to emotions than were the intricacies of political ideals and abstract philosophies of government.

In the heady, fume-filled dimness of grog-shop and tavern, packed with specimens of the recent arrivals in York, harbingers of new theories and opinions imperfectly understood, there must have been many scenes of bedlam around the town. The pot-valiant rantings and airing of views strongly held with that single-minded obstinacy that is the hallmark of the semiliterate would have made a scene to delight the cartoonist in a Rowlandson or Gilray, and perhaps a Hogarth. It was indeed the opinion of the aloof and austere Attorney-General, John Beverley Robinson, that Mackenzie himself was a ranter who belonged in the bedlam bin, and as such could be ignored with contempt.

Such was evidence of the misunderstandings that made a near-tragic farce out of Upper Canadian politics in the 1830s. Mackenzie, for all his ranting and his spiteful outbursts, belonged if anything to that school of democratic thinking whose best exponent was Robert Burns. He disliked hypocrisy, but his passionate insistence upon liberty did not make him hostile to authority, provided it was honest. Although he saw a good deal to admire in America, he was not at first, as many of his equally ranting detractors would have it, a republican desirous of seeing an end to the monarchy. Poor, sick, fever-haunted Mackenzie was like a Diogenes embarked upon the impossible hunt for an honest man.

As so often happens, the business of politics came down to a battle of personalities more than a clash of ideals. In the wake of irresponsible name calling and petty guttersnipe gibes, public excitement ran high. Mackenzie denounced 'irresponsible priests, placemen and pensioners.' When Simcoe's old friend John McGill died, the *Correspondent and Advocate* on 1 January, 1835, managed to imply a cheap insult in the announcement of his death:[267]

> DIED — Yesterday, the Honble. John M'Gill, an old Pensioner on his Majesty's Government.

The slighting jeer at 'pensioners' brought a long rebuttal from Peter McGill.

In return, Mackenzie was sneered at as the 'Dundee shop-boy,' and Jesse Ketchum was the 'Buffalo Tanner.' Mr. Andrew Heron labelled the Ryersons, whose only crime was an honest wish to see religion less Strachan-dominated, 'rebels'. At this Mackenzie's *Colonial Advocate* pointed out that Heron's own 'chief connexions male and female had long been on the Rochester side of the Niagara River.'[268]

Francis Collins, the editor of the *Canadian Freeman*, was taken to task by Mackenzie for sneering at 'Mr. Ketchum, the Tanner, Mr. Duggan, the Merchant, and Mr. Bishop, the Butcher — all good and respectable men, we [the *Freeman*] admit, in their own lines — but ill qualified for legislators.'[269]

Although the petty snobbery of these remarks was uncalled for, there was some merit in the assertion of their lack of qualificatons. Even Mackenzie had to admit: 'We want more legislators who are able to sign their own names and write three words following each other without misspelling, and we must allow them to get an education somewhere.'[270] The lieutenant-governors can hardly be blamed if at times they ignored the Legislative Assembly that, to their minds, must have contained many illiterate boors.

To be regarded as being inferior in education is always a stinging humiliation to the ambitious, and some native Upper Canadians were quick to shuffle the fault to others, as in an article on education that appeared in the St. Catharine's *Argus*: 'The too general apathy which prevails in the colony, in regard to this important subject, is not so much to be wondered at when we take into consideration the mixed character of the inhabitants, and the somewhat unsettled state of society, in consequence of the great influx of foreign emigrants, the majority of whom, it is to be feared, are wretchedly ignorant, and of a class who can not be considered, in any point of view, as an acquisition to the learning, wealth or respectability of the Province.'[271] Was this merely using newcomers as convenient scapegoats, or the self-congratulatory spoutings of the Scots merchant class in Niagara who were determinedly battering their way to the upper circles of society and 'respectability', Mackenzie's countrymen who had 'made it' to the top?

All of this Kilkenny-cat scratching and spitting was alien to those who had first settled around Simcoe's seat in Upper Canada and on Yonge Street. The emigrant ships, however, were now bringing their 'wretchedly ignorant' cargoes with their quotas of the dregs from the ugly social underside of the Industrial Revolution who would find occasion for a brawl in any event.

Typical of this breed was a great hulking, boozing, Irish-Catholic lout by the name of Nowlan, or Knowlan, who knocked down Mr. Dutcher, proprietor of the York Furnace; threatened Rogers the Hatter; accosted Mr. McDougal, a merchant, 'tore his vest and threatened him'; and 'threatended Paul Kane one night with a beating near Witman's, the chairmaker and acting constable.'[271] Nowlan was finally shot by a drunken Charles French, a youngster whose actions Mackenzie tried to justify, but with no success because Nowlan, said the disgusted Willie, would be 'sainted . . . by Collins [of the *Freeman*] because he died an Irish Catholic.'[272]

The memory of the River Boyne and 'the glorious twelfth' of July when 'King Billy slew the Papish crew' was like a religion flooded Styx running through the murky political scene. In a letter 'to the Irish Catholics of Upper Canada,' John Esmonde, who had been a supporter of William Lyon Mackenzie, said that he had turned against him because his attitudes were 'insulting to the Catholic religion.'[273]

It was an age when intolerance was no crime and was in some instances elevated to a virtue. Faced with rapid changes to their society, people were not much interested in debating political logic, but instead thrashed about on a thorn bed of general and unspecific discontent and prejudice. These they aired freely in the taverns, the rowdy shrines of roistering whose gospels would spread up Yonge Street from pothouse to pothouse with malted benediction. In York it was reported that 'a number of the cases upon which Coroners inquests have been summoned within the last few months have arisen from drunken revelry, riots in low houses, or in the streets, or from delay, or total neglect of attention, to persons who have been suddenly indisposed or injured.'[274]

In March 1832 there were riots in York, with so-called 'party' feeling running high between the Government, or Tory faction, and the anti-Government Reformers. Mackenzie and his followers, featured as 'The Younge Street Mob,' came to grief in a fracas at a meeting outside the court house: 'Mackenzie, Ketchum, Morison, McIntosh and others; had mounted into one of their Younge Street waggons opposite the Jail, and having collected their adherents who had been brought in from the country for the occasion, were doing the despicable mummery of resolving their old string of grievance resolutions. They had not proceeded far however in this silly mockery when some twenty or thirty Irish lads, who entertained no very favorable sentiments towards these patriots, ever since their gross and impudent insult upon the venerable Catholic Bishop, [Macdonnell] dashed into the middle of the Yonge street mob; seized the waggon and galloped off with it, patriots and all! to the utter consternation of the Younge streeters; who seemed petrified with astonishment; and to the infinite amazement of the multitude.'[275]

Newspapers carried accounts of the shoddy bickering under the head of THE YORK RIOTS:

> The following paragraph from the Courier will show that even means are taken to exasperate the farmers, by Sir John's administration and its adherents. A paper under the avowed patronage of the government, owned and edited by the confidential Secretary of the official addressing party, after witnessing the riots on Friday, amuses its fashionable readers by terming the manly yeomanry of this county "THE SWINE OF YONGE STREET."
>
> (From the Courier)
>
> Every wheel of their well organized political machine was set in motion to transmute country farmers into citizens of York; accordingly, about nine in the morning groups of tall, broad shouldered hulking fellows were seen arriving from Whitby, Pickering and Scarborough, some crowded in wagons and others on horseback, and Hogg the miller headed a herd of the swine of Yonge Street who made just as good voters at the meeting as the best shopkeepers in York.
>
> GEORGE GURNETT.[276]

To scrabble for a pun on Hogg and call the Yonge Street farmers 'swine' was scooping pretty low for the scrapings in the vocabulary of invective, and James Hogg snapped back with a sharp letter to Gurnett, the *Courier's* editor: 'Perhaps the insulted Swine of Yonge Street, stupid as they are, may have instinct enough, to pass the shops of those who avowedly belong to the Soup Establishment.'[277]

The spate of name calling and abuse displayed a preference for personal prejudices over particular principles. The soup-kitchen folk were collectively those whom the self-imagined Reformers considered the menials and scullions in the service of the lieutenant governor and his circle. Hogg was so incensed that he went so far as to challenge George Gurnett to a duel, which, in the end, didn't take place.

The sign of the Golden Lion Hotel carved by Paul Sheppard of Scarborough, 1st. from a pine stump; 2nd. from oak, with a putty mane.

The sign of the Golden Lion is displayed in the restored Gibson House, Willowdale, Ontario.

from a photograph in Richmond Hill Public Library

It is always easier to find something to gang up against than to unite in a positive common effort for some cause. The York officials were an easily recognizable group for attack, but the reasons for an attack were seldom held in common amongst their opponents, who fired off squibs at random. The sort of drivel that was dragged in to make a point is nowhere clearer than in a letter written by a Thomas Burrell; in the course of criticizing James E. Small on the counts of being a son of the clerk of the Executive Council and brother-in-law to T. G. Ridout, cashier of the government-instituted Bank of Upper Canada, Burrell wrote: 'A farmer when he comes to York and has to stop all night, can get no rest for carriages rattling about all the night long, going to and from each others houses to what they [the York officials] call pleasure parties.'[278] The taverns, presumably, were the while as quiet as the town churchyard.

A letter to the editor of the *Colonial Advocate* for 5 April, 1832, points up equally emotional and pointless attitudes on the part of all concerned:

FUN IN VAUGHAN

[At a meeting with 170 persons present, nine resolutions were taken, and at the voting on the third resolution] . . .a gentleman, by the name of Edward O'Brien, propped up by a Mr. Gapper (both Magistrates, or of Sir John's soup kitchen party) made the following remark; that he believed that the greater part of the Government officers were over paid, viz: (besides others) the Attorney and Receiver General in particular. On the other hand, he thought that Judges' salaries were insufficient to make them independent both of the people and Government which he thought they ought to be.

The resolution against high salaries for *all* officials was carried, as might be expected, with only two dissenting votes, O'Brien and Gapper, at which point Montgomery, the innkeeper upon whom the finer shades of democratic theory were lost, remarked that 'everyone is in favour of the resolution except the gentleman of the PAP SPOON.'

O'Brien's protests at this 'occasioned great laughter and fun to the Dutch farmers, on which Sergeant O'Brien got into a terrible fit of anger, and like a true knight of old, flung off his glove in imitation of a challenge.' He made a lot of unnecessary remarks about his uncle being First Lord of the Admiralty and that he would not be called a pensioner, because he had sold his pension. At that, Montgomery sneered, 'I suppose you have done like many a poor devil who was obliged to sell his pension in order to pay his debts, and now flatter and cringe so that you may be taken notice of by the Governor and get another grant of 500 acres of land.'

It ended with O'Brien having a fight with an 'enlightened Tailor' who beat him. Old Beaky would by no stretch have been amused by such capers. When the mob in London overturned his carriage, he had walked home although hurt, totally ignoring the plebeian tumult about him. His was a Stoic attitude to duty whereby matters had to be dealt with as seemed best, whether the result was popular or not. Such ways were not those of North America, however, where much ado was made about the privileges of 'free men'.

In a letter written to the *Colonial Advocate* on 1 July, 1830, a character from Thornhill who chose to call himself Humphrey Clod said in describing a meeting of the Home District Agricultural Society in May: 'Until the *gentlemen* shall please to remember that they are located in the midst of 10,000 North American Freemen, owners of the soil, and jealous of their liberties, agriculture in the Home District will benefit but little from such meetings as I faithfully described last week.'

This was the typical stand of the Yonge Street farmers: they were free men, entitled to have their views acted upon and to have their say, and they were not going to be pushed around by any governments, be they Tory, Reformer, or whatever.

It was the Tory group that won a majority in the Assembly in the 1831 elections, and Mackenzie, feeling ever more frustrated, made a trip to England in the summer of 1832 to present his grievances to the Colonial Office. The *Courier of Upper Canada* on 26 September, 1832, made sport of his efforts by predicting 'for the especial comfort of these Yonge Street Sages who first made, and then fell down and worshipped this Brazen Image,' that Mackenzie would ask for more money and donations from them to support his case in England, where he would spin out his stay.

Things didn't quite turn out that way, and Mackenzie returned to Upper Canada without getting any real satisfaction for his effort, although the Colonial Office was at least made aware that all was not well in Upper Canada. As the time came closer for the next election in 1834, so the Reform opposition became more determined, but Mackenzie's passions put off some of the more moderate among his followers. He became increasingly impatient, making ever more outspoken comparisons in favour of the way things were done in the United States as opposed to Upper Canada.

The Reverend Egerton Ryerson, who had at first supported Mackenzie, found this growing belligerence too much for his taste and withdrew his association in 1833 to the accompaniment of a wild blast from the irate crusader:

ANOTHER DESERTER!

The Christian Guardian under the management of our rev. neighbour Egerton Ryerson, has gone over to the enemy, press, types, and all, & hoisted the colours of a cruel, vindictive tory priesthood ....[279]

There were no two ways about it; Mackenzie imagined that whoever was not for him was agin him.

Although Mackenzie was lashing out like a windmill-baffled Don Quixote, the basic complaints of the Reformers remained much as they had long been[280] — that farmers and tradesmen were being kept down by taxes, that too much power was held by Strachan's church, and that the York officials enjoyed salaries that were too high, all to the detriment of roads and education. Moderate Reformers such as William Warren Baldwin, his son Robert, and Jesse Ketchum hoped that some advances toward a government more free from control by the lieutenant-governor might be made through recognized procedures of legislation, but they found it an uphill struggle.

The *Advocate* of 13 February, 1834, described a meeting in John Montgomery's tavern on Yonge Street above Eglinton at which the delegates were chosen for the County Conference to nominate candidates for the up-coming general election. Mr. David Gibson of Yonge Street was appointed as secretary of the meeting, and the delegates included Joseph Shepard, Jr., John Montgomery,

Joseph Cawthra, James Hogg, William Harrison of York Mills, Jesse Ketchum, John Rolph, and William Warren Baldwin. The meeting criticized Sir John Colborne as being 'unfit to govern freemen.'

The following week the *Advocate* triumpeted WHITCHURCH AWAKE! when the freeholders of the township held a meeting at Bogart's Mills with Isaac Playter as secretary and passed seven resolutions, of which the fifth stated that 'we view the proceedings of the present majority of the House of Representatives (the Assembly) as those of a band of determined enemies to the rights of freemen.'

Even the Quakers and some of their splinter groups such as the Children of Peace, although in general respectful of constituted authority, tended to a sympathy with the aims of the Reformers.[281] Joseph Milburne, who ran the tavern on the east side of Yonge Street at Thornhill, was typical of the Quakers who could be called staunch Reformers but who would have no part of anything that condoned violence in contradiction of their principles. David Willson's followers had some considerable debate on what course they should take, but in the end they were 'firmly united in the cause of [their] representative W. L. Mackenzie, so far as his means tends to equality and justice.'[282]

The push for reform had enough impetus from a variety of dissatisfactions that the Reformers won a majority in the Assembly in the October elections of 1834. In March of that year the York Incorporation Bill had been passed with twenty-two votes for and ten against changing the name of the newly incorporated city back to the old Toronto.[283] Swelled by the postwar emigration, the population of the town, excluding the garrison and the jail, had reached 7,473 in the summer of 1833.[284]

As a result of the first elections for the city council, Mackenzie became the first mayor of re-christened Toronto in 1834. Thanks now to the Reform majority in the Assembly, he was able to resume his seat in the legislature from which he had been expelled for libel on 12 December, 1831; despite four subsequent re-elections in 1832 and 1833, he had been promptly shown the door again on each occasion. His mayoralty lasted for the brief span of a year.

The Reform campaign now seemed to slacken, gathering second wind, and Mackenzie's less militant supporters grew lukewarm toward him. Hogg the Miller, for one, had had his fill of his countryman and was not reticent about giving the reasons for his disenchantment: 'A public dinner was given on Thursday evening, at Shepperd's tavern, Yonge Street, to Mr. Hogg, the unsuccessful candidate for the 1st Riding. About 60 sat down to a most sumptuous dinner provided for the occasion. Dr. Hamilton, [better known as the celebrated Guy Pollock] in the chair. An address of congratulation was presented to Mr. Hogg during the evening, to which that gentleman replied in the most happy terms; stating at length, his reasons for "quitting company" with Mr. Mackenzie. He said, that for a long time, he was impressed with the belief, that all he, Mr. Mackenzie, wanted or wished for, was a Constitutional Reform: — but now, when he, [Mr. Hogg] saw that it was Rebellion, anarchy, and bloodshed, which Mackenzie wished to introduce into the Province, he, Mr. Hogg, had turned his back on him forever. He, [Mr. Hogg] had broken the neck of the Revolutionists in that part of the country, and supported as he was, by the intelligent the respectable, and the really independent farmers of that Riding, he was quite certain, that on another occasion, it would be felt whether Mr. Mac. could longer prevail upon the intelligent farmers of that Riding to support him in his revolutionary designs . . . .

— A Mr. Cull said that "Mr. Gibson [on Lot 18 west side of Yonge and Representative of the First Riding of York in the 1834 Assembly] has, on all occasions, when requested to state his political creed, produced the Advocate newspaper, and when requested to state what grievances really exist, pulled out of his pocket Patrick Swift's Almanac. Mr. Gibson's qualification cannot therefore be his acquaintance with, and his ability to exhibit the real abuses in the Province".'[285] All well and good, but it was still Gibson who was elected to the Assembly.

The Mr. Cull referred to was probably James, a deputy provincial surveyor, who had also contracted to macadamize Yonge Street. He soon found, however, that he could not keep within his estimates, and although his work on the road was of a high quality, he had several wrangles with the penny-cautious trustees for the improvement of the highway. The bare fact of the matter was that Upper Canada simply could not yet afford a macadamized Yonge Street.

Money was a commodity in short supply, and although Mackenzie may have accused the Bank of Upper Canada of being a system of government robbery putting a credit squeeze on farmers for the benefit of its 'Family Compact' shareholders, Jesse Ketchum wrote this letter of appreciation to the bank. It appeared in the *Patriot* of 6 January, 1835: 'I feel happy that I can inform the President & Directors of the Bank of Upper Canada, that the road on Yonge Street is MacAdamised to the third concession. I think it will be gratifying to the Board that the money they have loaned has done a work of so much use to this City & its neighbourhood. I think that the country will feel thankful to the Bank for having afforded the means to make the road what it now is . . . .'

At the northern end of Simcoe's road, however, the campaign for improvement was still almost literally bogged down at the Holland Landing swamp. There any hope of a macadamized road must have seemed to be light years away: 'Notice. — At a Meeting of the Inhabitants of the Township of West Gwillimbury, held in James Evins' Tavern, Bradford, on the 24th day of October, 1835, it was unanimously resolved to apply to the Provincial Legislature, at their first meeting, to pass an Act imposing a tax of One Halfpenny in the Pound upon Rateable Property within the said Township, for the space of seven years from the time of the Act coming into operation, for the purpose of repairing and keeping in repair the Road between Yonge-street and the west end of the Causeway, in West

Gwillimbury; and any overplus of taxes, which may be after completing the said Road, to be laid out for the general improvement of the roads within the said Township; of which notice is hereby given to all whom it may concern.'[286]

For the people of that region there had always been hope that some benefit might result from the military establishment at Penetanguishene in the upkeep of the highway north. In 1828, Drummond Island had been given up to the Americans, the British garrison being removed from there to Penetanguishene, and there had been a brief anticipation that this might lead to some exertion to improve Yonge Street: 'The Detachment of 68th Regt., under command of Lieutenant Carson, has arrived at Penetanguishene, from Drummond Island. We mentioned in a former number the advantages which were likely to result to that part of the country, from the establishment of a Military Post. — The necessity of a good road from York to Penetanguishene presents itself with additional force. There is not perhaps in the whole Province, a road more travelled than Yonge Street, and it is very generally admitted we believe, that no where is improvement more required. The transport of Stores and materials, for the Military and Naval departments will no doubt be very considerable, and for this purpose, as well for the general convenience of the inhabitants, it is to be hoped that something will be done to put the Street in good repair. — The plan of making it a Turnpike, with Toll-gates, we are informed is not likely to succeed.'[287]

The great expectations were quickly disappointed, and in 1832, as the British government itself sought ways to save money, the naval establishment at Penetanguishene was cut back. The stores and cannon no longer required were hauled down Yonge Street over the corduroy roads with miserable, swampy stretches at places such as Elgin Mills, and between Richmond Hill and Langstaff. It was reported that sometimes as many as 'five span of horses [were needed] to drag the lumbering masses of iron out of the mud holes.'[288]

The naval ships at the base, a motley collection of the schooner *Tecumseth*, the gun-boats *Bee*, *Mosquito*, and *Wasp*, three batteaux and a 32-foot cutter were put up for public auction in the spring of 1832.[289] The *Tecumseth* and the brig *Newash* were in such poor shape that they eventually rotted and sank at their moorings in the harbour of Penetanguishene.

At the beginning of 1836, the naval stores at Penetanguishene were put up for sale, including 'Anchors, Wood and Iron stocked, (at Holland's Landing and Penetanguishene) from 35 Cwt to 1 Cwt. weight '[290] The monster 35 Cwt. anchor, however, obviously found no takers, still resting, as it does, in a public park at Holland Landing, an object of curiosity and wonder at how it ever got that far.

The army successors to the navy at Penetanguishene simply made the best of a bad job and transported stores, supplies, and troops however they could despite the condition of Yonge Street. A contract was let for the year 1836, covering all contingencies of supplying the post where a stone barracks would be completed in the summer of that year:[291]

ARMY CONTRACT.

The Assistant Commissary General at Toronto will receive Tenders on Monday the 19th of October next, at Noon, for the conveyance of Army Stores; for the supplying of means of Transport to Army Passengers; and for the Billeting Detachments of Troops on the March, between Toronto and Penetanguishene during the year 1836.

In the season of Navigation.

Means of Transport for Passenger, and Billetting for Troops, via Lake Simcoe, Barrie, and the Penetanguishene Road; also via Lake Simcoe, the Narrows, and Coldwater. — Conveyance of stores by the latter route.

During the close of the Navigation.

Conveyance of Stores, means of Transport for Passengers, and Billetting for Troops, via Innisfil and the Penetanguishene Road. The Contractor will be required to have Agents at the following places, vis:

TORONTO.
PENETANGUISHENE.
THE HOLLAND LANDING.
BARRIE.
THE NARROWS OF LAKE SIMCOE.
COLDWATER.

The civilian mind sometimes finds it difficult to understand the military way of doing things. If the road was rough, then bad luck; the army wasn't about to lay out money just to make it easier. In an emergency of war some panic solution could usually be found, but in peacetime it was 'Front and centre, Royals', pick up your bags, hammocks, muskets, and march. And if, as Kipling said, 'your 'eels get blistered, an' feels to 'urt like 'ell,' then that was Tommy's rotten-horrible luck and he could lump it. If farmers wanted wagon roads, then they could get on with it themselves and forget about any military interest in them.

At Bradford, it had also been hoped that the new steamboats on Lake Simcoe would boost the development of the village; its proprietors were advertising half-acre lots for sale and predicting that the steamboat would 'stop at Bradford every other night, and thus afford the means of communicating with York, from which it is distant only 60 miles.'[292] Bradford, however, was not quite in the line for ports of call, and the steamboat had to be a venture with at least some profit for those who had taken shares in it: Hon. P. Robinson, Edward O'Brien, W. B. Robinson, Samuel P. Jarvis, George Lount, Samuel Lount, George Playter, T. G. Ridout, James E. Small. A good deal of the active support that Mackenzie would get in 1837 was to come from the discontented in the areas of Bradford, Lloydtown, and Sharon at the Lake Simcoe end of Yonge Street where progress seemed to 'halt on palsied feet', and where the inhabitants felt neglected by the administration at Toronto.

In the world of suds and malt, however, there was one technical advance welcome to all:[293]

NEWLY INVENTED BEER PUMP.

The Subscriber is now making the above articles, which are on an entirely new plan, and warranted to surpass any Pump heretofore invented. Those who wish to purchase PUMPS are respectfully invited to call and examine before purchasing elsewhere.

H. PIPER,

No. 30, Yonge-street.

Toronto, June 6, 1835.

And there was plenty to discuss over the beverage pots in the new year of 1836. Sir John Colborne had been replaced by Sir Francis Bond Head, who arrived in Toronto on 23 January, 1836, with a reputation of being favourable toward reform. He soon showed that he wasn't. A very small man himself, he took a violent personal dislike to that turbulent titch, Mackenzie, who retaliated in kind.

Head followed the no-nonsense, discipline-the-louts approach inspired by his military training, and resented any attempts to thwart his own plans for the government of Upper Canada. When it appeared that he had no intention of considering even the least of the Reformers' complaints, or accepting any sort of advice from his appointed Executive Council, the latter resigned and the Reform Assembly refused to approve the budget for 1836. Head in a huff dissolved Parliament on 20 April.

Mackenzie himself, despairing of any corrective action being taken by authority in Britain, grew more blatantly radical, more darkly suspicious of favouritism, government by self-interest, and inefficient land development policies. The time of yelping and carping was over, and anyone with half an eye could see that the battle lines were being drawn for a bitter showdown.

Head had grounds enough for belief that he had sufficient support to ride roughshod over any opposition. Loyal addresses from Toronto with 1640 signatures and from Newmarket with 114, by showing disapproval of factious political efforts, bolstered his conviction of the correctness of his actions. From Yonge Street came an address: 'To his Excellency Sir FRANCIS BOND HEAD, Knight Commander of the Royal Hanoverian Guelphic Order, and of the Prussian Military Order of Merit, Lieutenant Governor of the Province of Upper Canada, & c. & c. & c.

'WE, the loyal inhabitants of Yonge Street, sensible of the many distinguished Privileges we enjoy by our Connexion with the British Empire, beg leave hereby to tender you our most sincere Thanks for and Approbation of your very independent and faithful Conduct since assuming the Government of this happy and thriving Colony, and particularly for the able, clear, and distinct Manner in which you have elucidated the Nature and Bearings of our well tried Constitution, to the Dismay and Discomfiture of a few political Partisans, who seek to destroy its nicely balanced Powers, by making every thing subservient to a dominant political Faction, than the which no greater Calamity could befall our adopted Country.' (155 Signatures)[294]

This doesn't smack much of the average Yonge Street farmer. The last remark about 'our adopted Country' hints that most of the feeling here came from those who had arrived from England after 1815.

Head was a man of several talents and achievements, but these certainly didn't include the tact to cope with political democracy or to handle an impassioned maverick such as Mackenzie. He succeeded in staging a Tory triumph at the polls in August 1836, going full ahead and damn the dissension, dismissing Dr. R. Baldwin, George Ridout, and J. E. Small from offices that they held on the charge that they had used 'disrespectful language' to his Head-ship.[295]

Feelings had now gone beyond the stage of invective or rowdy scrapping; frustration and bitterness were piling up behind closed doors and minds. A free-for-all has never been a novelty at any time in politics, and can often help to clear the air. Back in the relatively placid days of 1820, Ely Playter had recorded an election on 26 June when 'the people from Whitchurch came down in a body all for Robinson & Hawk — The Election commenced about ten some noise about the manner of Polling & much fighting out as the Stranging(?) party keep Possession of the Barn ....'[296]

Open fighting and some noise might have been no bad thing after the summer of 1836, but Head's bulldozing had pushed Mackenzie and his followers underground to secret meetings and clandestine resolutions. When public notice of the meetings was given, there was usually some sort of a tangle between the rival interests with whatever stray bully-boys they could rouse up for the occasion. An account of one such meeting was given in the *Patriot and Farmers' Monitor* of 22 August, 1837; it is a good example of how matters stood during that sullen summer of suspicion:

MEETING AT FINCH'S TAVERN, YONGE STREET.
The Radicals again defeated.
On Thursday the 17th Inst., in the afternoon, it was rumoured that a handbill was stuck up at Finch's Tavern, for a Public Meeting the following day, at Noon.
This is a copy of the handbill: —
YORK Township Meeting. THE GORE OF TORONTO MEETING that was to be held at CHARLES KING's Store, East Toronto, is postponed for a few days, then to be called in a more central situation. The Meeting of the Township of York, to choose Delegates, enrol the names of members of Societies, and take efficient steps for numbering and classing the Reformers, so that they may act with union and system

in their effort to get justice for Canada, will take place at FINCH'S TAVERN, MONTGOMERYTOWN, Yonge Street, at Noon, on Friday August 18th, 1837.

August 12th, 1837.

About 11 o'clock, the lovers of the British Constitution began to pour in from all quarters, the Destructive having ('tis supposed) some doubts about their reception, assembled at Davis's Tavern and sent on a party with a flag bearing the American Eagle, which flag, when brought near to Finch's Tavern, was instantly seized and torn to pieces. Shortly afterwards large bodies of respectable farmers came in, well known for their attachment to the Government; at two o'clock the assembly had increased to about 400, when word was brought that Mackenzie and Co. had left Davis's Tavern, and were going towards Toronto. The meeting having waited two hours beyond the appointed time, and no Radicals having appeared since the destruction of the flag, and Mackenzie and Co. having run away — Colonel Moodie was requested to take the Chair, and Mr. Boyd to act as Secretary. The following resolutions were put and carried unanimously, by the most numerous and respectable meeting ever assembled in Yonge Street: —

Moved by Mr. Hogg, and seconded by Mr. Thomas Shepperd, That this meeting is determined to support the British Constitution, & oppose with all its power the treasonable and destructive doctrines promulgated by Messrs. Hume, Mackenzie, Papineau, & party.

Moved by Capt. Stewart, and seconded by Dr. McCague, That experience has shown that peace and quietness are necessary for the prosperity of a country; and that agitation (by a disaffected set of men — whose sole object is to raise the standard of rebellion, for their own aggrandizement, at the expense of the hard working part of the community) will as certainly prove its ruin, if not put a stop to.

Moved by Mr. Jas. Gamble, seconded by Mr. Griffith, That this meeting deeply lament the injury done to this fine and thriving Colony, by which many of our most loyal and industrious countrymen are deterred from coming to settle among us.

Moved by Dr. McCague, seconded by Captain Stewart, That this meeting feel it their duty to return a vote of thanks to our excellent Governor, Sir F. B. Head, Bart., for his noble and patriotic exertions to promote the prosperity of this Province, during his administration. And that this meeting most cordially agree to co-operate with His Excellency in every laudable and lawful manner to extinguish the last scintillations of rebellion in this hitherto happy colony.

(Signed   ROBERT MOODIE,
Chairman.

Finch's Tavern, Yonge Street,
   18th August, 1837

It was pretty obvious who had signed the address from the 'loyal inhabitants of Yonge Street.' The degree of support ascribed to the farmers depended very much upon which party was describing events. The farmers, however, if not ecstatic over Mackenzie, by this time were not happy about Head, either.

In July Mackenzie had drawn up 'The Declaration of Independence of Upper Canada' at what were almost his headquarters — at the Sun Hotel at Dundas and Yonge, the Rebels' Corner. Although distinguished neither by voice nor presence, Mackenzie had harangued the York crowd from an upper window of this hotel after he had again won an election in January 1832 following his first expulsion from the Assembly. Much as he liked to 'sound off', the time for oratory was past by the summer of 1837.

The July meetings at the Sun were held to discuss resolutions for the support of Papineau's reform movement in Lower Canada. Secret Upper Canadian meetings were held at Lloydtown and at Doel's Brewery, which was well out in the suburbs at what is now Bay and Adelaide streets.

Throughout the summer and fall of 1837, their cause helped by the general discontent caused by the poor crops and low prices of that year, Mackenzie's Radical Reformers drummed up support across the countryside for a mass demonstration to be held in Toronto. This was tame stuff for Fighting Mac himself, who, by October, was arguing for a more forceful strike, venting frustrations in physical action against the government. He was encouraged in this by the fact that Bond Head, in response to requests for troops to intimidate the growing unrest in Lower Canada, sent all the available regular units out of Upper Canada. It was a deliberate taunt to the easily inflamed Mackenzie.

Head, making the best possible light of things in his official despatches, said: 'I in no way availed myself of the immense Resources of the British Empire; on the contrary, I purposely dismissed from the Province the whole of our Troops.'[297] And to give him the benefit of the doubt, there was some merit in his action. Upper Canada did not have the French-English feud of the lower province, and to loose trained regulars against an assortment of rioting civilians could have resulted in gory repression with long-lingering after-effects. Whether Head had the gumption to see this remains the question. The militia were at least going against people who were in many respects their kin, and whom they would not subject to the steady, murderous volleys followed by the bayonet, butt, and boot of the coldly drilled professional.

Mackenzie may have imagined that he had a greater following than events of rebels formed from the men at Dutcher's foundry at Yonge and King streets and at Armstrong's axe-makers. Here was a change from the myth of the trusty yeomen of Yonge Street upon whom Mackenzie claimed to rely. His shock troops were to be the roughnecks of the new iron age.

It was perhaps fortunate for Upper Canada that the yeoman was still the major figure in the daily life of the province, and that no great urban mass of industry-coarsened rabble existed for Mackenzie to work his oratory upon. What might have excited the back streets of Glasgow was not likely to have the same effect upon the shrewdly sceptical farmers of Yonge Street.

Mackenzie did present a way of airing deeply held grievances, however, and to prepare those who were ready to follow him to get some action out of an administration that they felt was indifferent to their needs, some drills and rifle practices were held under the guise of pigeon shoots.

The first spark of active rebellion came on 6 November in Lower Canada. At a meeting of the Upper Canadian Radicals later in that month a date was fixed for a march upon Toronto: 7 December, 1837. On 25 November, Mackenzie issued his Proclamation of Independence. It was too much for Hogg the Miller when he found a copy at his home, and he decided to warn Bond Head that an attack upon the city was planned.

If, in the opinion of Hogg and others, Head was making a bosh of the business by his theatrical indifference, Mackenzie was making an equally bonny mess at his end. The rebellion in Upper Canada might have been pure opéra bouffe, but the farce was marred by the tragedy of official retribution that took the lives of men whose only fault was to act upon principles held with honesty and courage. At the end, even their late opponents would speak in their behalf.

Mackenzie may have imagined that he had a greater following than events showed, but the crowd attracted by noisy eloquence will only act when convinced by some practical success — and that he didn't provide. Voltaire, when asked if he did not enjoy the crowd that had turned out to applaud one of his stage plays, remarked indifferently that they would come out in as great numbers to see him hanged. Yonge Street was to become the stage for a play such as Simcoe could never have imagined: rebellion. And although partisan crowds flocked to the show, there would have been a mammoth mob to see Mackenzie hung, had he been caught.

The general story is well known; how Samuel Lount and Anthony Anderson organized support in the areas of Bradford, Lloydtown, Sharon, and Holland Landing; how Dr. Rolph, who seems to have played an ambiguous role in the campaign, became windy at the news that the lieutenant-governor was at last taking some action and had issued a warrant for Mackenzie's arrest.

Rolph made a panic decision on 2 December in the absence of Mackenzie, who was rounding up support in the townships, and sent word to David Gibson, who had been the first city surveyor of Toronto, with a suggestion that the date be advanced from the seventh to the fourth, before a resistance could be assembled. Gibson relayed the message to Lount at Holland Landing, where about one hundred men were assembled and prepared to march by various routes to Montgomery's Tavern on Yonge just above Eglinton.

Mackenzie, when he heard of this from Gibson at the latter's house during Sunday, 3 December, wanted to countermand the order, but it was too late; Lount was on the march. Not unnaturally, all this shuffling around the countryside could not go unnoticed. In his autobiographical *Reminiscences of a Canadian Pioneer*, Samuel Thompson said that 'on Sunday, the 3rd, [December] we heard that armed men were assembling at the Holland Landing and Newmarket to attack the city, and that lists of houses to be burned by them were in the hands of their leaders; that Samuel Lount, blacksmith, had been manufacturing pikes at the Landing for their use ....'[298]

On the morning of the fourth, seeing some activity near his home in the area of Richmond Hill, Captain David Bridgford went over to Yonge Street to find out what was going on and met Lount with some of his followers. Bridgford, an 1812 veteran of the militia who had been dumped in a wheelbarrow for dead after being. knocked unconscious in the explosion of the York magazine, was arrested by Lount, but then released on Bridgford's word that he would go straight home and stay there. Ironic, perhaps, that Bridgford's son would later fight under Stonewall Jackson for a rebel Confederacy in the States.

Rumour piled upon rumour, and as alarm increased so did Bridgford's worry until on hearing that it was planned to burn Toronto he decided that he could no longer keep his word and went to see Colonel Moodie, who lived close by.

That old warrior was already discussing the situation with a number of concerned gentlemen, among them Captain Hugh Stewart, late of the Royal Navy, whose daughter was married to Colonel Halkett, A.D.C. to the Lieutenant-Governor. Those present have also included a Mr. G. Read, a Mr. Prime Lawrence, and a Daniel Brooke who may have been the same who had purchased the Pomono Mills in Thornhill from (Sir) Allan MacNab; the number and names of the company, however, will never be quite clear.

They were well aware of the serious turn of events and had sent a messenger named Drew to Toronto to warn the authorities of the imminent attack; he was captured by some of Mackenzie's men who had set up barricades across Yonge Street at what is now Eglinton Avenue. By evening Lount's force had arrived at Montgomery's Tavern to find no preparations made, no arms, no supplies, and no food.

Although Montgomery's Tavern had recently been leased to a Tory by the name of Linfoot who had only just moved into the place on 1 December, Montgomery still kept a room there. From his photographs, Montgomery looks a heavy, dour, straight-lipped sort of man with a strong streak of obstinacy in him. In the 1820s he ran The Bird in Hand Inn on Yonge Street just north of the Sun, and at some time had another inn just north of present-day Finch Avenue in an area then known as Montgomerytown, now Newtonbrook. Montgomery,

" assembled at about four o'clock in the evening of Monday, the 4th instant, as
rebels, at Montgomery's Tavern, which is on the Yonge Street Macadamized road, about
four miles from the city. As soon as they had attained this position, Mr. M'Kenzie
and a few others, with pistols in their hands, arrested every person. on the road, in
order to prevent information reaching the town.......

Colonel Moody, a distinguished veteran officer, accompanied by three gentlemen
on horseback, on passing Montgomery's Tavern, was fired at by the rebels, and
I deeply regret to say that the Colonel, wounded in two places, was taken
prisoner into the tavern, where in three hours he died, leaving a widow and
family unprovided for. " (from The Narrative of Sir Francis Bond Head; ed. S.F. Wise, p. 143).

although a Reformer, was not happy with Mackenzie's latest stunt, and probably
told him so in no uncertain language, as Wee Mac shrilled about the tavern that
Montgomery had built north of Eglinton in 1830.

Not far south of Montgomery's, at Shepard's Mills on the west branch of the
Don River, Thomas and Michael (the sons of old Joseph Shepard who had died in
1837 before the Reform, which he had long supported, came to the boil) were
making bullets for Lount's chilled and empty-bellied troops. After their miserable
trek from the north these troops were not in much of a mood for fighting, and they
would be further discouraged by the developments during that night of Monday, 4
December.

Upon hearing of Drew's capture, Colonel Moodie, fired with brandy and a
sense of duty, determined to go himself to Toronto, despite the opposition of his
wife who saw no sense at all in the idea. He set out with Captain Stewart and
Captain Bridgford. The stories of who and how many accompanied him are

somewhat garbled. By some versions they fell in with Brooke, Lawrence, and Read in the course of Yonge Street.

They passed the first picket of rebels at Montgomery's Tavern but were stopped at the second, so firing up the Scots wrath of the old Colonel, who was not accustomed to being interfered with; 'Wha daur meddle wi' me?' as the ancient Scots version of *Nemo me impune lacessit* runs. These were not the soldierly Canadian stalwarts of his 104th, but a bunch of importunate louts bent upon defiance of the laws of young Queen Victoria who had come to the throne in June 1837.

A pot-valiant roar of 'Who are you to stop me on the Queen's Highway?' could be heard as Moodie discharged his pistol. A flurry of shots followed and, in the words of Sir Francis Bond Head's official report: 'Colonel Moodie, a distinguished Veteran Officer residing in Yonge Street, accompanied by Three Gentlemen on Horseback, on passing Montgomeries Tavern was fired at by the Rebels, and I deeply regret to say that the Colonel, wounded in Two Places, was taken Prisoner into the Tavern, where in Three Hours he died, leaving a Widow and Family unprovided for.'[299] These were three long hours of agony for the colonel, and the sounds of his slow death had an unnerving effect upon the gathering at the tavern.

Captain Stewart was captured and held in the tavern, but Bridgford successfully dodged the rebels and reached Toronto. In his despatch of 19 December the lieutenant-governor said that he was awakened by Alderman Powell with the news of what had taken place, but Mackenzie in his account said that he believed the bearer of the information to have been 'Captain Bridgford. He [Head] had the bells set a ringing, took up his abode in the city hall; delivered out a few rusty guns, made speeches and was in great trouble,'[300] which was about the closest Wee Mac came to being funny on the subject of the rebellion.

In Richmond Hill Historical Society — *Scrapbook* — Microfilm Roll No. 4, Richmond Hill Public Library: The *Liberal*, 'No. 17 — Col. David Bridgford,' relates that Bridgford, after Col. Moodie's death, managed to get around the picket and back on to Yonge Street south of Montgomery's Tavern. Here he met Powell and told him to hurry to the city to warn the lieutenant-governor.

The whole thing was rather like a poor replay of Paul Revere's ride. Samuel Thompson remembered that 'at eleven o'clock on Monday night, the 4th of December, every bell in the city was set ringing, occasional gun-shots were fired, by accident as it turned out, but none the less startling to nervous people . . . . presently the sound of horse's hoofs was heard, echoing loudly along Yonge Street. With others I hurried out, and found at Ridout's corner (King and Yonge hardware store) a horseman, who proved to be Alderman John Powell, who told his breathless listeners, how he had been stopped beyond the Yonge Street toll-gate, two miles out, by Mackenzie and Anderson . . . . how he had shot Anderson and missed Mackenzie; how he had dodged behind a log when pursued;

and had finally got into town by the College Avenue.'[301]

Mackenzie later recounted that he had been riding down Yonge Street between eight and nine o'clock on the night of the fourth with Anthony Anderson of Lloydtown, one of the Shepards, and two unnamed. They had met with Powell and an Archibald McDonald, and made both of them prisoners. Powell, who had managed to hide two pistols on his person, suddenly drew and fired at Anderson, then broke away at a gallop to make his escape to the city.[302]

While Sir Francis continued to make light of the approaching crisis, Mackenzie organized the supply of provisions from a Loyalist butcher two miles north of Montgomery's on Yonge through the agency of Linfoot, to whom business was still business regardless of politics. Thus fortified to make the attempt, they decided in the morning to start the advance on the city.

According to one story, the rebel force arrived about eleven in the morning at the house of the postmaster, Howard, who was absent in the city, and demanded to be fed. Mackenzie, having had a bad fright after the encounter with Powell, was parading around like a stuffed Napoleon with ample padding against bullets beneath his coat, gibbering and gesticulating at an unimpressed Mrs. Howard.

The pressure was beginning to tell upon him, and Mackenzie, if he did not know of it already, was quickly learning Napoleon's maxim that an army marches on its stomach. He was determined that they should be fed at Howard's, and his men set about preparing what they could find: 'A baking of bread just made was also cut up and confiscated by a tall thin man, named Eckhardt, from Markham.'[303] Here was the long shadow of discontent from one of Berczy's old settler families.

When satisfied, the mob thundered off at about two o'clock in the afternoon to march down Yonge Street. They were forming up to split into two groups at Gallows Hill when a flag of truce was seen being carried up the hill followed by a crowd of intrigued spectators.

The truce team of Robert Baldwin and Dr. Rolph, of all people, brought a message from the lieutenant-governor, who perhaps was stalling for time with his offer of an amnesty. Mackenzie in turn sensibly asked that the offer be put into writing, but also demanded a national convention to consider their grievances. This was a gloriously tactless choice of words, because if anything sparked a panic it was the word 'convention', which had been made notorious by the French Revolution.

French Canada may have sneezed first in 1837, but Head was damned if he was going to catch any cold. Although he seems to have confused the order of events in his 19 December despatch, perhaps purposely for effect, the determination not to compromise was still there; and it was not simply a pose. Sir Francis Bond Head had no authority whatsoever to grant political concessions in Upper Canada, even had he wished to, and his flat answer, if it now seems overbearing, was correct: '[Mackenzie] replied to my Admonition by a Message that he would only consent that his Demands should be settled by a National Convention; and he insolently added, that he would wait till Two o'clock for my Answer, which, in One Word, was "NEVER!" '

So spake brave Horatius, but there was now help arriving in quantity to help him hold the bridge. On the afternoon of Tuesday the fifth, a steamboat from Hamilton brought Allan MacNab's contingent of sixty-five Loyalists, his 'Men of Gore'. Rolph and Baldwin went back up Yonge Street with the lieutenant-governor's blunt refusal and met Mackenzie and Lount who by now had led their men as far as the Bloor tollgate.

There could now be no more parley, and the messengers returned again to the city. Mackenzie, determined to make some showing to impress his followers, burned the nearby house of Dr. Horne, partly because of his association with the Bank of Upper Canada, but also, Mackenzie claimed, because Rolph before leaving had quietly suggested it to him; for this there can never be any proof one way or the other. Having made a braw bonfire for the boys, all trooped back to the Howard home about half-past three in the afternoon, when Mackenzie again cavorted about like a rabid Rumpelstiltskin, confronting Mrs. Howard with the spectacle and threat of Horne's burning house.

The whole gang encamped on the Howards' grounds until six o'clock in the evening, when Lount set out with a few hundred men to advance down Yonge Street. After a speed-the-boat harangue from the Dundee Danton at the Bloor tollgate, they marched on, three abreast, but with their resolve still unfirmed. Samuel Thompson had this story from a farmer on Yonge Street who watched them pass by: 'While a detachment of rebels were marching southwards down the hill, since known as Mount Pleasant, they saw a waggonload of cordwood standing on the opposite rise, and supposing it to be a piece of artillery loaded to the muzzle with grape or canister, these brave warriors leaped the fences right and left like squirrels, and could by no effort of their officers be induced again to advance.'[304]

The whole show finally came to grief when they ran into an equally twitchy picket under Sheriff Jarvis near the present-day Maitland Street. The picket loosed off some shots and then fell back, but Lount's front row, after firing, dropped down in military fashion to allow the line behind a clear field of fire. A number of people in the rear thought that the front rank had been killed and they broke up in confusion. In the flustered exchange, however, one of Lount's men was killed and two others from East Gwillimbury wounded, to die later in hospital.

An account of the incident appeared in the *Patriot and Farmers' Monitor* of 8 December, 1837: 'Colonel Cameron and son have been made prisoners. . . .Two small parties, under Mr. Sheriff Jarvis and Mr. Cameron, (no relation of the other two) advanced last evening (5th) a short distance up Yonge-street, and had some skirmishing with the Rebels, of whom one was killed and two others wounded; the rest, number not known, taking to their heels with most hearty good-will.

Near to the body of the dead Rebel were found a fowling-piece and two pikes about ten feet long, manufactured with punctilious regard to destructiveness: the blade stuck into the shafts, which are of hickory, are spear-shaped, sharply-pointed, and double-edged, calculated for thrusting and ripping up bellies, no doubt the contrivance of the bloody-minded villain, Mackenzie. Last evening a three-pounder cannon, made for the Rebels, was seized at Norton's foundry, just dry from painting, and was to have been delivered this morning. (6th) . . . .The number of the marauders has not been ascertained: it has been variously estimated at from four to six hundred, and they are said to be generally young ruffians from twenty to thirty years of age, with some scattering hoary villains among them. . . .Mr. Gibson, the Carpenter (not to be confused with David Gibson the Surveyor) has been arrested.'

Mackenzie, faced with this rout, is described by Thompson as doing his best 'to induce his men to advance on the city that evening; (5th) but as most of his followers had been led to expect that there would be no resistance, and no bloodshed, they were shocked and discouraged by Col. Moodie's death, as well as by those of Anderson and one or two others.'[305] It was no go; Wednesday, 6 December was a day of indecision and disorganization as the shaken forces fell back to regroup and lick their wounds at Montgomery's Tavern. The only positive action was taken when Mackenzie and Lount with a few men held up the westbound mail stage that morning on Dundas Street and made it turn off to Montgomery's.

There were several prisoners being held by now in the ballroom of the tavern. On Tuesday some sixty of these had been put in the charge of David Gibson and used to give an exaggerated impression of the force that had trooped down to Gallows Hill, although they probably got more out of the show than ever did the rebels.

Among those who had been captured was David Bridgford, who had ridden north to raise volunteers after relaying the news of Moodie's death to the city, but was less successful in avoiding his opponents this time. Mackenzie wanted to hang him as a spy, but Gibson intervened to have him held merely as a prisoner-of-war. With the events of the Tuesday, however, Mackenzie became completely unstuck and decided that Bridgford should be shot on Wednesday afternoon — by which time, Bridgford is reported to have told him 'you will then have enough to do to look after your own neck without attending to mine.'[306]

The two Camerons mentioned as prisoners by the *Patriot* of 8 December were the veteran, Colonel Duncan Cameron, C.B., and his son, Archibald. The Rebels had called at his home on Yonge Street at York Mills, demanding firearms, but they were out of luck. His nineteen-year-old son tried to ride into town to give warning, but was stopped at Montgomery's Tavern, where he was made a prisoner.

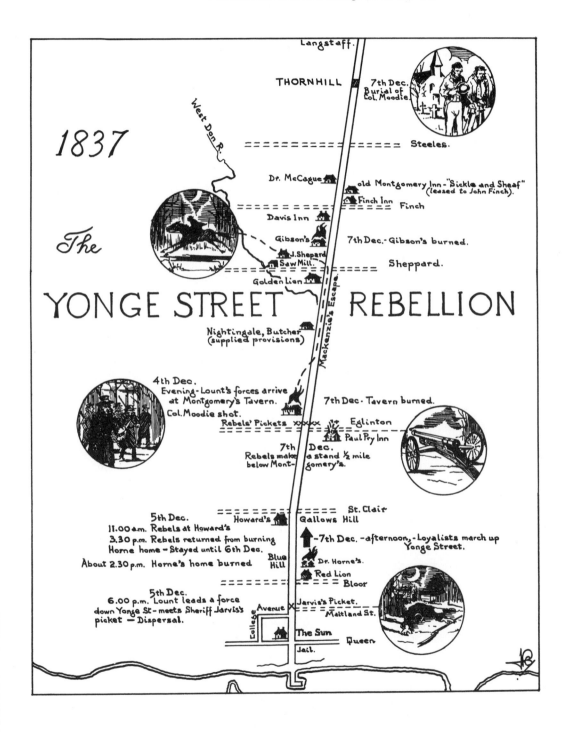

Langstaff.

THORNHILL

7th Dec. Burial of Col. Moodie.

West Don R.

1837

Steeles.

Dr. McCague

old Montgomery Inn - "Sickle and Sheaf"
(leased to John Finch).

Finch Inn   Finch

Davis Inn

The

Gibson's   7th Dec. - Gibson's burned.

J. Shepard
Saw Mill.   Sheppard.

Golden Lion

YONGE STREET REBELLION

Mackenzie's Escape.

Nightingale, Butcher
(supplied provisions)

4th Dec.
Evening - Lount's forces arrive   7th Dec. - Tavern burned.
at Montgomery's Tavern.
Col. Moodie shot.
Rebels' Pickets xxxxx   Eglinton
                              Paul Pry Inn
7th Dec.
Rebels make a stand ½ mile
below Mont- gomery's.

5th Dec.   St. Clair
11.00 a.m. Rebels at Howard's   Howard's   Gallows Hill
3.30 p.m. Rebels returned from burning   -7th Dec. - afternoon, - Loyalists march up
Horne home – Stayed until 6th Dec.   Yonge Street.
About 2.30 p.m. Horne's home burned   Blue   Dr. Horne's.
                                      Hill   Red Lion
                                              Bloor
5th Dec.
6.00 p.m. Lount leads a force   Jarvis's Picket.
down Yonge St - meets Sheriff Jarvis's   Avenue X
picket – Dispersal.   Maitland St.
                              College
                                        The Sun
                                        Jail.   Queen

On Wednesday it became clear that the demoralized force was going to remain at the tavern, having no stomach for further attacks on Toronto. Sir Francis, who had at first declared that the rebels must come to fight him on his own ground, was now encouraged to take the initiative with the arrival of more reinforcements in Toronto. A number of Toronto radicals who had been hanging around the Sun Hotel on Tuesday waiting for the coup to take place had faded away when it did not appear, no doubt to declare that their sympathies were with the government.

In the brilliantly clear light of the sunny afternoon of 7 December, the loyalist forces set out for an assault upon the rebel stronghold. At the front was the diminutive 'Galloping' Head, in civilian clothes, but so hung about with pistols as to look like a Texas Ranger's Christmas tree. With some 900 loyalists and militia under Colonel Fitzgibbon, including MacNab's men and Captain McLean's hundred from Scarborough, as well as with a battery of two guns under Major Carfrae, a brave show marched north from the city. The force was accompanied by two bands, supposedly playing, if it can be believed, 'Yankee Doodle'.[306]

Colonel Fitzgibbon must have been in his element that day. A colourful Irishman renowned as a riot-breaker, who owed his advancement from the ranks to Brock's notice, he had been of great help once before in dealing with Mackenzie during the wagon-toppling riot at York on 23 March, 1832. Rightly regarding Wee Mac as the source of much of the mischief on that occasion, Fitzgibbon forcibly shut him into his house, there to stay until the hullabaloo had died down.

On the day of the assault on Montgomery's Tavern, Colonel Moodie was buried at Holy Trinity Church, Thornhill. So tense was the atmosphere on Yonge Street that most of those present carried swords, pistols, fowling pieces, and even pitchforks, much to the displeasure of the minister holding the funeral service.

The long-awaited old soldier-farmer, Anthony van Egmond, had finally arrived at Montgomery's on Wednesday morning and a council-of-war was held with Mackenzie, Lount, and Gibson. Van Egmond was a Dutchman who had served as a colonel in Napoleon's army, but after the emperor's first exile to the island of Elba, he joined the Allies against Napoleon, holding officer rank in one of the Belgian regiments at Waterloo: not a very glorious attachment when the record of the Belgian troops, who broke and ran, is considered.

He certainly wasn't sympathetic to Mackenzie's plans for further action, and harsh words passed between them. Mackenzie, however, had no military experience whatsoever and in the end it was decided to make some sort of a stand about half a mile south of the tavern. Lount and van Egmond went with some 150 men into the woods on the west side of Yonge and a small force made a stand at the Paul Pry Inn on the east side.

The engagement, when it came, was brief and decisive. The first shots from the cannon of the loyalists killed Ludovic Wideman of Stouffersville (Stouffville), an old militia veteran of 1812 who supported Mackenzie only out of disgust at the manner in which the 1836 elections were conducted. The second cannon fired a round through the roof of the Paul Pry Inn. Two more cannon balls whistled through Montgomery's spacious tavern and Mackenzie's forces scattered to the breeze, to be searched out by the pursuing militiamen. It was all over, bar the flights and the retribution.

Mackenzie's Highland grandfather had been 'out' in the 'Forty-Five Rebellion' in Scotland to follow the boozy, charismatic figure of Bonnie Prince Charlie, whose venture ended with a bloody mess at Culloden, 'The Skye Boat Song', and Charlie-boy in full flight with a price on his head. A chorus of tear-blotted balladry then slopped enough romance over his scruffy, unco-operative Highlanders to give heroic proportions to the tale. Compared with this the rebellion in Upper Canada had been a tame sort of a show, but there was at least some excitement in the escapes that followed it.

No romance and no heroic myths came out of the Yonge Street fray of 1837. Head simply made bonfires of Montgomery's Tavern and David Gibson's house on Lot 18 on the west side of Yonge at Willowdale, and then got on with the chase. Like Mackenzie and Lount, Gibson had to flee for the border; their way was threatened by large rewards for their capture: 'a Reward is . . .offered of ONE THOUSAND POUNDS, to any one who will apprehend, and deliver up to Justice, WILLIAM LYON MACKENZIE; and FIVE HUNDRED POUNDS to any one who will apprehend, and deliver up to Justice, DAVID GIBSON — or SAMUEL LOUNT — or JESSE LOYD — or SILAS FLETCHER — '[307]

David Gibson was a Scot from Forfarshire who arrived in Markham during 1826 as a trained land surveyor. In 1829 he bought 105 acres of land for $400 on the south half of Lot 18 on the west side of Yonge. He was a member of the Reform Assembly in 1834, representing the First Riding of York and giving strong support to Mackenzie. When it was first proposed in the summer of 1834 to build a railway from Toronto to Lake Simcoe, he worked as a deputy to the surveyor of the line, Thomas Roy, who considered him 'a rather unreliable individual', who made a general hash of his job and then resigned.[308] Gibson escaped successfully to New York State and settled near Lockport, working for a time as an engineer on the Erie Canal.

Old Ely Playter, who had moved for an unstated but possibly political reason to the area of Buffalo at the end of the 1820s, made a brief diary entry without any comment on 5 September, 1839: 'The Judge sent me again to the Gd Jury room where I spent the day. Spent the evening with Mr Gibson — a Mr Cannady [Edward Kennedy?] & Henderson [Thomas Anderson?] Radicals from Canada.'[302]

Although pardoned in 1843, Gibson did not return to Canada until 1849, when he built a brick house to replace the old frame home burned in 1837 on Lot 18, where the restored brick building still stands.

There is a story that Mrs. Gibson, who fled with her children to a neighbour's

David Gibson 1804-1864

This building, a good example of an early Victorian farm-house
was completed in 1851 by David Gibson. Born in Glamis
Parish, Forfarshire, Scotland, Gibson emigrated to Upper Canada
where, in 1825, he was appointed a Deputy Land Surveyor.
He was an ardent supporter of William Lyon Mackenzie, and was
twice elected as a Reform member to the provincial parliament.
One of Mackenzie's chief lieutenants in the unsuccessful
Rebellion of 1837, he fled to the United States. His house was
burned by order of the Lieutenant-Governor, Sir Francis Bond
Head, and his property was made subject to forfeiture. Fully
pardoned, he returned in 1848, and resumed his profession
as surveyor. Later he was appointed as Inspector of Crown
Land Agencies and Superintendent of Colonization Roads.
Erected by the Archaeological and Historic Sites Board
Department of Public Records and Archives of Ontario.

house when their home was burned, managed to save David's surveying
instruments, and also the clock face and works that can still be seen in the
grandfather clock on the second floor of the restored house.

Mackenzie made an escape that had almost as much colour and legend in it as
Bonnie Prince Charlie's. He got on to Yonge Street after leaving the tavern and
rode north to the Golden Lion where he passed the elderly van Egmond and
almost immediately turned west, closely pursued, toward Joseph Shepard's mills.
Mackenzie doesn't mention it himself, but it is said that Mrs. Shepard delayed the
militia soldiers with talk while he got clear away.

MACKENZIE'S RIDE.

"At the Golden Lion, ten miles above the city, I overtook Col. Anthony Van Egmond, a Dutch officer, of many years' experience under Napoleon. .... .. The Colonel was a man of large property, old, and known to be opposed to Head's party ...... Finding myself closely pursued and repeatedly fired at, I left the high road with one friend (Mr. J.R.) and made for Shepard's Mills ......the official party were so close upon us that I had only time to jump off my horse, and ask the miller (himself a Tory) whether a large body of men, then on the heights, were friends or foes, before our pursuers were climbing up the steep ascent almost beside me."

(Mackenzie's Account from The Life and Times of William Lyon Mackenzie by Charles Lindsey, Vol. 2, p.103 – Coles Reprint.)

From there on it was touch and go to the United States border, with 'Mackenzie stopped here' becoming part of local feature stories. He is supposed to have hidden beneath a 'pot-ashery' at Gorham's Mills, Lot 93 east on Yonge at Newmarket.[310] At Oakville it is said that he disguised himself in women's clothing obtained from sympathizers, although one unlikely version suggests that the disguise came from the baggage of a lady who had been in the mail stage captured on 6 December[311] — shades of Betty Burke, the long-striding Irish maidservant who was in reality Bonnie Prince Charlie. Mackenzie may not have matched the 'over the sea to Skye' performance, but he did manage a melodramatic, musket-range departure by rowboat across the Niagara River to the American side at Black Rock just north of Buffalo, on Monday, 11 December, 1837.

His escape successful, he proceeded to organize himself on Navy Island in the Niagara River with the aid of American sympathizers, and with the hasty heart of the prideful Scot to delcare himself in arms against 'Miss Victoria . . .and her baneful domination'.[312] The *Patriot* of 19 January, 1838, made much sport of his situation, not without some picturesque humour: '[Mackenzie] with whom the Frontier Belles [of Buffalo] have fallen so desperately in love, whom they have so pinked out in ruffles, epaulettes, and sash, that were he riding around a circus-ring on a Shelty, he would not be known from Dandy Jack.'

From Navy Island he issued a proclamation:[313]

PROCLAMATION

THREE Hundred Acres of the most valuable Lands in Canda will be given to each Volunteer who may join the Patriot Forces now encamped on Navy Island, Upper Canada. Also, 100 Dollars in Silver, payable on or before the 1st of May next.

By Order of the Committee of the Provincial Government,
(Signed) W. L. MACKENZIE,
Chairman, pro tem.

Navy Island, Tuesday, 19th Dec. 1837.

Nice touch, that 'pro tem.' but Mackenzie probably didn't see much that was funny in it, the Scots reputation for pawky humour being at short stay on occasions like this. There was little to laugh at in the aftermath.

Poor old van Egmond was not so lucky. Slowed by his sixty-seven years he was soon apprehended by the militia and thrown into jail, where his aged constitution could take no more; the *Patriot* announced on 5 January, 1838, that 'GENERAL Van Egmont died this morning in our City Hospital!' A prosperous farmer himself, he had supported Mackenzie's movement because of dissatisfaction with the low status of farmers in general throughout the province.

The most tragic circumstances were those of Samuel Lount and Peter Matthews. Their efforts to reach the sanctuary of the United States were unsuccessful and they were put on trial and sentenced to death by hanging in April 1838 for treason.[314] It was a sorry verdict, and at the trial in January Captain Stewart and Archibald McDonald who had been prisoners at Montgomery's Tavern came forward to testify 'to the humanity of the General, (Lount) which, they emphatically said, they did with heartfelt pleasure, declaring that it was their full and entire conviction that, but for the determined opposition both of Lount and Gibson, the whole of the prisoners would have been BUTCHERED IN COLD BLOOD BY MACKENZIE.'[315]

By the time of the hanging, Sir Francis Bond Head had left the province, his resignation having been tendered as early as September 1837 and announced in January 1838. He had been considerably miffed at instructions from the home government ordering that he restore Bidwell and Ridout to the Bench.[316]

He was consoled and speeded on his way by, among others, a letter of appreciation from his Yonge Street following, and it was duly sent on to Lord Glenelg: 'We the inhabitants of Yonge Street and its immediate Vicinity, learn with Feelings of heartfelt Sorrow, that your Excellency is about to leave us; to leave us at a Time when your Policy in the Management of the Government of this Province has led to the happiest Result.'[317]

Happy for some, maybe, but not for everybody by a long shot. Head's successor, Sir George Arthur, continued in the grim Roman way of 'gravitas' and duty without sympathy, although the death penalties, with the exception of Matthews' and Lount's were commuted to imprisonment for life. Sir George remained impervious to the pleas of Mrs. Lount and the petition with 5000 signatures that came down from Newmarket. As John Ryerson wrote to his brother Egerton in April 1838: 'There seems to be a determination on the part of certain persons connected with the executive to carry things to extremes.'

In the report of the trial of John Montgomery, the tavern-owner seems to have been his usual lumpy self in his dealings with Mackenzie while the latter was running his road-show on Yonge Street; but his non-co-operation and indifference to the antics of Wee Mac's troupe didn't carry much weight with the jury, nor did the Day of Judgement blast which he loosed at Chief Justice J. B. Robinson, who had the last word: guilty of treason, sentenced in April to be hung. Captain Bridgford's testimony against Montgomery was given much importance, although he seems to have had a personal quarrel with the accused; equally damning was Captain Stewart's statement that Montgomery had refused him pen and paper to write for a doctor to attend Colonel Moodie.[318]

The punishment was changed to imprisonment for life. Montgomery, with several others, was confined in Fort Henry at Kingson; from there he organized an escape with eleven prisoners including Michael and Thomas Shepard and Edward Kennedy to Rochester in New York State.[319]

Of all those arrested, the home district had by far the longest list, and upon it appear several old Yonge Street names from long-settled families. What was their reason for rebellion? Their efforts on Yonge Street had not been unsuccessful.

An interesting comment is made by Samuel Thompson. In much the way that the Clan Fraser had marched on to the field at Culloden to the skirl of bagpipes and banners, only to find that the battle was over, so in 1837, 'the day after the battle, six hundred men of Simcoe, under command of Lieutenant-Colonel Dewson, came marching down Yonge Street, headed by Highland pipers playing the national pibroch.'

They brought with them sixty prisoners, and, said Thompson, 'it was an extraordinary fact, that these poor settlers (from County Simcoe) living in contentment in their log cabins, with their potato patches around, should turn out and put down a rebellion originated among old settlers and wealthy farmers in the prosperous county of York.'[320]

What made the old settlers and farmers prone to rebel was perhaps not so much the question of constitutional changes advanced by liberal political theorists, but the dull, sullen nag of resentment. Those of American background and origin without Loyalist affiliations disliked the English influx that firmly shouldered them aside. They objected to the attitudes of the officials at York, and had a very real feeling that they were losing the privileges of 'free men', so dear to the American experience, to a group of people drawing their power from the lieutenant-governor.

The poor of County Simcoe had little, if anything, to lose; the long-settled farmers of Yonge Street, however, had their pride and their achievements slighted; never mind the jaw about political systems, it was the 'gentlemen of the Pap Spoon' who rubbed the Pennsylvania 'Dutch' farmers and the likes of a successful innkeeper such as Montgomery on the raw. As far as Yonge Street was concerned, the Rebellion of 1837 might in some ways be said to be a clash of cultures: American-English against British-English.

Certainly, among those indicted for treason or arrested for complicity, some old, familiar, Yonge Street names appear[321] — 'Aaron Munshaw, yeoman, indicted for treason' — and, in the long string of those arrested thanks to lists Mackenzie had made, of his supporters which were found among some of his belongings in Montgomery's Tavern:

William Ketchum, tanner, the son of Jesse Ketchum
Joseph Shepard, yeoman, the son of old Joseph Shepard the Indian trader.
Michael Shepard, yeoman,
Thomas Shepard, yeoman, the bullet makers.
John D. Wilson (Willson), yeoman of Sharon, who, on the evening of 6
    December, had brought a wagon-load of pikes, guns and provisions from
    Holland Landing to Montgomery's.
Jacob Shepard, yeoman.
Daniel Shepard, labourer.
John Shepard, labourer.

William Kendrick, labourer.
J. W. Kendrick, labourer.
Francis Lyons, labourer.
James Johnson, yeoman.
Joseph Johnson, yeoman.
John Devins.
Reuben Lundy.
William Rogers.
Peter Rogers.

Names and relationships, of course, are always difficult to establish without considerable research. What of William Heron, labourer, and Abraham Anderson? Were they related to the Scots families of those names settled on Yonge Street during its earliest years? And there were, of course, those who were sympathetic to reform, such as Hogg the miller, Joseph Milburne the Quaker innkeeper, and possibly Isaac Playter, although they drew the line at active revolt.

The reform, when it did result, was British in tone, handed down by Britain and geared to her political considerations. The old American settlers were firmly set aside, although for many years to come there would still be a resentment against the English attitudes and affectations that had been established.

Newspapers are always good for a clue to the ways of an age. With a sonorous rumble of opinion that would have brought him an 'A' for an essay on the Press, Dr. Johnson declared in an essay on the press: 'I never derive more benefit, or see more pleasure for the time, than in reading a Newspaper lately issues from the Press. I do believe that nothing adds so much to the glory of any country as a Newspaper. Liberty is stamped legibly upon its pages, and even the fold is marked with freedom.'

If anything was missing to emphasize the liberty of the Toronto papers of the day, it was Mackenzie's *Advocate*; with all its gossip and blistering broadsides, it made grand reading even if it didn't always go off with much accuracy of facts. And it had found readers enough if the willingness to place advertisements in it is any indication of popularity.

The draught that came in on the vanishing coattails of Wee Mac was the breeze that bent the barley, not the uprooter of tradition's old oaks. If it carried a tang of American ways, nobody cared to notice; the folds of the Toronto papers were now indelibly marked with, if anything, the brand of British ways.

In the *Patriot and Farmers' Monitor* for 19 February, 1839, John Mead of Yonge Street advertised 'Furs! Furs! Furs! for the Gentry of Toronto and its vicinity! . . .' This wasn't a rural, landed gentry. There were no Squire Westerns, no Pitt Crawleys, and none of Tennyson's pheasant lords mouldering since Egbert; rather, there was a gentry whose basis, though not openly acknowledged as much, was success in business, American fashion.

The few rural gentry such as the Hon. Aemilius Irving, all trot and sparkle, driving out of the gates of his estate at 'Bonshaw', or Captain Martin Macleod of Skye who had settled on Lots 60 and 61 to establish his estate of 'Dornoch', may have set a style, but it was not of a usual pattern.

Those who felt themselves to be a part of the gentry of Toronto and Yonge Street banded together in the way of that very English institution, the club. Theirs was a club dedicated to the continuation of British habits, and to join it they had paid their dues by deploring American influences and by giving a staunch allegiance to Britain. This allegiance carried with it the privilege of letting members criticize club policies if they felt like it, a privilege denied to outsiders.

The Home District Agricultural Society, in which Mackenzie had once found supporters, now reflected these club attitudes, and was, in fact, in many ways like a club by itself. At a meeting of this society club at Richmond Hill on 9 December, 1840, with the sheriff of home district in the chair, it was 'resolved that Upper Canada, being essentially an agricultural country, the due protection and encouragement of its farming interest ought to form a leading feature in its legislation, and the policy adopted by the Mother Country towards her Colony. That the little attention which the British Government has hitherto appeared to bestow upon this subject ...is altogether unaccountable.'[322]

Present at this meeting were such members of the old brigade as Captain Stewart and Messrs. Thorne, Gapper, Gamble, Kinnear, Van Nostrand, Edward O'Brien, W. B. Robinson, Charles Thompson, and John Comer — a loyal bandwagon. They didn't doubt, however, that their loyalty allowed them to state freely that as Britain was 'one great workshop of manufacturers' with a large population and an excess of labour, there should be an unrestricted interchange of goods between Canada and Britain. Canadian produce, they said, should be admitted free into Britain, and they voiced objection to wheat, flour, pork, and livestock being let into Canada from the United States free of duty.

In some ways there might seem to be a flavour of Mazo de la Roche's Whiteoaks to this group, but in another respect they showed an American get-up-and-go in their desire to see new ideas taken up, and an impatience to see rapid progress made in their province. And this interest could cut across the lines of politics and backgrounds, uniting people in partnership to promote the growth of Upper Canada.

As early as the summer of 1834, W. B. Robinson, Charles Thompson, Benjamin Thorne, and, interesting to note, Samuel Lount, had met with others to consider a canal or a railroad from Toronto to Lake Simcoe. The scarcity of money for investment and the lack of support during the depression of 1837 brought the company that was formed as a result, the City of Toronto and Lake Huron Rail Company, to a grinding halt, and attention again went back to the not-much-improved Yonge Street.

In September 1838 a concerned trustee for the Yonge Street Road wrote that 'A very serious accident has occurred at the embankment near Hogg's Hollow, by the upsetting of a waggon over the bank, by which 3 or 4 females have been severely injured — one not expected to survive.'[323]

Somewhere the British military tradition of a road as straight as a guardsman's back had died hard, and come what may, Yonge Street was to be cut through at Hogg's Hollow, and damn the expense. In 1844, the task fell to the provincial government of improving the road at the dreaded Hogg's Hollow, and in 1846 it was afflicted with the chronic handicap of keeping up the entire length of Yonge Street.

Reading descriptions of travel along Yonge Street at this time by a British army officer, Sir Richard Bonnycastle, anybody might believe that the entire development along that road was due solely to the enterprise and industry of the English. On a journey from Toronto to Penetanguishene and back in 1846, he had these observations to make: '[To Penetanguishene] the route is per coach to St. Alban's [Holland Landing] thirty and three miles, along Yonge Street, of which about one-third is macademized from granite boulders; the rest mud and etceteras, too numerous to mention. Yonge Street is a continuous settlement . . . .The first quarter of the route to St. Alban's is a series of country-houses, gentlemen's seats, half-pay officers' farms, prettily fenced, and pleasant to the sight: the next third embraces Thornhill, a nice village in a hollow; Richmond Hill, with a beautiful prospect and detached settlements: the ultimate third is a rich, undulating country, inhabited by well-to-do Quakers, with Newmarket on their right, and looking for all the world very like "dear home".'[324]

All jolly nice, says Sir Richard, if the influence is English, as at Dolby's Tavern, a low, one-storey frame building, the stopping place for coach horses at Richmond Hill: 'Attention, good fare, and neatness prevail. It is English.' And he makes quite a point of this distinction: 'If you find neatness at an hostel, it is kept by old-country people. If you meet with indifference and greasy meats, they are Americans. If you see the best parlour hung round with bad prints of presidents, looking like Mormon preachers, they are radicals of the worst leaven.' Bonnycastle's style, with his humorous way of expression, must have been highly entertaining to his readers, although no one with American connections was likely to find his English flippancy funny.

For all the appearance of 'dear home', however, he found that Yonge Street was 'still a tiresome journey', and stopped for the night at Holland Landing, 'where all was scrub forest in 1837' but by 1846 had been developed to the extent of 'a little street, a house of some pretension occupied by Mr. Laughton, the enterprising owner of the Beaver steamboat, plying on Lake Simcoe, and two inns.' At the steamboat wharf, two to three miles north of St. Alban's, 'flies, mosquitoes, ague, and other plagues, are so rife, that all attempts at settlement are vanity and vexation of spirit.'

The road from Kempenfeldt Bay to Penetanguishene he found 'much

THE DOAN HOUSE –AURORA.

The Doan House on Yonge Street was built by Charles Doan,
first Postmaster of Aurora, in the 1840s.
Ebenezer Doan, with his five sons and their families came from
the U.S.A. in 1805-1808, and settled on Yonge Street, north
of Aurora. His son, also Ebenezer, was the Master Builder of
the Sharon Temple.
Among the Reformers arrested in 1837 were Charles, Jesse and
Jonathan Doan.

improved' since 1837, but the latter place itself was 'a small village which has not progressed in the same ratio as the military road to it has done. It is peopled by French Canadians, Indians, and half-breeds, and is very prettily situated at the bottom of the harbour.' This reads as though the place had been dumped off the end of the jetty, but it wasn't as deadly as that. The advertisements for Penetanguishene read much like those for Yonge Street had about half a century earlier.[325] On town lot 25 in the village of Penetanguishene there was a '2 storey frame dwelling with Out-houses and Garden attached' and also a 'good Log Dwelling' on town lot 14; and close to the harbour, two miles from the village, was the Bay Farm of 129 acres, 'much of it cleared and cultivated' and a log dwelling, barn, and outhouses.

To scratch up the cash to pay for the Penetanguishene Road, the system of tolls was extended beyond the north end of Yonge Street at the Landing:

THE MAIN NORTHERN ROAD,
From Lake Ontario, at Toronto, to Lake Huron
The opening of this road efficiently, throughout, is considered highly
desirable, and strongly recommended, but the portion here more
immediately referred to, is from the termination of that undertaken by

the District, at the Holland Landing, to Barrie, which it is proposed to drain, form and plank, and to establish toll bars thereon: from thence to Penetanguishene, it is intended to improve.[326]

The above memorandum was submitted to the governor-general for formal approval.

On his return from Penetanguishene, stopping at Richmond Hill, Bonnycastle noted that the road 'will be macadamized some fine day; for the Board of Works have a Polish engineer [he was Casimir Gzowski] hard at work surveying it — of course no Canadian was to be found equal to this intricate piece of engineering — and I saw a variety of sticks stuck up, but what they meant I cannot guess at. I suppose they were going to *grade* it, which is the favourite American term —'

Owing his knighthood to the services that he had performed during the 1837 rebellion in Lower Canada, Sir Richard commented jauntily on Yonge Street's association with those troubled times in Upper Canada. David Wilson of the Temple of Peace at Sharon he regarded as a freak, 'a fraud of man.' 'Lount had the mind of an honest man in some things. . . ' 'Finch's Tavern . . . was formerly the Old Stand, as it was so called, of the notorious Montgomery, another general, a tavern general of Mackenzie's, who moved to a place about four miles from the city, where the rebels were attacked in 1837 . . . .It is now rebuilt on a very extensive scale; and he is again there, having been permitted to return . . .'

Continuing south from Richmond Hill to Toronto, Bonnycastle remarked that 'all of the macadamized portion of the road to Toronto' had been laid south of Thornhill. And on approaching Toronto, at the Blue Hill Ravine, he observed that 'large brick yards are in operation, and here white brick is now made, of which a handsome specimen of church architecture has been lately erected in the west end of the city. Tiles, elsewhere not seen in Canda, are also manufactured near Blue Hill.'

John Davis had come from England to the area of the Blue Hill in 1810, and five years later, following the example of John Humberstone, he set up a pottery works at what is now Yonge and Millwood Road. This has been described as 'one of the busiest industrial sites on Yonge Street . . . .There was a great open-air tank in which the clay was mixed, and a great wooden paddle was suspended over it. This paddle was turned by the efforts of a horse which walked around the tank. In the rear of the property three great firing kilns had been erected and in these sewer pipes and the flower pots and other forms of pottery were fired and made ready for commerce.'[327]

At this time in the 1840s an interesting visitor to Yonge Street, a shade from its past, was old Ely Playter; unfortunately, however, he made little, if any, comment upon the changes that he saw around him. Returning to Upper Canada in the summer of 1843, he explored his old haunts. A strong surge of sentiment and nostalgia tugged below the turgid stream of factual commentary in his diary as he passed by old Castle Frank on 7 June, laden with the memories of his early days in that area over a quarter of a century ago.[328]

At Newmarket on 17 June, he watched the militia training: 'The Rolls called — three Cheers for the Queen was about all. The Col gave them a glass of beer a piece and some of the Tee-Totallers were offended at that.'

In July he was back at Richmond Hill where he visited old cronies: the Arnolds, Langstaffs, Abm Johnsons, J. Cumer, and Mrs. Montgomery. On the sixteenth he lets the memories crowd back: 'I went to the new Church on the Concession Line near where [sic] I once owned land which I had laboured improved and lived now a part of the City suburbs — . . . .After noon I strolled on the old Don flatts — thot of the times and circumstances of by gone days and sceanes of Last War — 'His pilgrimage complete, he returned on the eighteenth to his home near Lewiston in New York State.

In the summer of the following year, however, he was back, and while on the steamer from Queenston to Toronto on 22 May he met 'an old acquaintance Saml Canady he had moved to Ohio, and as surprising as it was had become disaffected and Radical.' Old Ely didn't approve of radicals, moderate or otherwise. On 5 June, 1844, he read 'a pamphlet of a Reform Association Meeting in the City, inflammatory speeches by Baldwin, H. J. Boulton & others rampant Rebelism in my opinion.'

Although he visited Barrie and the Narrows in the schooner of his old friend, Eli Beman, and so must have seen the growth taking place there and met with people who were directly involved in pushing the new ideas for progress, Ely Playter made no comment, but simply noted how he passed the time of day: '16th June — . . .call'd at Frasier's Inn, went on board the Steamboat — Met Mr Charles Tompson and walked with him to Orillia House kept by a Mr. King.'

It would seem that old Ely had reached that saddest point in life when the new ceases to interest, and there remain only associations from the past, the doldrums of reflection. In February 1845 he was again back in Upper Canada, and 'heard of Ely Beman being in the City and looked for him came to Yonge Street and met Cozn George Playter.' Any changes that he might have noticed on Yonge Street, however, were only the prologue to a decade of rapid progress that would open an entirely new chapter in the road's story.

In December 1844 the scheme to construct a railroad north from Toronto was revived by William Allan, one of the city's leading businessmen. A depression during 1847, a lean year during which the Penetanguishene Road was at last considerably improved, combined with a dispute over where the rail terminus should be, brought the project to grief. The idea remained, however, almost as an obsession, an American determination to compel Destiny's compliance. Finally, on 11 October, 1849, the *Globe* carried copy of a complimentary address to the resourceful and aggressive Mr. Frederick C. Capreol for his sustained efforts in promoting the bill to enact the Toronto and Lake Huron Union Railroad. The construction of this railroad was begun in October 1851, and one year later the first locomotive, named the *Lady Elgin* after the Governor General's wife, was imported from Portland, Maine via schooner from Oswego.

Toronto, however, was not about to rely upon American industry and know-how to supply its machinery. The Toronto Foundry on Yonge Street near Queen, which under the Norton management had produced the never-delivered cannon for Mackenzie's patriots, now made a more significant contribution to progress under the management of James Good, who took over at the beginning of 1843. Toward the close of 1852, Good's Foundry contracted for a part of the locomotives for the Ontario, Simcoe and Huron Railroad — or 'Oats, Straw and Hay' Railroad, as the line was called — and advertised for 200 mechanics. On 19 April, 1853, the *Globe* announced that 'the first Locomotive and Tender . . .was yesterday removed from Mr. Good's Foundry.' The engine was subsequently named the *Toronto*.

After the Drawing by Stanley Turner, ARCA, OSA.

A Locomotive Boiler being drawn from Good's Foundry on Yonge Street,
c. 1855.

Contracts had been let in February of 1853 for the building of stations at Thornhill, Richmond Hill, Aurora (then Machell's Corners), New Market, Holland Landing (St. Alban's), Bradford, and Barrie. By the summer of 1853 the show was on the road:

ONTARIO SIMCOE
AND HURON RAILROAD
NOTICE

On and after MONDAY, 18 July, the Passenger Trains will run daily between Toronto and Bradford, as follows (Sundays excepted):
Express Train leaves Toronto, at 8 A.M.; arrives at Bradford, at 10.25, A.M.

Accommodation Train leaves Toronto, at 3.30, p.m.; arrives at Bradford, at 5.45, p.m.

. . . .

. . . .

ALFRED BRUNEL
Superintendent.[329]

A time of little over two hours from Toronto to Bradford was a miraculous New Iron Age leap in travel compared with the bungle and bounce of the previous horse, coach, and stage method. The railway line that had been opened to Aurora in May 1853 and to Bradford in the following month was eventually opened to Allandale in October 1854, so by-passing Barrie by a mile, to the loudly expressed outrage of its citizens. By the beginning of 1855 the railroad had reached its terminus at Collingwood on Georgian Bay – Lake Huron.

Steamer and stage now combined with the railroad to provide effective travel northward:[330]

THE STEAMERS

MORNING,

On Lake Simcoe, and the
KALOOLAH

On the Georgian Bay, to and from Sault Ste. Marie, will run in connection with the Northern Railroad Cars, as formerly advertised.

CHARLES THOMPSON.

Stages will leave daily, to and from Machell's Corners, at the usual hours.

ROBERT B. C. PLAYTOR.

Church Street,
Toronto, June 30, 1853

When the *Morning* was being built and her hull fitted out at Holland Landing, the machinery and engines had to be dragged up Yonge Street on tree-trunk rollers drawn by horses; it was a long, temper-trying haul before the railroad made freight carriage easier. But the iron rails of 1853 signalled the beginning of the decline of stages on Yonge Street.

It wasn't long before all the newspaper advertisements seemed to be for rail and steamship travel, and in a very short time trips became part of a treat and not the grimly necessary undertakings of the still recent staging days:

"Northern Route. Royal Mail Line, from Toronto to Sault Ste. Marie ......
The Steamer Morning, Captain Charles Bell, in connection with the above line of stages
and the Steamer Kaloolah on Lake Huron, will leave Barrie at 5 o'clock a.m. for
Bradford Landing as follows: Mondays, Wednesdays and Fridays via Beaverton ......
and on Tuesdays and Thursdays via Orillia and intermediate places. Returning from
Bradford Landing on the arrival of the stages from Toronto ......"

EXCURSIONS

Ontario, Simcoe and Huron Railway. — Notice
EXCURSION TICKETS FOR TRIPS
from Toronto to Lake Simcoe, making the circuit of the Lake, and
returning to Toronto the same day, are now issued at the Toronto
Ticket Office of the Company.

Price 12s. 6d. currency. Children half price.

A. BRUNEL, Superintendent.[331]

Stages ran 'to Thornhill and Richmond Hill Villages in connection with the
Trains.'[332]

Novel fun it might be, but God help anyone found interfering with the line.
The Company had become very sensitive about a reputation for safety after a
supposedly empty train-run in July 1853 bumped a cow near Thornhill and went
off the rails, injuring a ride-hopper; the company offered a price equal to that of
Mackenzie's scalp for mischief-makers:

$1,000 REWARD,

THE Ontario, Simcoe, and Huron Railroad Union Company will pay
the above Sum of "ONE THOUSAND DOLLARS" to any party who

will give such information as shall lead to the discovery, apprehension and conviction of the person or persons who placed a small TREE across the Track of this Road, about one mile North of the Richmond Hill Station, during the Night of Friday, the 19th day of August, instant.

A. BRUNEL,
Superintendent.[333]

During this same decade, safety would also become the cry of those who wanted to see improvements on Yonge Street, and the *Globe* of 20 October, 1849, carried the notice that 'the jurors of our Lady the Queen upon their oath present, that ...Yonge-street and Dundas-street, are now, and have been for some time in a most dangerous state ...and ....they are of the opinion that the said roads being within the liberties of the said City of Toronto ought to be repaired by the City authorities.'

Easy enough to make noises about who ought to do something, but by now the responsibility for Yonge Street was a buck to be passed around; it was an expensive buck at that, almost as though it was the pot in a game of liars' dice.

On Tuesday, 6 November, 1849, the *Globe* summed up the play in this eternally popular political game of catch-penny:

> THE CITY ROADS.
> The delay in repairing them has been caused by a doubt which exists as to the present ownership of the roads. The Government have been empowered to transfer them to the City Corporation on certain terms, but a difficulty has prevented the title being transferred. While the title is in abeyance the Government has declined laying out any money, as the benefit is to pass to the City so soon: and the Corporation have also refused to lay out money on roads which are as yet not their property. The result has been that the roads have been allowed to go to wreck and the City has suffered severely in consequence ....His Excellency the Governor General has been pleased to instruct the Commissioner of the Board of Works to arrange with the City Council for the performance of the repairs — on the condition that should any obstruction occur to prevent the transference of the roads the Provincial Government will bear the expense of the work, but that should the transference be completed as anticipated the city will pay the cost of the repairs.

There's a familiar ring to this, all right, beneath the prosaic phrases. And schemes to make the road pay were limited to the old, hackneyed route of putting up the toll rates, which the commissioners of the Home District Turnpike Trust did in an effort to make their charge show profit. It was probably with a near-giddy relief that the contract to keep up Yonge Street was sloughed off in a private sale in 1849 to Mr. James Beatty, a city councillor and leather merchant in

Toronto, who hoped with some of his associates to operate a profitable toll company. A booster shot from a government grant in 1850, however, brought about Bonnycastle's prophecy that Yonge Street would be macadamized 'some fine day' along its entire length to Holland Landing. With the aid given in that year the final push from just south of Richmond Hill was started northward to the Landing.

Among his sprightly comments en passant, Bonnycastle threw in the observation that 'the vice of Canada is, however, drink'.[334] Here he was strongly supported by William Harrison, the historian of Richmond Hill, who continually deplored in his writing the destructive influence of the barley brew. Boozy enthusiasms weren't a peculiarly Canadian phenomenon, but resulted more from the type of people required to lay roads and railways, the rough-going navigators, or 'navvies', so prominent in the history of the nineteenth century's labour force.

In his article, 'Our Hotels',[335] William Harrison said that in the improvement of the Yonge Street road northward from Richmond Hill, 'a large number of men were employed, and many of these, navvies of various nationalities,' boarded at a hotel in the village: 'the drinking and fighting was something extraordinary. The men were paid their wages on Saturday afternoons and most of it was spent in a general carousal on Saturday night and Sundays.' If, as Kipling said, 'blood be the price of admiralty', then drunken sprees were the price of Yonge Street, from the days of the Queen's Rangers on.[336]

In a second article on the area's hotels, Harrison chronicled a tale of woe with some of the following highlights for the Richmond Hill area of Yonge Street in the 1850s: 'One young man was so drunk that he fell under the wheels of his wagon and was killed. An ostler (once a businessman) took laudanum and committed suicide, as did a young girl seduced. In one of the hotels a man fell downstairs and broke his neck. Another died after being flung head-first out of a bar. A young man broke his mother's heart and "died a sot." And all of it owing to the demon drink, that 'heart's delight of the old, bold mate of Henry Morgan.'

Harrison's most dramatic reminiscence, however, is of a crime unrelated to alcohol: the Kinnear murders of 28 and 29 July, 1843. Both victims and their killer were known to Harrison when he was a small boy. The *Globe* newspapers between 28 July and 7 August are missing, but on the eighth of August the following report appeared:

> Since our paper was ready for press, D. Bridgeford, Esq. Coroner, H[ome] D[istrict] has obligingly forwarded the following particulars of the inquest on Mr. Kinnear, and his house-keeper, Nancy Montgomery. The jury on the death of Thomas Kinnear, Esq., return as their verdict, "Wilful Murder" against James M'Dermot. The jury on the death of Nancy Montgomery, return as their verdict "Wilful Murder," against James McDermot and Grace Marks. After rendering

THE KINNEAR MURDER.

"In the evening somewhat late the Captain returned from the City. Driving to the stable he left the horse and went to the house to inform his man. McDermot met him as he came in at the door and fired. The ball went thru his heart and lodged in the skin of his back. He staggered and fell, exclaiming, "Oh my God, I am shot!" On Grace Marks expressing her horror at the deed, McDermot immediately pointed the gun at her and fired again, saying "If you ever tell, your life will not be worth a straw."

(Written by William Harrison for the Newmarket Era, 30 July, 1908 - 65th anniversary of the murder)
Richmond Hill Public Library - Microfilm.

their verdict, the Jury unanimously passed the following resolutions, viz:

1. The Coroner's Jury holding the inquest on the bodies of Thomas Kinnear and Nancy Montgomery, cannot part without expressing their high approbation of the prompt and efficient manner in which Francis Boyd, Esq, Mr. J. Newton, Geo. Gurnett, Esq., F. C. Capreol, Esq, and Mr. Kingsmill acted in bringing to justice the miscreants charged with this shocking murder —

An account of this 'shocking murder' appeared in 'Recollections of the Kinnear Tragedy' written for the *Newmarket Era* on 30 July, 1908, by William Harrison,[337] whose family had settled on a farm about two miles north of Richmond Hill, opposite Kinnear's on Lot 48 in Vaughan. 'Captain' Kinnear was described as a gentleman of aristocratic bearing, and Hannah Montgomery, known as Nancy, his housekeeper, as a woman 'of medium height, a well built, happy tempered woman, who was always cheerful and very neighbourly.' She was often to and fro the Harrison's farm, where the young William remembered how their hired man, Joe, in response to a dare, 'took her up on one of his brawny arms, her full pail in the other hand, carried them across Yonge St., (then knee-deep in mud) and set her down at her master's gate. Nancy thanked him and went home laughing.' And high jinks were to see the end of her.

To complete Kinnear's household there were two servants, both recently from Ireland: James McDermot, the stable-boy, and eighteen-year-old Grace Marks who helped Nancy with the housework. Grace Marks seems to have been a very pretty sort of a wench, though a saucy colleen through knowing it; McDermot was a surly cuss, supposed to be a deserter from the British army, although that in itself was no great damnation in those days.

Kinnear's relationship with his housekeeper can be left to the imagination and conjecture, but she enjoyed a position of familiarity and authority that Grace Marks, sure in the knowledge of her own attractions, resented. As for McDermot, a lazy, sullen lout, he no doubt had a similar chip at the 'Captain's' easy situation and ready supply of cash.

It was Kinnear's custom to ride into Toronto on a Friday to the bank when he required money, and to return on the following day. During such an absence on the evening of Friday, 28 July, 1843, there was some high-spirited skylarking in the house, according to Harrison, with the fun well-flavoured by drink from the 'Captain's' larder.

In the course of this horseplay, which seems to have been part of a well-staged scheme, a towel was thrown around Nancy's neck, she was then strangled and her body thrown down the cellar steps, to be hidden later under a meat tub. Other Lizzie Borden-style stories say that she was hit with an axe before being dumped downstairs, where she was later found, still conscious, by the McDermot-Marks pair who finished her off with more axe-blows and cut up the body, whose parts were then hidden under the tub.

On the following day, McDermot borrowed a double-barrelled gun 'to shoot pigeons with' from a man called Harvey who lived in a log hut on the Newberry farm directly across from Kinnear's. When the 'Captain' returned home that Saturday evening, as he came into the house from the stable, intending to send McDermot out to his horse, he received a blast in his chest from the gun and fell with the superfluous exclamation, 'Oh my God, I am shot'.

Marks was more upset by Kinnear's death than by Nancy's, and McDermot fired a warning shot at Grace as a threat to keep quiet before the 'Captain's' body too was thrown down the cellar.

The culprits then took off swiftly from the scene, and the bodies were found by two Sunday-afternoon callers, Captain Francis Boyd and Mr. James Newton, Sr. A somewhat bizarre memento of the event, says Harrison, was kept by Colonel Bridgford, who took the towel that had been used to strangle Nancy and hung it on a tree in his orchard, 'where wind and time shredded it.'

The news of Kinnear's murder sent up a great hue-and-cry among those of the club, the 'Esqs.' of the gentry, who spared no effort to bring McDermot and Marks to book; this included a strenuous personal chase by Frederick Capreol that would have made Tam O'Shanter's witch, Nanny, look like a lame tortoise.

The fleeing pair was caught soon enough without Capreol's midnight extravaganza. McDermot performed his last jig on the end of a rope. Grace Marks was sentenced to a life of prison labour, which she managed to dodge with a convincing display of insanity resulting in her transfer to a less physically taxing asylum, until a doctor wise in the ways of the deranged saw through her act. She was eventually released and, by one way of it, ended her days in the United States where she married and settled down to disappear in obscurity.

Yonge Street itself would now suffer death of a sort, if death can be a matter of degree. The Simcoe dream of a great military and trading road north to a base at Penetanguishene had become a brief reality only to be dissipated by the decision in 1852 to withdraw the military garrison on Georgian Bay. The latter's isolation had made it an unpopular spot with the soldiery, and one society-deprived subaltern left a poetic lament on the lack of social diversions in the ironic key of Auld Lang Syne:

> With beavers take a hand at whist,
>   And gallopade and waltz —
> With shaggy bears, who, when you roam
>   Afar in forest green
> Remind you that your nearest home
>   Is Penetanguishene.[338]

No. Toronto had much more to offer the young sparks who would be sent out to Upper Canada for a tour of duty, and Penetanguishene lapsed into an isolated backwater as prosperity and population followed the line of the railway. Parallel to Yonge Street it went, crossing the road in three places, as far as Holland Landing, and then to Bradford, passing close by Barrie and on to Collingwood for

*Timothy Eaton's store at Yonge and Queen Streets, 1869.
and a gas-lamp, first used on Toronto's Streets in 1842.*

the lake steamers. It was along this line that a special train was run from Toronto
for the visit of Albert, Prince of Wales, on 10 September, 1860.

Eighteen-sixty was the magic year when the land blossomed at last beyond the
bog at the end of Yonge Street. Bradford shipped 155,000 bushels of wheat by rail
to Toronto that year and doubled the amount before the decade was halfway
through.[339] Added to the lumber boom, it all made for a considerable increase in
the populations of Bradford and Barrie. The railway was the way to go.

Poor old Johnny Simcoe: the American influences that he had so despised and
feared were becoming a part of the business life of Yonge Street, a dash of
initiative not often to be found in the cramped Dickensian counting houses of
England. It was not the American way to be reticent in promoting and advertising
business, and this flavour announced the appropriately named American Hotel on
the northeast corner of Yonge and Front streets:

AMERICAN HOTEL,
Corner of Yonge and Front Streets,
TORONTO.
N. F. PEARSON
(from dunkirk, n.y.)

Begs to announce that he has re-painted, papered and fitted the above
House with new Furniture of the latest taste and fashion, and is now
ready to receive guests. The House is very near the wharves, and the
Terminus of the Northern Railroad, and in the immediate vicinity of
the Banks and business part of the city. The balcony commands a

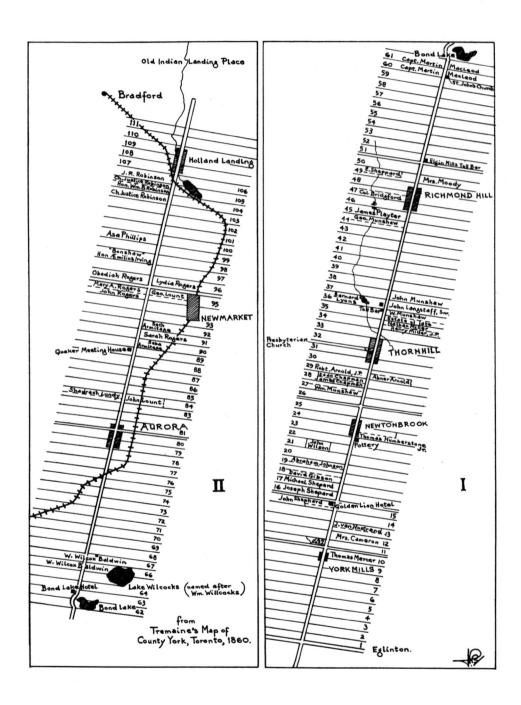

from
Tremaine's Map of
County York, Toronto, 1860.

complete view of the beauties of the bay. The proprietor has had much experience in his business, and he proposes that the American Hotel shall be worthy of being ranked as a first-class house.
Toronto, June 24th, 1853.[340]

What say to that, Bonnycastle? He'd probably have dismissed it as typical Yankee slickness; it showed a sharp business sense, however, stressing the advantages of nearby steamboat wharves and the railroad, the way of the future for commerce and travel. Whether or not it reminded anyone of 'dear home' didn't matter very much, sentiment having no partnership in business.

Practical progressives soon shifted their attention from Yonge Street, which was again taken over by the provincial government in 1863, but to keep it patched up, not to promote it. The novelty of harnessed steam, the noise and power of the railroad, now caught the imagination of the new age with visions of opening up a continent, and beside this the glamour of the bumpy Yonge Street highway to strategic military outposts fast faded as the latter disappeared.

The road had had its mettlesome youth of wars, rebellion, loud politics, and intemperance, and could now settle to the steady pace of mundane respectability. With hard-working Quaker farmers at one end and ambitious businessmen at t'other, its mien was now that of sober broadcloth and mutton-chop whiskers: no more frontier rigs and certainly no dandy checks and Dundreary — sedate, not sporty.

If anything, however, the road was essentially Canadian. Of a length not then to be found anywhere in England's neatly embroidered countryside, running through rich agricultural land to connect two massive lakes that were virtually inland oceans, exposed to extremes of heat and cold and pounding rains, Yonge Street was no mean triumph in its time. The dream of an Englishman, its development was largely owing to people already used to the ways of pioneer life in America. It may only have stretched from lake to lake, but in its conception was the spirit of the Great Canadian Dream of a continent spanned from sea to sea.

But the last word had to come from a Scot, no doubt in the Rob Roy Hotel on the southeast corner of Yonge and Queen streets, a noted rendezvous for Scots immigrants and the Canadian equivalent of the 'Hielan' Man's Umbrella' at Glasgow Central Station in Scotland. With the Rob Roy's whisky at twelve-and-a-half cents a gallon, it was the nearest thing to an expatriate's national dream, or dram if you want to be funny about it. Perhaps refreshing himself after travelling the road in a dusty summer, and no doubt with his own Edinburgh in mind, he declared, 'Aye, yon's a Royal Mile, a'richt — it's nought but a string o' them a'together — an endless bluidy succession!'

Postlude

T. S. Eliot, in that opaque way of his, wrote that 'Time present and time past —
are both perhaps present in time future,' so giving his own particular flick to the
perpetual spin of history's wheel and its eternal cycle where 'in the end is the
beginning.'

The 1860s were an end to one era of Yonge Street, but simultaneously a
beginning to a new epoch in travel by rail and steamship. In Toronto itself, the
street was also overshadowed as one magazine noted: 'Toronto possesses but two
principal streets — Yonge and King. . . .The buildings on King Street are grander
and greater than their neighbours on Yonge, the shops are larger and dearer; and
last, though far from being least, King street is honoured by the daily presence of
aristocracy, while Yonge is given over to the business-man, the middle class and
the beggar.'[341] The end of a dream, a street of tradesmen. How Simcoe would
have detested that, the nadir of his dreams in an age when tradesmen were told to
call at the back door and smarted at being tolerated as necessities.

In addition, the 'National Obsession', Confederation, dominated not only the
1860s but a century of Canadian history books, dropping Yonge Street to the
footnotes as east-west trade routes were heralded as the harbingers of a nation
stretching from sea to sea, linked by railways and steamers that made the old
fur-trade routes unnecessary. Yonge Street became merely an appendage to
Toronto, itself a provincial capital in small letters; Montreal held sway as the
doyen of business in the budding nation.

The railway, however, in turn declined as improved roads and increasingly
reliable and fast automobiles brought back the popularity of the highway. The
present saw Yonge Street become synonymous with Highway 11, rolling into a
distance beyond even the remotest contemplation of the street's founders, for
whom Penetanguishene was the ultimate terminus.

If the automobile restored much of the street's importance as a thoroughfare, it didn't do much for its history, a subject that that crusty old king of the crank-handle empire, Henry Ford, had declared to be bunk anyway. The automobile's only salute to Yonge Street's history has been a cloud of dust or a shower of spray as it whizzes past the historic marks along the way, its driver itching to be clear of the restrictions of each passing town, his eyes intent for the welcome 'Maximum 80 km/h' signs.

Whoever walks along parts of the street will find ample reminders of its past in the markers for the site of Montgomery's Tavern, the restored Gibson House, the scene of the de Puisaye settlement, the place where Colonel Moodie's house once stood, the old Quaker Meeting House, the massive anchor that never got past Holland Landing, and the Yonge Street Cairn itself between Richmond Hill and Aurora, to name a few.

As 'Muddy York' matured into Toronto, its reach stretched ever farther up Yonge Street, taming Hogg's Hollow to a mere winter nuisance of fog-filled cavity, grading and paving to a degree that might have stilled the disparaging Bonnycastle chatter. High-rises replaced the forested flanks, and shopping plazas obliterated the trace of blacksmith and harness-maker. Yet once beyond Holland Landing and Bradford, and avoiding Barrie, some of civilization's closeness recedes and the sweep of Nature's threatening grandeur that so impressed the hedgerow-cloistered English beholder remains to make the blasé driver wary.

Notes

[1] *Simcoe Correspondence*, Vol. 1, ed. Brig. Gen. E. A. Cruikshank, Charles Stevenson to Simcoe, 12 July, 1793.

[2] *Ibid*, p. 199; Simcoe to Alured Clarke, 20 August, 1792.

[3] *Simcoe Correspondence*, Vol. 2, pp. 66, 69; Simcoe to Evan Nepean, 28 September, 1793.

[4] *Ibid.*, Vol. 1, p. 29; Simcoe to Henry Dundas, 30 June, 1791.

[5] *Simcoe Correspondence*, Vol. 1, pp. 71, 75; Yonge to Simcoe, 21 September and 7 October, 1791.

[6] Although the Americans received this territory at the 1783 Treaty of Paris, the British did not evacuate the posts on the excuse that the Americans violated the agreement on the fate of the Loyalists. The forts were finally evacuated in tardy fashion after the settlement of Jay's Treaty, 19 November 1794; the evacuation was not completed until 1796.

[7] *Simcoe Correspondence*, Vol. 1; Simcoe to Nepean, 3 December, 1789.

[8] *Niagara Historical Society, Transactions*, No. 39, 1928: 'Records of Niagara, 1784-7,' ed. E. A. Cruikshank, p. 66; Benjamin Frobisher to Lieutenant-Governor Hamilton, 2 May, 1785.

[9] *Simcoe Correspondence*, Vol. 2; Simcoe to Hammond, 24 August, 1793.

[10] *Canadian Institute*, Transactions, 4th Series, Vol. 2, 1890-1: 'The Administration of Lieut.-Governor Simcoe, Viewed in His Official Correspondence,' E. A. Cruikshank, p. 288.

[11] *Simcoe Correspondence*, Vol. 1, p. 247; Simcoe to Dundas, 4 November, 1792.

[12] *Mrs. Simcoe's Diary*, ed. Mary Quayle Innis, p. 105.

[13] *Simcoe Correspondence*, Vol. 1, pp. 338-342; Simcoe to Clarke, 31 May, 1793.

[14] *Simcoe Correspondence*, Vol. 2, p. 2; 4 August, 1793.

[15] *Ibid.*, Vol. 1, p. 338, and Vol. 2, p. 39; Simcoe to Dundas, 23 August, 1793.

[16] *Mrs. Simcoe's Diary*, pp. 104-5: *cf. Simcoe Correspondence,* vol. 2, p. 36; Simcoe to John King, from 'York (late Toronto) Upper Canada, August 22nd, 1793.' On 26 August, 1793, over the signature of E. B. Littlehales, major of brigade, was issued an official order that Toronto would be changed to York, effective 27 August, 1793, when a 21-gun salute would be fired.

[17] *Simcoe Correspondence*, Vol. 2, p. 62; Simcoe to Dundas, 20 September, 1793.

[18] *Canadian Historical Review*, Vol. LIII, No. 2, June, 1972: 'Fortress Ontario or Forlorn Hope? Simcoe and the Defence of Upper Canada,' Malcolm Macleod.

[19] *An Historical Sketch of the County of York*, Wm. Canniff, p. v.

[20] *The Tiger of Canada West*, W. H. Graham, p. 79.

[21] *Mrs. Simcoe's Diary*, pp. 80-81, 97, 107, 150.

[22] *Ibid.*, p. 13.

[23] *Ontario History*, Vol. XXXIX, 1947. 'The Toronto Carrying Place and the Toronto Purchase,' P. J. Robinson.

[24] *Niagara Historical Society*, Transactions, No. 39, 1928. 'Records of Niagara; 1784-7,' ed. E. A. Cruickshank.

[25] *The Chevalier de Rocheblave and the Toronto Purchase*, P. J. Robinson, p. 135.

[26] *The Town of York; 1793-1815*, ed. Edith G. Firth, p. 6: Extract from the *Upper Canada Gazette*, 1 August, 1793.

[27] *The Queen's Rangers in Upper Canada*, H. M. Jackson, p. 45.

[28] *The Diary of Mrs. John Graves Simcoe*, ed. J. Ross Robertson, p. 196.

[29] *Simcoe Correspondence*, Vol. 2, pp. 70 ff; Alexander Macdonnell's Diary.

[30] *Ibid.*, pp. 90-1; Simcoe to Dundas, 19 October, 1793.

[31] *Ibid.*, Vol. 3, p. 227, Simcoe to the Privy Council for Trade and Plantations, 20 December, 1794.

[32] *Ibid.*, Vol. 2, pp. 70 ff; Alexander Macdonnell's Diary of the Journey to Matchedash.

[33] *Simcoe Correspondence*: Vol. 2, pp.90-91; 19 October, 1793.

[34] Some degree of confusion exists on this matter: The Ontario Archives *Report*, 1929, p. 152, says that on 20 September, 1793, Simcoe informed the Executive Council that Yonge Street was then open from York to Gwillimbury (Holland Landing). In Vol. 2 of *Simcoe Correspondence*, pp. 70 ff, there is a footnote on the 'new route' that Yonge Street had just then (Oct. 1793) been opened to the old pine fort by the Rangers.

[35] *Simcoe Correspondence*, Vol. 2, pp. 51-52; Simcoe to Dundas, 16 September, 1793.

[36] *The York Pioneer*, 1974: 'Simcoe's Yonge Street and the Laying Out of the York County Reserve Lands,' Leo A. Johnson, pp. 35-36.

[37] *St. Andrew's College Review*, May, [939]: Simcoe's Yonge Street, 1793,' Percy J. Robinson.

[38] *Simcoe Correspondence*; Vol. 2, p. 180; Simcoe to Dorchester, 14 March, 1794.

[39] *Ibid.*, p. 358. — With the Posts being in the territory held by the Americans, it would in any event be only a matter of time before they were given up, peacefully, it was to be hoped. The island near Old Michilimackinac was Mackinac Island.

[40] *Simcoe Correspondence*, Vol. 2, pp. 136-7; Dorchester to Simcoe, 27 January, 1794.

[41] Simcoe was not impressed by the Militia — *Simcoe Correspondence*, Vol. 3, p. 40; Simcoe to Dorchester, 5 September, 1794 — 'As the Canadian Milita in general has shown a very improper disposition . . .'

[42] *Ontario Historical Society, Papers and Records*, Vol. VII, 1906 — 'The First Chapter of Upper Canadian History;' Avern Pardoe, p. 7. *Mrs. Simcoe's Diary*; ed. Mary Quayle Innis; 15 March, 1794.

[43] *The Canadian Historical Review*, Vol. LIII, No. 2, June, 1972 — 'Fortress Ontario or Forlorn Hope? Simcoe and the Defence of Upper Canada;' Malcolm MacLeod, p. 166.

[45] See letter in Archives of Ontario, Toronto — *Berczy Papers* — Wm. Berczy (son) to Chevalier Hulseman, Austrian Chargé d'Affaires in U.S.A., 22 August, 1847 — no satisfactory evidence seems to have been produced in reply.

[46] Details of Berczy's background and career are amply provided in *William Berczy: Co-founder of Toronto*; John André — see also *Ontario History*, Vol. LVII, 1965, 'Genesis of an Early Canadian Painter: William Von Moll Berczy,' Lita-Rose Betcherman.

[47] *Simcoe Correspondence*; Vol. 2, pp.109-10.

[48] *Ibid.*

[49] *William Berczy: Co-founder of Toronto*; John André, p. 32 — Mention of a previous winter visit is also made in Simcoe's letter to Dorchester, 2 December, 1793 — *Simcoe Correspondence*, Vol. 2, pp. 109-110.

[50] *Berczy Papers*; Archives of Ontario, Toronto.

[51] *Simcoe Correspondence*, Vol. 2, pp. 190-1; Simcoe to Dorchester, 16 March, 1794.

[52] *Berczy Papers* — Archives of Ontario — Minutes of Council at the Council Chamber in Newark, County of Lincoln, 17 May, 1794.

[53] *Simcoe Correspondence*, Vol. 2, p. 237; Berczy to Simcoe, 18 May, 1794.

[54] *Berczy Papers* — Archives of Ontario — Berczy's *Narrative*.

[55] *Berczy Papers* — Archives of Ontario — Berczy's *Narrative*.

[56] *Simcoe Correspondence*, Vol. 2. pp. 257, 278; Simcoe to Dorchester, 2 June, 1794, and 17 June, 1794.

[57] *Berczy Papers* — 'Sketch of the Life and Times of William Berczy,' J. M. Walton, J. P. County of York.

[58] *Simcoe Correspondence*; Vol. 3, p. 24; William Chewett to E. B. Littlehales.

[59] *Simcoe Correspondence*, Vol. 3, p. 24.

[60] *Berczy Papers* — Archives of Ontario.

[61] *Simcoe Correspondence*, Vol. 2, p. 341.

[62] *The Positive Side of John Graves Simcoe*; Mattie M. I. Clark, pp. 50-51.

[63] *Simcoe Correspondence*, Vol. 2, p. 323; 15 July, 1794 — Acting Surveyor General, Upper Canada.

[64] *The Positive Side of John Graves Simcoe*; p. 89.

[65] *Berczy Papers* — Archives of Ontario, Toronto — 'Anecdote B.'

[66] *Berczy Papers*.

[67] *Simcoe Correspondence*, Vol. 4, p. 282; Report of the Committee of the Executive Council, Upper Canada, 15 July, 1796.

[68] *St. Andrew's College Review*, May, 1939: 'Simcoe's Yonge Street, 1793,' Percy J. Robinson: also — *Berczy Papers*, Berczy to David Smith, 30 November, 1794.

[69] *William Berczy: Co-founder of Toronto*; John André, p. 35.

[70] *Simcoe Correspondence*, Vol. 3, pp. 58-60; Simcoe to the Committee of the Privy Council for Trade and Plantations, 1 September, 1794.

[71] *Berczy Papers*; Berczy to Surveyor General's Office — Received 2 September, 1794.

[72] *Berczy Papers*.

[73] *Ibid.*

[74] *Simcoe Correspondence*, Vol. 3, p. 179.

[75] *Simcoe Correspondence*, Vol. 3, p. 226; 20 December, 1794.

[76] *Ibid.*, pp. 52-69, 1 September, 1794.

[77] *Berczy Papers*.

[78] *Simcoe Correspondence*, Vol. 3, p. 192; Letter from a gentleman in New York, 20 November, 1794.

[79] *Berczy Papers — Narrative*.

[80] *Ibid.*

[81] *William Berczy: Co-founder of Toronto*; John André, p. 44.

[82] *Simcoe Correspondence*, Vol. 4, p. 199; Petition of Berczy to Simcoe, 23 February, 1796.

[83] *Berczy Papers — Narrative*.

[84] *The Town of York; 1793-1815*; ed. Edith G. Firth, p. lii.

[85] *Simcoe Correspondence*, Vol. 4, p. 282; 15 July, 1796.

[86] *Simcoe Correspondence*, Vol. 1, pp. 377 ff; Simcoe to Dorchester, 10 November, 1793.

[87] *Land Policies in Upper Canada*; Lillian F. Gates, pp. 33-4.

[88] *Mrs. Simcoe's Diary*; ed. Mary Quayle Innis, p. 170.

[89] *Simcoe Correspondence*, Vol. 4, p. 177.

[90] *Ibid.*, p. 201.

[91] *St. Andrew's College Review, May, 1939*; 'Simcoe's Yonge Street, 1793,' Percy J. Robinson.

[92] *150 Years at St. John's, York Mills*; M. Audrey Graham, p. 3.

[93] *Mrs. Simcoe's Diary*; ed. Mary Quayle Innis, pp. 175, 176, March 1796.

[94] *Land Policies in Upper Canada*; Lillian F. Gates, p. 41.

[95] *Berczy Papers* — Archives of Ontario, Toronto — 'Anecdote B.'

[96] *Berczy Papers* — Archives of Ontario, Toronto — *Narrative*.

[97] *The Valley of the Humber; 1615-1913*; K. M. Lizars, p. 48.

[98] *The Town of York; 1793-1815*; ed. Edith G. Firth, pp. 35-6; Letter of 7 September, 1796.

[99] *Ontario History*, Vol. XLVIII, 1956; 'The Administration of Peter Russell, 1796-1799,' Edith G. Firth.

[100] *Simcoe Papers* — Archives of Ontario, Toronto.

[101] *A History of Vaughan Township*; G. Elmore Reaman, p. 232.

[102] *The Town of York; 1793-1815*; ed. Edith G. Firth, (Documents, p. 50).

[103] *A Willson Memorandum*; compiled by Hildred G. Pinfold, p. 92.

[104] *Infant Toronto as Simcoe's Folly*; John André, p. 62.

[105] *Ibid.*, pp. 63 *ff.*

[106] See *The Liberal*, 12 November, 1975 — 'Thornhill's first woman settler in 1793' — Yesterdays — by Mary Dawson.
Historical Sketch of Markham Township, 1793-1950; A. D. Bruce.

[107] *Coventry Papers* — Public Archives of Canada — 'The Reminiscences of Captain Dittrick:' — 'we had to content ourselves with a hollow stump to pound our grain in, which was done with a cannon ball, fastened to a cord or bark of a tree, and affixed to a long pole which served as a lever.'

[108] *History of Toronto and County of York*; Vol. 1, p. 126. (He built a small gristmill in the following year.)

[109] *Ibid.*, p. 115

[110] *The Liberal*, 29 October, 1975 — 'Nicholas Miller first Thornhill settler' — Yesterdays — by Mary Dawson.

[111] *Historical Sketch of Markham Township, 1793-1950*; A. D. Bruce; p. 11.

[112] *Observations on Professions, Literature, Manners and Emigration in the United States and Canada in 1832*; the Rev. Isaac Fidler, pp. 269-70.
A History of Vaughan Township; G. Elmore Reaman, p. 60, thinks that the lady might have been the widow of Balser Munshaw (or was it Jacob Munshaw?).

[113] *Old Toronto*; ed. E. C. Kyte, p. 14.

[114] *The Valley of the Humber; 1615-1913*; K. M. Lizars, pp. 107-8.

[115] 'The Chevalier de Rocheblave and the Toronto Purchase,' Percy J. Robinson.

[116] There seem to have been two separate Munshaws:
(i) Balthasar Mundschauer from Pennsylvania, later Balsar Munshaw, who settled on Lot 35 east on Yonge, next to his friends Miller and Lyons.
(ii) Jacob Munshaw, U.E.L., came from Pennsylvania during the American War and settled in Canada. He received a grant of land on Yonge Street and his son, also Jacob, erected a large frame building on the hill just south of Thornhill, at Lot 27 west on Yonge.
See — *Pioneer Life on the Bay of Quinté*: ed. W. F. E. Morley, p. 557 and *Thornhill 1793-1963: The History of an Ontario Village*; Doris M. Fitzgerald, p. 19 — There is also Berczy's List of Settlers provided at Newark, 4 Nov. 1796 — Archives of Ontario, Toronto.

[117] *Infant Toronto as Simcoe's Folly*; John André, p. 109.

[118] Information on these various individuals may be found in *Pioneering in North York*; Patricia W. Hart: — *150 Years at St. John's, York Mills*; M. Audrey Graham: — *The Town of York*; ed. Edith G. Firth.

[119] For details on de Puisaye, see *A Colony of Emigrés in Canada*; Lucy Textor.

[120] *Salute to Canada*; Sister M. Annette, p. 11.

[121] *A Colony of Emigrés in Canada*; Lucy Textor, p. 27.

[122] *Ibid.*, p. 29, 1 November, 1798.

[123] *A Colony of Emigrés in Canada*; Lucy Textor, p. 27 — and letter from Russell to the Duke of Portland, 21 November, 1798.

[124] *Upper Canada Gazette*: 7 December, 1796 — 'McEwen, who stands indicted for the murder of the late acting chief of the Massasaga tribe of Indians, will take his trial at the next court of general goal [sic] delivery, which is to be beholden in this town, on Tuesday next.'
14 December, 1796 — '. . . . . . the grand jury in the case of McEwen found no bill, it not having been proven that the chief, with whose murder he was charged, is dead.'
The trial, it could be said, was a farce.

[125] *Upper Canada Gazette*, 30 December, 1797, and 13 January, 1798.

[126] *York Pioneer and Historical Society*; Annual Report, 1912: 'French Refugees on Yonge Street.'

[127] *Women's Canadian Historical Society of Toronto*; Transactions, No. 3, 1899: 'Recollections of Mary Warren Breckenridge,' Catherine F. Lefroy.

[128] *Upper Canada Gazette*; 4 January, 1800, and 11 January, 1800.

[128a] *The Russell Papers*, 1720-1811, Archives of Ontario, Toronto. (Microfilm).

[129] *Upper Canada Gazette*; 1 March, 1800, 18 October, 1800, and 21 February, 1801.

[130] *Ibid.*, 24 September, 1803.

[131] *Ibid.*, December, 1800.

[132] *Upper Canada Gazette*; 10 August, 1799.

[133] *York Pioneer and Historical Society*; Annual Report, 1912; 'French Refugees on Yonge Street.'

[134] The *Upper Canada Gazettes* for the early 1800s almost regularly carried lengthy advertisements by Quetton St. George.

[135] *Simcoe Correspondence*, Vol. 1, pp. 151-4; 7 May, 1792.

[136] *History of Toronto and County of York*; pub. C. Blackette Robinson, Vol. 1, p. 15. — Stegmann was a former lieutenant of the Hessian Regiment of Lassberg. He was lost in the wreck of the *Speedy* in October 1804.

[137] *Upper Canada Gazette*; 20 December, 1800 — 'The Oracle': In *Toronto of Old*, Henry Scadding (ed. F. H. Armstrong) p. 286, says that Simcoe's projected east-west road, Dundas Street, when it reached the centre of Toronto at Yonge, followed the route of Queen (Lot) Street.

[138] *Upper Canada Gazette*; 12 March, 1801.

[139] *Sketches of Old Toronto*; Frank Norman Walker, p. 20.

[140] Historical Plaque Descriptions, 14 October, 1958 — Archives of Ontario, Toronto: *Journal of Timothy Rogers*, (Microfilm, section D-2-8) — Archives of Ontario.

[141] *Upper Canada Gazette*, 4 October, 1806.

[142] *Timothy Rogers' Journal* — (Microfilm, D-2-8, Quaker Archives) — Archives of Ontario, Toronto.

[143] *Statistical Account of Upper Canada*; Robt. F. Gourlay, Vol. 1, pp. 459-60.

[144] See *A String of Amber*; Blodwen Davies.

[145] *Robertson's Landmarks of Toronto*; Archives of Ontario, Microfilm — Reel 3, Chapter IX, p. 20.

[146] *Thornhill, 1793-1963*; Doris M. Fitzgerald, p. 19, note 2.

[147] The Annual Bounty, or Presents, system to keep the Indians loyal to Britain seems to have been begun about 1755. The Indian Reserve Policy was started in 1830.

[148] See *Upper Canada Gazettes* — December, 1799; July, 1802; June, 1807; November, 1807.

[149] Vol. 2, p. 137.

[150] *Simcoe Correspondence*, Vol. 2, pp. 119-20, 14 December, 1793.

[151] *The Town of York, 1793-1815*; ed. Edith G. Firth, p. 154 — Memorial of 5 November, 1810.

[152] *History of Toronto and County of York*; pub. C. Blackett Robinson, Vol. 1, p. 95.

[153] *Old Toronto*; ed. E. C. Kyte, p. 67.

[154] *History of Toronto and County of York*; Vol. 1, p. 13.

[155] See *Old Toronto*; ed. E. C. Kyte, p. 67: *History of Old Toronto*; C. Blackett Robinson, Vol. 1, p. 16: *Canadian Historical Review*, Vol. XXIV, 1943, 'Yonge Street and the North West Company,' Percy J. Robinson.
Sketches of Old Toronto; Frank Norman Walker, p. 20:
McGillivray, Lord of the Northwest; Marjorie Wilkins Campbell, p. 97.

[156] Vol. 1, p. lxi.

[157] *Simcoe Correspondence*, Vol. 2, p. 115.

[158] *Les Bourgeois de la Compagnie du Nord-Ouest*; L. R. Masson; Vol. 2, p. 172, 'An Account of Lake Superior, 1809.'

[159] *The Fist in the Wilderness*; David Lavender, p. 57.

[160] *Ibid.*, p. 62.

[161] *The Correspondence of the Honourable Peter Russell*; ed. E. A. Cruikshank and A. F. Hunter; Vol. 3, 1798-9.

[162] *The York Gazette*, 9 December, 1807.

[163] *Ibid.*, 16 March, 1808.

[164] *The Liberal*, 24 December, 1975 — 'Markham Loyalist first settled Yonge' — Yesterdays — by Mary Dawson.: *Upper Canada Gazette* 3 November, 1804, for an account of the loss of the *Speedy*.

[165] *Canadian Historical Review*; Vol. XXIV, 1943; 'Yonge Street and the North West Company,' Percy J. Robinson.

[166] *The Town of York, 1793-1815*; ed. Edith G. Firth, pp. 154-6.

[167] See, for example, the letters of John Askin, Jr. 13 January, 1808 and 17 June, 1808, in 'Yonge Street and the North West Company,' by Percy J. Robinson.

[168] *The John Askin Papers*; ed. Milo M. Quaife, Vol. 2, p. 688.

[169] 'Mr. McIntosh' was Angus McIntosh of the N. W. Coy who went back to Scotland in 1830 to be Chief of the Clan McIntosh — See *The Mackintosh Papers*, Archives of Ontario, Toronto.

[170] Quoted in 'Yonge Street and the North West Company' from *Ten Years in Upper Canada*; Matilda Edgar.

[171] p. 282, note 3: Henry Scadding in *Toronto of Old* (1873) p. 300, quotes from D. W. Smith's *Gazetteer* of 1799 — '(Yonge Street) is thirty miles from York to Holland's river, at the Pine Fort called Gwillimbury, where the road ends; from thence you descend into Lake Simcoe, and, having passed it, there are two passages into Lake Huron; the one by the river Severn, which conveys the waters of Lake Simcoe into Gloucester Bay (Matchedash); *the other by a small portage, the continuation of Yonge Street, to a small lake, which also runs into Gloucester Bay.*' This 'small portage' was the Indian trail which later became the old Coldwater Road. : p. 499, he says: 'A continuation of Yonge Street in a more perfect sense, was at a later period surveyed and partially opened by the military authorities, from a point on Kempenfeldt Bay, a little east of the modern Barrie, in a direct line to Penetanguishene; but the natural growth of the forest had in a great degree filled up the track.'

[172] *Ely Playter Diary*, — Archives of Ontario.

[173] *Recollections of the American War; 1812-14*; Dr. Dunlop, p. 47.

[174] 'An Episode in the War of 1812: The Story of the Schooner *Nancy*, by Lieut.-Col. E. A. Cruikshank in *Ontario Historical Society, Papers and Records*, Vol. IX, 1910.

[175] *The York Gazette*, 4 July, 1807.

[176] *Select British Documents of the Canadian War of 1812*; ed. William Wood, Vol. 1, p. 169 — 25 February, 1812.

[177] 'Major-General Sir Isaac Brock, K.B.,' by J. A. Macdonnell, K.C., in *Ontario Historical Society, Papers and Records*, Vol. X, 1913.

[178] *The Hero of Upper Canada:* W. Kaye Lamb, p. 15.

[179] *Select British Documents of the Canadian War of 1812*; ed. William Wood, Vol. 1, p. 396.

[180] *Ibid.*, Vol. 1, p. 352: Brock to Prevost, 12 July, 1812.

[181] 'A Study of Disaffection in Upper Canada,' E. A. Cruikshank — in *The Defended Border*: ed. Morris Zaslow.

[182] *The Liberal*, 26 November, 1975, 'Veterans of Bunker Hill at Fort York in 1812,' — Yesterdays — by Mary Dawson.

[183] *Toronto of Old*; Rev. Henry Scadding; ed. F. H. Armstrong, p. 315.

[184] *The Town of York, 1793-1815*; ed. Edith G. Firth, p. 293 — 5 Dec. 1813.

[185] *Ibid.*, p. 300 — 5 May, 1813.

[186] *Ibid.*, p. 315 — 28 June, 1813.

[187] *Select British Documents of the Canadian War of 1812*: ed. William Wood, Vol. 1, p. 352 — Brock to Prevost, 12 July, 1812.

[188] *The Town of York, 1793-1815*; ed. Edith G. Firth, pp. 282-3.

[189] *The Town of York, 1793-1815*; ed. Edith G. Firth, p. 320.
Note: The *Upper Canada Gazette*; 18 Month, 1830 — Statement of the Militia Pension List includes 'Joseph Shepard — Wounded at York.'

[190] *The Liberal*, 29 October, 1975 — 'Nicholas Miller first Thornhill settler,' — Yesterdays — by Mary Dawson.

[191] *A History of Vaughan Township*; G. E. Reaman, p. 28 and *Toronto of Old*; Henry Scadding, p. 430.

[192] *Illustrated Historical Atlas of York County, Ontario*, Toronto, 1878, p. XI.

[193] *Simcoe County Pioneer & Historical Society Papers*, No. 5, 1912: A. C. Osborne, pp. 12-13.

[194] 'An Episode in the War of 1812. The Story of the Schooner *Nancy*,' *E. A. Cruikshank in Ontario Historical Society; Papers and Records*; Vol. IX, Toronto, 1910.

[195] *Ibid.*

[196] *Select British Documents of the Canadian War of 1812*; ed. William Wood, Vol. 3 Pt. 1, p. 266 — Drummond to Prevost, 28 January, 1814.

[197] *The John Askin Papers*; ed. Milo M. Quaife, Vol. 2, p. 789.

[198] *Recollections of the American War; 1812-14*; Dr. Dunlop, p. 60.

[199] *Select British Documents of the Canadian War of 1812*; ed. William Wood, Vol. 3, Pt. 1, p. 272 — McDouall to Drummond, 26 May, 1814.

[200] *The Fist in the Wilderness*; David Lavender, p. 204.

[201] 'The Story of the Schooner *Nancy*,' E. A. Cruikshank.

[202] *Recollections of the American War: 1812-14:* Dr. Dunlop, pp. 90, 95.

[203] *Forest Scenes and Incidents in the Wilds of North America*; George Head, Esq., pp. 178-185. George (later Sir George) Head was the brother of Sir Francis Bond Head, Lieutenant-Governor of Upper Canada, 1836-38.

[204] *The York Gazette*; 4 July, 1807, and 11 November, 1807: — A number of 'public-spirited people' gathered to cut a route down the hill at Frank's Creek, and Lt.-Gov. Gore on hearing of this sent a person with $50 to assist in improving Yonge Street.

[205] *The Town of York: 1815-1834*; ed. Edith G. Firth, p. 36. In the *History of the Town of Newmarket*, Ethel Warren Trewhella, p. 29 quotes Joseph Bouchette who, in 1815, speaks of improvements to Yonge Street '*of late* effected by the North West Company.'

[206] *Ely Playter Diary* — Provincial Archives of Ontario.

[207] P. 486.

[208] *Ely Playter Diary; —* Provincial Archives of Ontario.

[209] Some details of this family may be found in the *History of Newmarket* by Ethel Warren Trewhella.

[210] *Life and Journals of Kah-ke-wa-quo-na-by (peter Jones)* — Thursday, 14 August, 1828. — Provincial Archives of Ontario.

[211] *History of the Town of Newmarket*; Ethel Warren Trewhella, p. 135.

[212] *The Women's Canadian Historical Society*, Transactions, No. 12, 1912-13.

[213] *A History of Simcoe County*; A. F. Hunter, Part 2, p. 13. Matters cannot have gone too well, because the *Upper Canada Gazette* of 16 August, 1802 lists Lewis Algeo, 'late of the Township of West Gwillimbury' as 'an absconding or concealed debtor.'

[214] *Ibid.*, Part 2, p. 22.

[215] *Surveyor-General's Office: Letters Received Oct. 1797 – June 1798;* p. 188: — Provincial Archives of Ontario.

[216] *The Journals of Mary O'Brien, 1828-1838*; ed. Audrey S. Miller, p. 59

[217] *Observations on Professions, Literature, Manners and Emigration, in the United States and Canada in 1832*; the Rev. Isaac Fidler, pp. 270-1.

[218] *Statistical Account of Upper Canada*; Robert Gourlay, Vol. 2, p. 312.

[219] *Upper Canada Gazette*, 10 April, 1817.

[220] *Ibid.*, 1 February, 1811.

[221] *Observations on Professions, etc.*; the Rev. Isaac Fidler, p. 351.

[222] *Observations on Professions, etc.*; the Rev. Isaac Fidler, p. 327.

[223] *Ibid.*, p. 461.

[224] *A History of Vaughan Township*; G. Elmore Reaman, p. 59.

[225] *Statement Showing the Name, Age and Residence of Militiamen of 1812-1815*: Morgan, Roger & Co., Ottawa, 1876 — Prov. Archives of Ontario.

[226] *The Journals of Mary O'Brien 1828-1838*; ed. Audrey S. Miller, p. 21.

[227] The name is sometimes spelled wrongly, as was so often the case in those days, as 'Moody' and should not be confused with the Moody family that petitioned for a Yonge Street Lot in May, 1798.

[228] *The Liberal*, 3 March, 1976 — "Grand Vaughan mud folly was accursed" — Yesterdays — by Mary Dawson.

[229] *Upper Canada Gazette*, 6 March, 1823.

[230] 31 January, 1828.

[231] *Observations on Professions, etc.*; the Rev. Isaac Fidler, pp. 222-3.

[232] *Upper Canada Gazette*, 27 June, 1833. (U. C. Gazette 20 Mar. 1934 — Peacetime fine reduced from 20/- to 10/- (£5 in war).)

[233] *Journals of Mary O'Brien 1828-1838*; ed. Audrey S. Miller, p. 49

[234] *Aspects of Nineteenth-Century Ontario*; ed. F. H. Armstrong, H. A. Stevenson, J. D. Wilson, p. 221.

[235] *Upper Canada Gazette*, 19 July, 1817.

[236] *The Loyalist*, 30 August, 1828.

[236a] *The Journals of Mary O'Brien, 1828-1838*; ed. Audrey S. Miller, pp. 15 and 41.

[237] *Ibid.*, p. 25 — 21 November, 1828.

[238] Public Archives of Canada, Series 'C,' Vol. 1268 — Letter Book, Military Secretary's Office, Kempt to Murray, 11 June, 1829.

[239] *The York Gazette*, 9 June, 1810.

[240] *Upper Canada Gazette*, 30 August, 1832.

[241] *Ibid.*, 5 September, 1834.

[242] *Narrative of a Second Expedition to the Shores of the Polar Sea (1825, 1826, and 1827)*; Capt. John Franklin, R.N. — M. G. Hurtig, Ltd., Edmonton.

[243] *The Journals of Mary O'Brien, 1828-1838*; ed. A. S. Miller, p. 20.

[244] *The Journals of Mary O'Brien, 1828-1838*; 27 February, 1829 — p. 43.

[245] *Colonial Advocate*, 14 April, 1831.

[246] *The Journals of Mary O'Brien, 1828-1838*; ed. Audrey S. Miller, p. 158.

[247] *The Journals of Mary O'Brien, 1828-1838*; ed. Audrey S. Miller, 22 February, 1834, p. 224, and 18 May, 1836, p. 249.

[248] 'The Reverend Newton Bosworth: Pioneer Settler on Yonge Street,' by F. H. Armstrong in *Ontario History*, Vol. LVIII, 1966.

[249] Advertisement in the *Colonial Advocate*, 19 August, 1830: — see also 26 April, 1827 — Jackes's Hotel, the Rising Sun, corner of Dundas and Yonge.

[250] Richmond Hill Historical Society — 'Scrapbook' — Richmond Hill Public Library — The *Liberal*, No. 28 — 'Our Hotels.'

[251] *The Banished Briton and Neptunian*; Robert F. Gourlay, No. 22, p. 238: Harvard Univ'y Library.

[252] *Statistical Account of Upper Canada*; Robt. F. Gourlay, Vol. 1, pp. 458-60.

[253] *Life and Journals of Kah-ke-wa-quo-na-by (Peter Jones)*, — Thursday, 31 January, 1828: — on p. 222 for Friday, 12 June, 1829, at a meeting with Sir John Colborne and Dr. Stuart, Lord Bishop of Quebec, Jones was pleased to note of the Lieut.-Gov. that 'His Excellency was so free from sectarian prejudices' in the matter of converting the Indians.

[254] 27 February, 1834.

[255] *Upper Canada Gazette*, 22 May, 1832.

[256] The *Colonial Advocate*, 19 April, 1832; The *Courier of Upper Canada*, 15 February, 1832.

[257] *Ely Playter Diary*, — Provincial Archives of Ontario — 12 and 13 June.

[258] 7 November, 1832.

[259] *Courier of Upper Canada*, 21 October, 1834 — see 21 April, 1835 for the sale of the boat.

[260] *The Journals of Mary O'Brien, 1828-1838*; ed. Audrey S. Miller, p. 201 — 23 October, 1832.

[261] *The Advantages of Emigration to Canada*; William Cattermole (1831): Coles Reproduction (1970) : pp. 49, 62-3, 113, 164-5, 186-7.

[262] For the political overtones in the Society, see 'Yonge Street Politics 1828 to 1832,' by Audrey S. Miller in *Ontario History*, Vol. LXII, 1970.

[263] Reprinted in the *Colonial Advocate*, 7 January, 1830.

[264] Imperial Blue Books, Provincial Archives of Ontario; — Head to Lord Glenelg, 16 July, 1836.

[265] 'The Stormy History of the York Roads, 1833-35,' by Michael S. Cross in *Ontario History*, Vol. LIV, 1962.

[266] 20 August, 1829.

[267] *The Patriot and Farmers' Monitor*, 20 January, 1835.

[268] 9 December, 1830.

[269] *Colonial Advocate*, 20 March, 1828.

[270] *William Lyon Mackenzie: Rebel Against Authority*; David Flint, p. 17.

[271] Quoted in the *Advocate*, 6 February, 1834.

[271] *Colonial Advocate*, 12 June, 1828.

[272] *Ibid.*

[273] *The Patriot and Farmers' Monitor*, 17 June, 1834.

[274] *The Courier of Upper Canada*, 19 October, 1832.

[275] *The Patriot and Farmers' Monitor*, 3 April, 1832, quotes from the *Courier*.

[276] *Colonial Advocate*, 28 March, 1832.

[277] *Ibid.*, 26 April, 1832.

[278] *Colonial Advocate*, 3 April, 1828.

[279] The *Colonial Advocate*, 26 October, 1833.

[280] There is a long article on this subject in the *Colonial Advocate*, 9 June, 1831.

[281] The *Colonial Advocate*, 20 March, 1828 — describes how the Government took cattle and horses from the Quakers as militia fines, and then sold them at 3 or 4 Dollars a head.

[282] 'Yonge Street Politics, 1828 to 1832,' by Audrey S. Miller, in *Ontario History*, Vol. LXII, 1970.

[283] *The Patriot and Farmers' Monitor*, 7 March, 1834.

[284] *Ibid.*, 16 August, 1833.

[285] The *Courier*, 21 Oct. 1834 — quoting from Toronto *Recorder*.

[286] The *Upper Canada Gazette*, 3 December, 1835.

[287] The *Loyalist*, 25 October, 1828.

[288] Richmond Hill Historical Society — 'Scrapbook' — Richmond Hill Public Library — The *Liberal*, No. 10 — 'John Stegman P.L.S., and Yonge Street' (Microfilm Roll No. 4).

[289] The *Courier of Upper Canada*, 15 February, 1832.

[290] The *Patriot and Farmers' Monitor*, 15 January, 1836.

[291] *Ibid.*, 29 September, 1835.

[292] The *Courier of Upper Canada*, 24 February, 1832.

[293] The *Patriot and Farmer's Monitor*, 1 December, 1835.

[294] *Despatches from Sir F. B. Head* — Provincial Archives of Ontario — Enclosures with letter from Head to Lord Glenelg, 21 April, 1836.

[295] *Ibid.*, — Head to Lord Glenelg, 16 July, 1836.

[296] *Ely Playter Diary* — Provincial Archives of Ontario.

[297] *Despatches from Sir F. B. Head* — Provincial Archives of Ontario — Head to Lord Glenelg, 19 December, 1837.

[298] p. 83.

[299] *Despatches from Sir F. B. Head, etc.*; Provincial Archives of Ontario — Head to Lord Glenelg, 19 December, 1837.

[300] The *Patriot and Farmers' Monitor*, 16 February, 1838 — Reprint of Mackenzie's Narrative which he had sent to the editor of the *Jeffersonian*.

[301] *Reminiscences of a Canadian Pioneer*; p. 84.

[302] The *Patriot and Farmers' Monitor*, 16 February, 1838.

[303] *Reminiscences of a Canadian Pioneer*; Samuel Thompson, p. 91.

[304] *Reminiscences of a Canadian Pioneer*; p. 85.

[305] *Reminiscences of a Canadian Pioneer*; Samuel Thompson, p. 85.

[306] *The Liberal*, 14 April, 1976, 'Secret signal worked,' — Yesterdays — by Mary Dawson.

[307] *The Lives and Times of the Patriots*; Edwin C. Guillet, p. 24.

[308] The *Patriot and Farmers' Monitor*, 8 December, 1837.

[309] 'Toronto's First Railway Venture, 1834-38,' by F. H. Armstrong, in *Ontario History*, Vol. LVIII, 1966.

[310] *Ely Playter Diary*, — Provincial Archives of Ontario — (Microfilm — Reel No. 2)

[311] *History of the Town of Newmarket*; Ethel Warren Trewhella.

[312] *Reminiscences of a Canadian Pioneer*; Samuel Thompson, p. 86.

[313] The *Patriot and Farmers' Monitor*, 19 January, 1838.

[314] *Despatches from Sir F. B. Head, etc.*; Head to Lord Glenelg, Enclosure, 28 December, 1837.

[315] An account of the hanging is given in the *Patriot and Farmers' Monitor*, 13 April, 1838.

[316] The *Patriot and Farmers' Monitor*, 19 January, 1838.

[317] *Despatches from Sir F. B. Head, etc.*; p. 458.

[318] *Ibid.*, Enclosure with letter of 20 March, 1838.

[319] The report of Montgomery's trial can be found in the *Patriot and Farmers' Monitor*, 13 April, 1838.

[320] The details of this are given in *The Life and Times of William Lyon Mackenzie*, by his son-in-law Charles Lindsey, Vol. 2. : also, 'The Trials of John Montgomery,' by E. A. Lacey in *Ontario History*, Vol. LII, No. 3, 1960.

[321] *Reminiscences of a Canadian Pioneer*, pp. 89, 93.

[322] These lists appear in *The Life and Times of William Lyon Mackenzie*; Charles Lindsey, Vol. 2, pp. 376-389 (Coles Reprint) and *The Lives and Times of the Patriots*; Edwin C. Guillet, pp. 251-3.

[323] The *Patriot and Farmers' Monitor*, 15 December, 1840.

[324] 'The Stormy History of the York Roads, 1833-35,' by Michael S. Cross in *Ontario History, Vol. LIV, 1962.*

[325] *Canada and the Canadians*, Sir Richard Bonnycastle, Vol. 1, pp. 111*ff*

[326] The *Patriot*, 11 February, 1842.

[327] The *Patriot*, 31 August, 1841.

[328] 'The Davisville Pottery', by Jean Bacso in *The York Pioneer*, 1975.

[329] *Ely Playter Diary* — Provincial Archives of Ontario.

[330] The *Daily Leader*, 18 July, 1853.

[331] The *Daily Leader*, 11 July, 1853.

[332] The *Daily Leader*, 24 August, 1855.

[333] *Ibid.*, 7 September, 1855.

[334] *Ibid.*, 23 August, 1853.

[335] *Canada and the Canadians*, Vol. 1, p. 154.

[336] Richmond Hill Historical Society — 'Scrapbook,' — Microfilm Roll No. 4, Richmond Hill Public Library.

[337] See the *Russell Papers*, — Provincial Archives of Ontario, — D. W. Smith to Russell, 22 April, 1799; — '. . . the Rangers, . . .vanishing to carouse upon S. Georges day . . .'

[338] Richmond Hill Historical Society — 'Scrapbook' — Microfilm Roll No. 4 — Richmond Hill Public Library.

[339] *Women's Canadian Historical Society of Toronto*; Transactions, No. 4, 1899.

[340] 'The Northern Railway: Its Origins and Construction, 1834-1855,' by Russell D. Smith in *Ontario History*, Vol. XLVIII, No. 1, 1956.

[341] The *Daily Leader*, 13 July, 1853.

[342] *Toronto; A Pictorial Record, 1813-1882*; Charles P. de Volpi; — Plate No. 66, from the 'Canadian Illustrated News', 3 September, 1870.

Bibliography

André, John. *Infant Toronto as Simcoe's Folly*. Toronto: Centennial Press, 1971.

André, John. *William Berczy: Co-founder of Toronto*. Toronto: Ortoprint, 1967.

Annette, Sister M., C.P.S. *Salute to Canada*. Winnipeg: Canadian Student Yearbooks, Ltd., 1967.

Armstrong, F. H., et al. *Aspects of Nineteenth-Century Ontario*. Toronto: University of Toronto Press, 1974.

Armstrong, F. H. 'The Rev. Newton Bosworth: Pioneer Settler on Yonge Street'. *Ontario History*, Vol. LVIII, 1966.

Armstrong, F. H. 'Toronto's First Railway Ventury, 1834-38'. *Ontario History*, Vol. LVIII, 1966.

Armstrong, F. H. 'The York Riots of March 23, 1832'. *Ontario History*, Vol. LV, No. 2, 1963.

Basco, Jean. 'The Davisville Pottery'. *The York Pioneer*, 1975.

Berczy, William von Moll. 'Narrative re an Expedition in U.C. for Settling Part of that Province with Germans from Europe'. *Berczy Papers*, Archives of Ontario.

Betcherman, Lita-Rose. 'Genesis of an Early Canadian Painter: William Von Moll Berczy'. *Ontario History*, Vol. LVII, 1965.

Bonnycastle, Sir Richard Henry, Kt. *Canada and the Canadians*, 2 Vols. London: Henry Colburn, Publisher, 1849.

Breithaupt, W. H., C.E. 'First Settlements of Pennsylvania Mennonites in Upper Canada'. *Ontario Historical Society — Papers and Records*, Vol. XXIII, 1926.

Breithaupt, W. H., C.E. 'Some Facts About the Schooner "Nancy" in the War of 1812'. *Ontario Historical Society — Papers and Records*, Vol. XXIII, 1926.

Bruce, A. D. 'Historical Sketch of Markham Township, 1793-1950'. Unionville Centennial Library, Unionville, Ontario.

Burkholder, L. J. 'A Brief History of the Mennonites in Ontario'. Mennonite Conference of Ontario, 1935.

Burkholder, Mabel. 'Palatine Settlements in York County'. *Ontario Historical Society, — Papers and Records,* Vol. XXXVII, 1945.

Campbell, Marjorie Wilkins. *McGillivray, Lord of the Northwest.* Toronto: Clarke, Irwin and Company, Ltd., 1962.

Canniff, Wm. *An Historical Sketch of the County of York.* Toronto: Miles and Co., 1878.

Canniff, Wm. *History of the Settlement of Upper Canada.* Toronto: Dudley and Burns, 1869.

Cassels, Hamilton, Jr. 'York Mills, 1800-1955'. *Ontario History,* Vol. XLVII, 1955.

Cattermole, William. *The Advantages of Emigration to Canada, being the Substance of two lectures.* London: Simpkin and Marshall, 1831. (Toronto: Coles Reproduction, 1971).

Clark, Mattie M. I. *The Positive Side of John Graves Simcoe.* Toronto: Forward Publishing Company, Ltd., 1943.

Coles, Harry L. *The War of 1812.* Chicago: University of Chicago Press, 1965.

Cross, Michael S. 'The Stormy History of the York Roads, 1833-35'. *Ontario History,* Vol. LIV, 1962.

Cruikshank, Lieut.-Col. E. 'An Episode of the War of 1812. The Story of the Schooner "Nancy" *Ontario Historical Society — Papers and Records,* Vol. IX, 1910.

Cruikshank, Brig. Gen. E. A., ed *The Correspondence of Lt. Gov. John Graves Simcoe, 1791-96,* 5 Vols. Toronto: The Ontario Historical Society, 1923.

Cruikshank, E.A., ed. 'Records of Niagara; 1784-7'. *Niagara Historical Society Transactions,* No. 39, 1928.

Cruikshank, E. A., and A. F. Hunter, eds. *The Correspondence of the Honourable Peter Russell,* Vol. 3, 1798-99. Toronto: The Ontario Historical Society, 1936.

Davies, Blodwen. *A String of Amber; the Heritage of the Mennonites.* Vancouver: Mitchell Press, Ltd., 1973.

Doane, Gilbert James. 'An Experience in Genealogy'. *The York Pioneer,* 1964.

Dunlop, Dr. William. *Recollections of the American War, 1812-14.* Toronto: Historical Publishing Co., 1905.

Fidler, the Rev. Isaac. *Observations on Professions, Literature, Manners and Emigration, in the United States and Canada in 1832.* London: Whittaker, Treacher and Co., 1833.

Firth, Edith G. 'The Administration of Peter Russell, 1796-1799'. *Ontario History,* Vol. XLVIII, 1956.

Firth, Edith G., ed. *The Town of York; 1793-1815.* Toronto: The Champlain Society, 1962.

Firth, Edith G., ed. *The Town of York; 1815-1830.* Toronto: The Champlain Society, 1962.

Fitzgerald, Doris M. *Thornhill 1793-1963; The History of an Ontario Village.* Thornhill: 1964.

Flint, David. *William Lyon Mackenzie: Rebel Against Authority.* Toronto: Oxford University Press, 1971.

Franklin, Captain John, R.N., F.R.S. *Narrative of a Second Expedition to the Shores of the Polar Sea in the Years 1825, 1826 and 1827.* Edmonton: M. G. Hurtig, 1971.

Fretz, J. Winfield. *The Mennonites in Ontario.* Waterloo, Ontario: Mennonite Historical Society of Ontario, 1967.

Gates, Lillian F. *Land Policies of Upper Canada.* Toronto: University of Toronto Press, 1968.

Gillham, Elizabeth McClure. *Early Settlements of King Township, Ontario.* Published by the Author, 1975.

Goldie, John. 'The Tramp of a Botanist Throuth Upper Canada in 1819'. *The Women's Canadian Historical Society, Transactions,* No. 12, 1912-13.

Gourlay, Robt. F. *The Banished Briton and Neptunian: a Record of the Life, Writings, Principles and Projects of Robert Gourlay,* (Issues #1-#16, #39). Boston: S. N. Dickinson, 1843. — In Toronto Metropolitan Library. — Issue #22 in the collection of Harvard University Library.

Gourlay, Robt. F. *Statistical Account of Upper Canada, Compiled with a View to a Grand System of*

Emigration. 2 Vols. London: Simpkins and Marshall, 1822.

Graham, M. Audrey. *150 Years at St. John's, York Mills*. Toronto: General Publishing Company, Ltd., 1966.

Graham, W. H. *The Tiger of Canada West*. Toronto: Clarke, Irwin and Company, Ltd., 1962.

Gray, L. R., ed. 'From Bethlehem to Fairfield, Part 1'. *Ontario History,* Vol. XLVI, No. 1, 1954. (this has a good section on Berczy and the early settlement at Williamsburg.)

Guillet, Edwin C. *The Lives and Times of the Patriots*. Toronto: Thomas Nelson and Sons Ltd., 1938.

Guillet, Edwin C. *The Pioneer Farmer and Backwoodsman*. 2 Vols. Toronto: The Ontario Publishing Company, Ltd., 1963.

Guillet, Edwin C. *Pioneer Inns and Taverns*. 5 Vols. Toronto: The Ontario Publishing Company, Ltd., 1964.

Harrison, Wm. 'French Refugees on Yonge Street'. Synopsis of an Address — *York Pioneer and Historical Society, Annual Report,* 1912.

Hart, Patricia W. *Pioneering in North York*. Toronto: General Publishing Company, Ltd., 1968.

Head, Sir F., B. Bart, K.C.H. *Despatches Relative to Canada; with Answers from the Secretary of State*. — Ordered, by the House of Commons, to be Printed, 22 March, 1839. Imperial Blue Books, Archives of Ontario.

Head, George, Esq. *Forest Scenes and Incidents in the Wilds of North America*. London: John Murray, Albemarle Street, 1829.

Hitsman, J. Mackay. *The Incredible War of 1812*. Toronto: University of Toronto Press, 1965.

Humphries, Charles W. 'The Capture of York'. *Ontario History,* Vol. LI, No. 1, 1959.

Hunter, Andrew F. *A History of Simcoe County,* in 2 Parts. Barrie, Ontario: Historical Committee of Simcoe County, 1948.

Innis, H. A. *The Fur Trade in Canada*. Toronto: University of Toronto Press (Rev. Edn.), 1962.

Innis, Mary Quayle, ed. *Mrs. Simcoe's Diary*. Toronto: Macmillan, 1965.

Jackson, H. M. 'The Queen's Rangers; 1st American Regiment' *Bridle and Golfer,* October, 1933. Archives of Ontario.

Jackson, Lt. Col. H.M. *The Queen's Rangers in Upper Canada*. Montreal; 1955.

Jefferys, C. W. *The Picture Gallery of Canadian History,* 3 Vols. Toronto: The Ryerson Press, 1945.

Johnson, Leo A. 'Simcoe's Yonge Street and the Laying Out of the York County Reserve Lands'. *The York Pioneer,* 1974.

Jones, the Rev. Peter. *Life and Journals of Kah-ke-wa-quo-na-by*. Toronto: Anson Green, Wesleyan Printing Establishment, 1860.

Kyte, E. C., ed. *Old Toronto*. Toronto: The Macmillan Company of Canada, Ltd., 1954.

Lacey, E. A. 'The Trials of John Montgomery'. *Ontario History,* Vol. LII, No. 3, 1960.

Lamb, W. Kaye. *The Hero of Upper Canada*. Toronto: Rous and Mann Press, Ltd., 1962.

Lavender, David. *The Fist in the Wilderness*. New York: Doubleday and Company, Inc., 1964.

Lefroy, Catherine F. 'Recollections of Mary Warren Breakenridge'. *Women's Canadian Historical Society of Toronto, Transactions,* No. 3, 1899.

Lindsey, Charles. *The Life and Times of William Lyon Mackenzie,* 2 Vols. Toronto: P. R. Randall, 1862. (Toronto: Coles Reproduction, 1971.)

Lizars, K. M. *The Valley of the Humber; 1615-1913*. Toronto; Coles Publishing Company, Ltd., 1974.

Locke, G. N., and Margaret Ray. 'The Queen's Rangers'. — Pamphlet issued to Toronto Public Library, 1924.

Luck, John. *Newmarket Centennial; 1857-1957*. Newmarket, Ontario: Newmarket Era and Express Ltd., 1957. — Archives of Ontario.

Macdonnell, J. A., K.C. 'Major-General Sir Isaac Brock, K. B.'. *Ontario Historical Society —Papers and Records* Vol. X, 1913.

McFall, Jean. 'Elmer Starr of Yonge Street'. *The York Pioneer,* 1959.

McFall, Jean. 'Samuel Lount'. *The York Pioneer,* 1974.

MacLeod, Malcolm. 'Fortress Ontario or Forlorn Hope? Simcoe and the Defence of Upper Canada'. *Canadian Historical Review,* Vol. LIII, No 2, June, 1972.

MacLeod, Malcolm. 'Simcoe's Schooner "Onondaga." '*Ontario History,* Vol. LIX, 1967.

Masson, L. R., ed. *Les Bourgeois de la Compagnie du Nord-Ouest.* 2 Vols. New York: Antiquarian Press, 1960.

Middleton, Jesse Edgar. *The Municipality of Toronto; A History.* Vol. I. Toronto: The Dominion Publishing Company, 1923.

Middleton, Jesse Edgar. *Toronto's 100 Years.* Toronto: The Centennial Committee, 1934.

Milani, Lois Darroch. *Robert Gourlay, Gadfly.* Thornhill, Ontario: Ampersand Press, 1971.

Miller, Audrey S., ed. *The Journals of Mary O'Brien, 1828-1938.* Toronto: Macmillan of Canada, 1968.

Miller, Audrey Saunders. 'Yonge Street Politics, 1828-1832'. *Ontario History*, Vol. LXII, 1970.

Morley, W. F. E., ed. *Pioneer Life on the Bay of Quinté.* Belleville, Ontario: Mika Silk Screening Ltd., 1972.

Muggeridge, John. 'John Rolph — A Reluctant Rebel'. *Ontario History,* Vol. LI, No. 4, 1959.

Newlands, David L. 'The Yonge Street Friends Meeting House, 1810-1975'. *The York Pioneer,* 1975.

Osborne, A. C. 'Old Penetanguishene'. *Simcoe County Pioneer and Historical Society Papers,* No. 5. Barrie, Ontario, 1912.

Pardoe, Avern. 'The First Chapter of Upper Canadian History'. *Ontario Historical Society —Papers and Records,* Vol. VII, 1906.

Pinfold, Hildred G. *A Willson Memorandum.* Richmond Hill Public Library, Richmond Hill, Ontario. 1974.

Quaife, Milo M., ed. *The John Askin Papers.* 2 Vols. Detroit: Detroit Library Commission, 1928.

Reaman, G. Elmore. *A History of Vaughan Township.* Toronto: University of Toronto Press, 1971.

Reaman, G. Elmore. *The Trail of the Black Walnut.* Toronto: McClelland and Stewart, Ltd., 1957.

Rempel, John I. 'A Brief History of "Dead Houses" Along Yonge Street'. *The York Pioneer,* 1965.

Robertson, J. Ross. *Robertson's Landmarks of Toronto; A Collection of Historical Sketches of the Old Town of York from 1792 until 1833; and of Toronto from 1834 to 1898.* Toronto: 1898. — Archives of Ontario.

Robertson, J. Ross, ed. *The Diary of Mrs. John Graves Simcoe.* Toronto: William Briggs, 1911.

Robinson, C. Blackett, publisher. *History of Toronto and County of York.* Vol. 1. 1885.

Robinson, P. J. 'Yonge Street and the North West Company.' Canadian Historical Review, Vol. XXIV, 1943.

Robinson, Percy J. 'The Chevalier de Rocheblave and the Toronto Purchase'. Ottawa: *Royal Society of Canada,* 1937.

Robinson, Percy J. 'Simcoe's Yonge Street, 1793'. *St. Andrew's College Review,* May, 1939.

Robinson, Percy J. 'The Toronto Carrying-Place and the Toronto Purchase'. *Ontario History,* Vol. XXXIX, 1947.

Robinson, Percy J. *Toronto During the French Régime.* Toronto: University of Toronto Press, 1933.

Scadding, Dr. Henry, D.D. *Toronto of Old.* Toronto: Adam, Sevenson and Company, 1873. — Archives of Ontario.

Scadding, Henry, D.D. *Toronto of Old,* ed. F. H. Armstrong. Toronto: Oxford University Press, 1966.

Scott, Duncan Campbell. 'John Graves Simcoe'. *The Makers of Canada Series,* Vol. IV. Toronto: Oxfort University Press, 1926.

Smith, Russell D. 'The Northern Railway: Its Origins and the Construction, 1834-1855'. *Ontario History,* Vol. XLVIII, No. 1, 1956.

Stacey, Col. C. P. 'The Battle of Little York', written for the *Toronto Historical Board,* 1963.

Textor, Lucy E. *A Colony of Emigrés in Canada, 1798-1816.* Toronto: University of Toronto Studies, 1904.

Thompson, Samuel. *Reminiscences of a Canadian Pioneer for the last fifty years (1833-1883).* Toronto: Hunter and Rose, 1884. (Reprint, Toronto: McClelland and Stewart, 1968.)

Trewhella, Ethel Warren. *History of the Town of Newmarket* — in Richmond Hill Public Library, Richmond Hill, Ontario.

Upton, L.F.S., ed. *Issues in Canadian History* — *The United Empire Loyalists: Men and Myths.* Toronto: The Copp Clark Publishing Company, 1967.

Van Steen, Marcus. *Governor Simcoe and His Lady.* Toronto: Hodder and Stoughton, 1968.

de Volpi, Charles P., F.R.P.S.L. *Toronto; A Pictorial Record, 1813-1882.* Montreal: Dev-Sco Publications, Ltd., 1965.

Walker, Frank Norman. *Four Whistles to Wood-up.* Upper Canada Railway Society, Incorporated, 1953.

Walker, Frank Norman. *Sketches of Old Toronto.* Toronto: Longmans Canada, Ltd., 1965.

Walker, Dr. Frank N., and Mrs. Walker. 'The 'Northern' — York County's First Railroad'. *York Pioneer and Historical Society,* Annual Report, 1951.

Wise, S. F., ed. *Sir Francis Bond Head: A Narrative.* Toronto: McClelland and Steward, Ltd., 1969.

Wood, William, ed. *Select British Documents of the Canadian War of 1812.* Vols. 1, 2, and 3 (Parts 1 & 2). Toronto: The Champlain Society, 1920.

York Pioneer, The (1965). 'The Society of Friends (Quakers) Yonge Street Meeting, 1807'.

Zaslow, Morris, ed. *The Defended Border; Upper Canada and the War of 1812.* Toronto: The Macmillan Company of Canada, 1964.

Ms Collections/Family Records:

Berczy — *The Berczy Papers, 1794-1897.* Archives of Ontario.

Coventry — *The Coventry Papers.* Public Archives of Canada, Ottawa.

Playter — *Ely Playter Diary, Feb. 1801 — Dec. 1853.* Archives of Ontario.

Reesor — *The Reesor Family in Canada,* Genealogical and Historical Records, 1804-1950. Archives of Ontario.

Rogers — *Journal of Timothy Rogers, 1783-1813, 1827.* The Archives of the Religious Society of Friends (Quakers). Archives of Ontario.

Russell — *The Russell Papers, 1720-1811.* Archives of Ontario.

Miscellaneous:

Historical Plaque Descriptions. Archives of Ontario.

Scrapbook — Flashbacks and Window on the Past — Richmond Hill Public Library, Richmond Hill, Ontario.

Surveyor-General's Office: Letters Received, October 1797 — June 1798 #7. Archives of Ontario.

Illustrated Historical Atlas of York County, Ontario. Toronto: Miles and Co., 1878. (Belleville, Ontario: Mika Silk Screening, Ltd., 1972).

Explore Centennial Richmond Hill. Richmond Hill Public Library, Richmond Hill, Ontario.

York/Toronto Newspapers — Canadian Library Association — Ontario Legislative Library. Archives of Ontario.

The Colonial Advocate
The Courier of Upper Canada
The Daily Leader
The Globe
The Loyalist
The Patriot and Farmers' Monitor
The Upper Canada Gazette or American Oracle/The York Gazette
Current Newspapers:
The Liberal, Richmond Hill editions, — 'Yesterdays' by Mary Dawson — 1975-1976.

Index